EMOTIONS IN CRISIS

Youth and Social Change in Spain

Nina Margies

BRISTOL
UNIVERSITY
PRESS

First published in Great Britain in 2024 by

Bristol University Press
University of Bristol
1–9 Old Park Hill
Bristol
BS2 8BB
UK
t: +44 (0)117 374 6645
e: bup-info@bristol.ac.uk

Details of international sales and distribution partners are available at bristoluniversitypress.co.uk

© Bristol University Press 2024

British Library Cataloguing in Publication Data
A catalogue record for this book is available from the British Library

ISBN 978-1-5292-3503-6 hardcover
ISBN 978-1-5292-3504-3 ePub
ISBN 978-1-5292-3505-0 ePdf

The right of Nina Margies to be identified as author of this work has been asserted by her in accordance with the Copyright, Designs and Patents Act 1988.

Cover design: Lyn Davies Design
Front cover image: Stocksy/Wizemark
Bristol University Press use environmentally responsible print partners.
Printed and bound in Great Britain by CPI Group (UK) Ltd, Croydon, CR0 4YY

FSC
www.fsc.org
MIX
Paper | Supporting responsible forestry
FSC® C013604

Contents

Acknowledgements

This journey was not possible without all the support, advice and encouragement of many people in durable as well as fluid encounters.

First and foremost, I would like to thank all the young people who shared their stories, thoughts and feelings with me. Without your openness, hospitality and knowledge, this book would not exist. Many thanks also to all (expert) interviewees who took the time to explain the young people's situation in post-crisis Spain and served as gatekeepers.

My utmost gratitude goes to Talja Blokland for your trust, support and inspiring conversations. I learned from you how to look at things through the 'sociological glasses'. I am also indebted to Åsa Wettergren for your guidance and encouragement. Our many discussions helped me to find a structure and clarify my thoughts.

I am grateful for the time and valuable advice by Emma Jackson, Helena Flam, Virág Molnár, Hanna Hilbrandt, Penny Travlou and to my feeling community and partners in crime: Hannah Schilling, Daniela Krüger, Eleni Triantafyllopoulou and Katharina Knaus.

There were numerous spaces that were crucial for the making of this book. First and foremost, the Institute of Urban and Regional Sociology at the Humboldt University of Berlin with the wonderful colleagues and an atmosphere of mutual trust.

Another important space was the Department of Sociology at the Universidad Complutense de Madrid. I am thankful to Jesús Leal, Margarita Barañano Cid, Marta Domínguez Pérez and Daniel Sorando for inviting me as guest researcher at your department. Rubén Díez García, Elena Casado, Eduardo Crespo, Pablo López Calle, Alberto Riesco, Amparo Lasén and Pedro Uceda, our discussions about young people in Madrid, the Spanish labour market and the role of emotions in all this were extremely valuable for my research.

An important testing ground of first analyses was the ESA Research Network RN11 – Sociology of Emotion, which is not only a wonderful platform for academic exchange but also a small community of committed and warm-hearted people. Thank you Monika Verbalyte for taking me on and into the RN11 board.

I am very grateful for the wonderful work places I was able to use during the work on the book: the Georg-Simmel Center for Metropolitan Studies, the Institut Français Madrid and the Bürogemeinschaft Lottumstraße.

Without the generous financial support I received, it would not have been possible to focus on the research to such an extent. Therefore, I am grateful to the Studienförderwerk Klaus Murmann, the Casa de Velázquez (EHEHI), the German Academic Exchange Service (DAAD) and the Department of Social Sciences at the Humboldt University of Berlin.

Also, many thanks to Esther Rupérez Pérez, Marta Mitjans Puebla and Natalia Pérez Ramos for interview transcription, and Tom Hillstead for English proofreading.

I also wish to thank Bristol University Press for the guidance throughout the publication process (in particular, Shannon Kneis, Emily Watt, Emily Ross, Anna Richardson and Amber Lanfranchi) and Newgen Publishing UK (in particular Lee-Ann Ashcroft).

Last but not least, my infinite gratitude goes to my family and friends: Juli, Marv, Bonny, Aliénor as well as Bianka and Andreas, Lena, Christiane, Dietlind, Vitalija and Nicolas for the good vibes, your constant encouragement and for being the 'back office'.

Introduction

No home, no job, no pension, no fear. (Juventud sin Futuro, 2011)

'Of course, I'm worried, because without work there is no future. Because I do have the training for it, I'm prepared, I've done my vocational training … and I'm also doing a degree … but no matter how much training I do, if I don't have a job, what are all these certificates good for?' (Belén[1] in 2017, 26)

'It makes you anxious. Anxiety, depression … You watch as the years go by and realise that your future prospects aren't going to materialize. I'm going to remain stuck like 10 years ago, when I was 17 years old. Am I going to be studying all my life? I want to escape.' (Mateo in 2017, 29)

'What happens when you look for lots of ways out but don't find any? Well, ultimately you end up feeling frustrated.' (Alfonso in 2018, 18 years old)

'What scares me the most is being dependent, even at my age, on my parents, you know? It's awful, just awful. And you say: "Fuck, I'm working, I'm doing everything at once, how can I still be dependent?"' (Alberta in 2017, 27)

'When you look to the future, you always view it more pessimistically and with a certain amount of anxiety because you just never know.' (Petra in 2016, 35)

In 2008, the financial crisis hit Spain hard, bringing the country in many respects to its knees. The economy collapsed, millions of people lost their jobs, public sector and infrastructure investments were massively cut, the poverty rate increased and the traditional two-party system began to crumble. Trust in the political and economic system was severely shaken. Against this backdrop, protests were launched and people across the country began to stand up and to mobilize themselves. On 15 May 2011, mass demonstrations were held all over Spain and people occupied the central square, Puerta del Sol, in the capital Madrid. It was the start of a social movement (15M)[2] whose participants called themselves the 'Indignados' (the indignants) and voiced their criticism, raising social, economic and political grievances. Young people in particular took their discontent to the streets, organized campaigns such as *No+ becas x trabajo* (No more internships for work) or *No es ciudad para jóvenes* (This is not a city for young people) and formed collectives such as Juventud sin Futuro (Youth without a Future). They saw themselves as a generation with no future prospects and no general access to housing, work or pensions. Their criticisms highlighted a particular state of feeling that young people seemed to share across the country which was characterized by insecurity, hopelessness, indignation and outrage (van de Velde, 2011).

In October of the same year, sociologist Zygmunt Bauman commented on this social movement in the major Spanish newspaper *El País*. He described it as 'emotional', and said that it 'lacks thinking' (Verdú, 2011). He believed that the indignation that people had carried into the public sphere would evaporate in the same way as emotions typically do in what he called *liquid modernity* (2000).[3] 'Emotion', as he argued, 'is unstable and unsuitable for shaping anything coherent and lasting' (Verdú, 2011).

Yet the frustration, despair and indignation did not disappear. They persisted, as we can see from the statements made by some of the young people in 2016 and 2017 at the beginning of this introduction. Almost ten years after the crisis began and five years after the social movement emerged, young people were still talking about feeling forgotten and betrayed, and were not seeing any serious prospects for the future, leaving them feeling anxious, frustrated and angry. It seems that their emotions were by no means a short-lived phenomenon or a spontaneous outburst, but had rather developed into a structural phenomenon shaping the young people's daily lives.

This book is about those emotions. It captures narratives of young people in Madrid in the aftermath of the economic crisis (2016–18) and their emotional accounts of change. The hypothesis is that upheavals and profound changes translate into emotions in individuals. What people feel is an indicator not only of what is going on *inside* of them but also *outside* of them – for example, to participate in everyday life and have access to resources and opportunities. The emotions the young people experienced and expressed are indicators of a society in transition in which parts of processes and possibilities that had been taken for granted were subject to change. Their accounts demonstrate that they were not able to enter or navigate their way through the labour market in the way that they had expected. The labour market had been hit hard by the crisis, and jobs were scarce. The currency of education had lost its value, and instead of being able to gain employment by means of educational qualifications, they talked about how they found themselves in a state of dependency and dead ends. The connection between the changed structural conditions and the new challenges and constraints on young people's individual agency was expressed through their worries, anxieties and frustrations. Their emotions can be seen as an interface between what was happening at the societal level and how it translated for the young people in their everyday life. They were therefore not only personal sensations and psychologically explicable, but also inherently social, structuring and structured by social interactions and processes (Barbalet, 1998: 6). Many scholars in the sociology of emotion have demonstrated that emotions connect structure and agency (Kemper, 1978; Hochschild, 1979; Collins, 1981; Gordon, 1990; Barbalet, 1998; von Scheve, 2009). The aim of this book is therefore not only to show *that* emotions connect structure and agency, but also to further demonstrate *how* they do this.

The questions that will guide this book are the following: what are the emotions that shape the experiences of young people in post-crisis Spain? How can we explain their emergence and persistence? How do young people express, interpret and deal with their emotions? What role do emotions play in dealing with crisis and change? And, more generally, how can an emotions-based perspective help us to understand crisis and social change more broadly?

To answer these questions, the book draws upon a qualitative case study carried out in Madrid, Spain between 2016 and 2018. During a total of 19 months of fieldwork, I talked to youth organizations, trade unions, associations supporting the development and reintegration of young people at risk and/or social exclusion, local authorities and conducted semi-structured in-depth interviews with 68 young people. They were between 18 and 35 years old, equal in numbers with respect to gender, and their levels of education ranged from primary school to university degree. Most of them were born in Spain, but some of them came from Latin America and Africa. What they all had in common was their work situation that reflected the different forms of (non)work that were subject to or expression of the changing labour conditions during the economic crisis: they were in temporary work, in several part-time jobs at the same time, were unemployed or in (further) education loops.

Emotions, crisis and change: the research field

The interest in change and the way it translates into people's experiences, including their feelings, can be traced back to the beginning of sociology as a discipline. While systematic concepts of emotion were rarely developed, sociologists observed how the profound transformations of industrialization and the division of labour in the 18th and 19th centuries also changed the structures of emotions and thus the nature, expression and interpretation of emotions (see, for example, Smith, 1812; Durkheim, 1893; Elias, 1939). Simmel (1903), Weber (1934) and Elias (1939), for example, described the emotional regime of the emerging industrial capitalism as an increasing rationalization of emotions. They observed that both the expression and management of emotions changed substantially, and interpreted this as shifting from instinctive and affect-driven to continuous emotional self-control. In addition, Elias (1997: 341, 410) argued that the arenas of social tensions moved from an external stage to an internal one, resulting, for example, in fewer exterior fears of physical violence and more interior ones. In this context, a new form of self-control developed in which emotions such as fear, lust or disgust, which had previously been freely expressible, became subject to social taboos and were internalized. External constraints turned into self-constraints, and emotions such as shame and embarrassment became central to how social control worked (Elias, 1997: 408–9). But sociologists not only observed changes at the level of individual emotion management. Durkheim (1893) demonstrated how the profound transformations equally affected collective emotional structures. He saw the specialization and subdivision of functions and occupational groups as the reason for a general fragmentation of the collective consciousness in (Western) society. Feelings were increasingly limited to individual circles or social spheres and so it became more difficult to develop a collective emotional force or collective effervescence. Durkheim also argued that rapid changes within the labour market and a volatile economic situation, such as in times of crisis, could lead to emotional disorientation. This is especially the case when individuals' expectations of their economic situation and social position could no longer be met. Then, he argued, cultural and emotional norms become disordered and plunge the individual into (deep) dissatisfaction or even lead to suicide if feelings of dissatisfaction no longer find a social corrective (Durkheim, 1897).

We find also the idea of disharmony between individual agency and structural conditions creating a particular 'structure of feeling' (Williams, 1977) in later studies on crises and profound transformations. Walkerdine and Jimenez (2012), for example, demonstrate how the way in which people in former coal mining areas in South Wales had coped with chronic insecurity over generations was no longer helpful when faced with changes in a deindustrializing labour market. The closure of factories, the departure of people and thus new spatial and temporal rhythms of everyday life disrupted the way in which social and affective relations were organized and consequently produced considerable amounts of anxiety and fear. The authors highlight 'the complex psychosocial character of this "disembedding"' (Walkerdine and Jimenez, 2012: 75) in which the habitual collective emotion management could no longer be carried out in the same way and contributed to the emergence of a new emotional landscape.

For Sennett (1998), who studied similar economic developments in the context of the US, they resulted in a certain structure of character. The long-term emotional experiences that make up character, as Sennett argues, are increasingly marked by a sense of drift and the illegibility of risk. He observed a mismatch, structuring people's experiences, between the ideas and aspirations of their life biography on the one hand and the working conditions and lived reality on the other.

What is evident in these studies is that structural change not only brings shifting conditions of existence but also involves the destabilization of references, imaginaries or explanatory frameworks. Positional suffering can be the consequence, as Atkinson (2013) points out in the context of the 2008 financial crisis in the UK. Maintaining a certain standard of living proved to be increasingly difficult for the people he interviewed and involved a lot of emotional pain. He speaks of the symbolic violence, in this case, that people suffered when they were unable to attain the forms of recognition they were used to receiving. This is how a society in crisis can translate into a 'crisis of the subject', as Mbembe and Roitman (1995: 327) argue. Using Cameroon as an example, they show how the economic crisis in the 1980s and 1990s led to profound changes not only in the spatial, social and economic structure of the country, but also in the mental structure. The 'lack of coincidence between the everyday practice of life (facticity) and the corpus of significations or meanings (ideality) available to explain and interpret what happens' (Mbembe and Roitman, 1995: 324) generated a considerable sense of uncertainty. They demonstrate how, for example, the mass dismissals had such an impact that the young and educated generation in particular developed a constant fear that they would lose their job (Mbembe and Roitman, 1995: 350). This climate of anxiety, the authors argue, shaped everyday public and private life, and contributed to a new emotional landscape that saw a 'rise in domestic conflict, the rapidity with which people resort to anger, verbal abuse and physical violence … aggravated by new forms of urban violence, inspired either by the quest for subsistence or attempts to eradicate the very sources of perceived anger' (Mbembe and Roitman, 1995: 351).

The phenomenon of disharmony between the changing environment and an individual has been sociologically conceptualized by Bourdieu (1979). Labelled *hysteresis*, this notion captures the embodied experience of change that is generated by a structural mismatch between a field and a person's habitus and has emotional consequences for the individual. Bourdieu repeatedly used this concept as a template to explain people's profound experiences of transformation and crisis, such as in his studies on Algeria (Bourdieu, 1977) and the French education system (Bourdieu, 1979).

This book builds on these studies and ties in with Bourdieu's idea of hysteresis. The changes in work and education in post-crisis Spain formed the basis for the systemic production of mismatch, a wide divergence between young people's expectations and the opportunities they actually had to fulfil them. Against this background, this book will not only show that hysteresis leads to emotions, but will also demonstrate how. Unlike in many studies in sociology, emotions are not considered here as a byproduct, but are the actual object of study and analysis.

Studying emotions

But how should emotions be studied empirically, given their often episodic nature and low visibility? Long treated as a black box in the social sciences and rarely the direct object of empirical research, little attention has been paid to methodological procedures that make it possible to explore emotions systematically (Kleres, 2011: 182). In manuals on qualitative social research, they often appear only in the context of emotional challenges for the researcher during fieldwork (see Lofland and Lofland, 2006: 54ff; Kvale, 2007: 34f; Sherman Heyl, 2007: 374f). In recent years, however, the topic has attracted growing interest and has generated a number of reflections on how to study emotions by surveying, observing, interviewing and reading them through visual or textual material (Kleres, 2011; Flam and Kleres, 2015; Barchard, 2017; Loughran and Mannay, 2018). For my research, in which (emotional) experiences and their interpretation were at the forefront, I opted for researching emotions through 'face-to-face bodily and verbal communication' (Flam, 2015: 2), in which I concentrated on my interviewees' narratives and the language, practices and bodily expressions that accompanied them.

'Most of what people do when they make meanings, negotiate about meanings, and use cultural resources in their meaning-making happens in language. People talk about what they have done and why; they discuss with others how a thing should be understood; they think about what things mean to them' (Magnusson and Marecek, 2015: 6). Emotions can hence be captured or made tangible through the spoken word. This becomes clearest through overt linguistic markers at the lexical and syntactical level (Kleres, 2011: 194). Direct emotion words (for example, fear, happy) or whole sentences (for example, "I'm extremely angry") can be used to express emotions. In addition, indirect references such as exclamations (for example, "No way!, What an idiot!"), modal words (for example, luckily, hopefully), rhetorical questions, metaphors or irony provide information about emotional evaluations of an action, person or event (Kleres, 2011: 194–5). Yet we can analyse not only *what* people say, but also *how* they say it. We can find additional clues through phonetics that can indicate emotional states. The voice may provide this information, for example, if what is said is accompanied by a giggle, if someone's voice cracks or if it is trembling. The emphasis of individual words, the volume with which certain elements are delivered or the hesitation and pauses in speech can also offer situated clues about a speaker's feelings (Kleres, 2011: 195). According to Kleres (2011: 183), the various elements of a narrative episode constitute an emotional experience. Emotions, he suggests, have a narrative character and narratives are emotionally structured. The events that the interviewees described during the interview, the actors they mentioned and the meaning they attached to them are all part of an emotional experience that was expressed in their narrative.

Another way to identify implicit emotions, according to Scheer (2012, 2016), is to look not only at the 'sayings' but also at the 'doings'. When people act in a certain way (for example, slamming the door or avoiding walking somewhere at night) they convey, consciously or unconsciously, a certain attitude towards an event, place or actors involved. Scheer calls these *emotional practices*, building on Bourdieu's theory of practice. Consuming media (for example, a film, music or a book) or drugs, or writing a diary or a politician's funeral speech following a tragic event are all examples of practices in which mobilizing, naming, communicating and regulating emotions take place (Scheer, 2012: 209–17).

Ultimately, we can gain empirical access to emotions through bodily expressions. Emotions need a medium, the body, in order to be experienced, interpreted and expressed. Such an emotional expression may occur through facial expressions and gestures, through body postures or 'manifestations such as tears, changing skin colour, or heavy breathing' (Scheer, 2012: 214). It may happen consciously, as a signal or means of exchange, or unconsciously. By observing, it is possible to capture these forms and expressions of emotions, even if the person being observed does not notice or name them as such. The main access to the young people's emotions in this book was thus the spoken word and their narratives, through which I was able to identify both emotion words (I was angry) and emotional practices (I smashed the door). In addition, I based my analysis on observations of the young people's bodily expressions and gestures during the interview situation. A clenched fist, a trembling voice, silence or tears pointed to emotional experiences and when combined with the narratives helped me to gain a more nuanced understanding.

Yet I could only draw on what the young people themselves talked about, which might prompt the question of how we can be sure that the feelings they expressed were genuine and authentic. The answer here is probably rather sobering: we can never know with certainty. If we adopt Goffman's dramaturgical approach (1959), then our daily social interactions are first and foremost a theatre play in which we give a role-specific performance on the stage. Other scholars believe that in the process of civilization and the emergence of capitalism, the state and the market have gradually altered what was once seen as our true inner feelings or instincts (see Elias, 1939;

Illouz, 1997, 2006; Flam, 2009). Hochschild (1983) even speaks of alienation in this context, which has resulted from the commodification of emotions in the capitalist system, especially in the service sector. 'This centuries-long emotions management', as Flam (2015: 5) thus sums up, 'made it impossible to posit any clear-cut difference between "authentic", subjective feelings, and the prescribed emotions.'

So perhaps the question of emotional authenticity is much trickier than the answer to it. To begin with, this question is inherently normative. Warner and Shields (2009: 97) argue that 'an observer's judgement about another's emotional authenticity is fundamentally a social judgement. It is connected directly to how the observer construes the actor's emotion in terms of normative social standards'. The idea of authenticity thus already includes ideas about what feelings would be appropriate in a given situation and in what intensity and form they should be expressed. They are thus closely linked to the feeling rules described by Hochschild (1979).

The social judgement over someone's emotional authenticity also entails the question of legitimacy and thus of value. Recognizing someone's feelings as sincere and genuine provides them with value. When I question the emotional truthfulness of my interviewees, in a way, I write off the validity of their emotions and consider them as less worthy of my (scientific) attention. 'Challenges to emotional authenticity', as Warner and Shields (2009: 99) aptly note, 'are, in effect, disputes about who has claims to selfhood.' In other words, it is about whose emotions are taken seriously and whose are not. It goes without saying that inequalities of power and status play an essential role in this decision. Questioning the female perception of pain is a case in point. Several studies (Ruiz and Verbrugge, 1997; Samulowitz et al, 2018) show how the (emotional) representation of women's physical suffering is more likely to be interpreted as emotional, hysterical, inexplicable or psychosomatic and therefore, in conventional Western medicine, as invalid for physical medical treatment. Often the recommendation for further treatment is to see a psychologist or psychiatrist and to work on their emotions to cure the 'imagined' physical pain. Calling women's emotional authenticity into question when it comes to pain can be seen as an act of symbolic violence (Bourdieu, 1979), an act that often has real consequences. Gender bias in medicine and healthcare has led, among other things, to diseases being overlooked or treated differently from those of men, and to fewer investments in research and medicine production to fight diseases that are more common in women (García Dauder and Pérez Sedeño, 2017).

Hence, the question of emotional authenticity is always a contested one. Therefore, perhaps it is more helpful to shift the focus from factual accuracy to the very social relations in which emotional authenticity is performed and negotiated (see also Rosenwein, 2010: 21). As such, I was not asking about the 'truth' of my interviewees' emotions. Rather than asking whether they really felt the way they described it, I was concerned with the questions of how and why the young people I had interviewed mobilized and drew on certain feelings in their accounts. This allows us to see how people place themselves and are placed by others. Naming, communicating and regulating emotions (Scheer, 2012) depend on where we are in social space. Naming and communicating emotions, for instance, relies on being able to put a name to the feeling in a way that people (the recipients) will understand. It also implies being recognized and entitled to be affected in this particular way. If this is not the case due to issues of class, gender or race, regulating emotions becomes crucial. If a young woman in the interview does not express any anger about her clearly precarious and exploitative work situation, although she would 'objectively' have good reason to do so, then the absence of anger does not make her emotional experience inauthentic. We may also explain it by her (low) gendered position of status and power and thus the impact of social categories and their intersections, which made her feel (not) entitled to express anger. In this book, I have therefore tried to ask what it meant when young people referred (or did not do so) to certain emotions. By looking at how they refer to emotions, we can learn about how people see themselves as actors in society, how they perceive their room for manoeuvre, but also how they are shaped by societal expectations and norms.

Before we move on to the context in which the experiences and emotions of the young people in this book emerged, let me mention a final but important aspect. With regard to the interpretation and analysis of the young people's stories, it is worth highlighting that both tend to 'freeze' certain aspects of particular interest and to reduce complexity. As I present the analysis in the following chapters, the young people's narratives are chopped up into excerpts that work to corroborate my analytical findings. Some of them appear more prominently and so we get to know their stories and hear their voices. Nevertheless, the stories, experiences and emotions of all 68 interviewees have been included in the reflections and are representative of the patterns that emerged across the interviews. It is also worth mentioning that the insights into the interviewees' worlds are in a way ideal-typical. None of the young people, for example, felt only anger and frustration or dealt with emotions in an exclusively individual or collective way alone. Thus, when I refer to certain experiences, perceptions or interpretations, it is because they illustrate a certain aspect of the analysis particularly well.

Young people in post-crisis Spain

In order to understand the context in which the experiences and emotions of the young people in this book emerged, I take a closer look at the social and economic situation in Spain that has shaped the country in recent years. In the following section, I will briefly elaborate on the economic crisis of

2008 and the resulting Great Recession, and will highlight the consequences they had on work and education for young people, even many years after the crisis.

The economic crisis and the Great Recession

When the economic crisis of 2008 spread throughout the world, it hit Spain particularly hard. A number of external and internal factors led to the collapse of large parts of the Spanish economy and to social bankruptcy. It all started with the bursting of the real estate bubble (which had been inflating for years), which caused property prices to plummet. This affected the financial sector first of all, but also subsequently other parts of the Spanish economy. There was mass unemployment as approximately 3.7 million jobs were lost between 2008 and 2013 – that is, almost one in five jobs were affected (Campos, 2018: 49). Unemployment was skyrocketing, particularly among young people, as we will see later. All these developments ultimately resulted in a sharp decline in public revenue, which in turn caused the public deficit to rise swiftly (Banyuls Llopis and Recio, 2012: 209).

In response to the crisis, the socialist government (PSOE) under José Luis Rodríguez Zapatero initially introduced tax cuts and policies for sustaining expenditure (Banyuls Llopis and Recio, 2012: 208–9). However, as the recession continued to snowball and following growing pressure from the European Union and the International Monetary Fund (IMF), it increasingly relied on stricter austerity policies, which were continued and intensified under the conservative government of Mariano Rajoy, who was elected to power in 2011 (France, 2016: 179). Spain thus adopted what Clarke and Newman (2012) identified as a general trend: instead of identifying the dysfunctional financial system as the core problem, politics refocused its attention on the public budget and expenses by individuals, which were both presented as being far too excessive and as causing debts that could only be reduced by cutting public spending and increasing privatization. This is why Ortiz and Cummins (2012) also speak of a second crisis, brought on by the severe austerity measures that many countries consequently adopted. And indeed, for Spain, the economic crisis quickly transformed into a social one (Navarro, 2013) that led to a great recession in many areas of society. The austerity programme included a 5 per cent reduction in public sector salaries, a freeze on pensions, a sharp drop in the number of people employed by the state, an increase in the retirement age to 67 and the suspension of child benefits (Banyuls Llopis and Recio, 2012: 209–11; France, 2016: 179). In addition, the national government transferred responsibilities for education, social services and health to the Autonomous Regions, thus shifting the financial burden onto their shoulders. As a result, in Madrid, for example, public services such as hospitals, banks and the airport were privatized.

The comprehensive austerity programme had numerous consequences for the population and caused a considerable rise in poverty. The average disposable income in Spain dropped, with the poorest 10 per cent of the population seeing their income fall by 13 per cent per year (France, 2016: 220). Personal bankruptcies increased fivefold compared to pre-crisis levels (France, 2016: 179). Moreover, the measures placed additional pressure on families and kinship networks that often functioned as (the only available) safety nets, whereby private savings were used up to 'provide basic security for the individual in case of financial hardship' (Blossfeld et al, 2011: 19).

Spain also experienced a wave of evictions due to the fact that tenants and homeowners were unable to pay their rent or mortgages. From 2008 onwards, the number of evictions increased steadily and between 2011 and 2016, there continued to be more than 60,000 a year (*La Vanguardia*, 2017).[4] For young people, all these developments had drastic consequences: the labour and housing markets had become increasingly inaccessible to them, precariousness and marginalization were on the rise, it was becoming ever more difficult to convert educational qualifications into paid work, and the difficulties of emancipating from the parental household increased conditions of (semi-)dependency (Moreno Mínguez et al, 2012: 39).

Consequences on the labour market: unemployment and precarious work

Let us first take a closer look at the labour market where the massive swathe of job losses heavily affected the young population. Between 2008 and 2011, 1.5 million jobs occupied by young people disappeared. This meant that 71 per cent of the jobs generally lost in Spain during this period were those held by young people (Fundación 1° de Mayo, 2012: 62). Accordingly, youth unemployment grew from 17 per cent before the economic crisis to 55.5 per cent in 2013, although in some regions that figure was much higher (Eurostat, nd). In early 2013, Andalusia, Extremadura and the Canary Islands recorded rates of between 66 per cent and 70 per cent (Consejo de la Juventud de España, 2013b, 2013c, 2013d), making them the unfortunate frontrunners not only within Spain but also in Europe (France, 2016: 200).

In order to combat high youth unemployment, the government implemented a series of labour market reforms, primarily aimed at further flexibilizing and deregulating employment, and granted employers a number of powers. The Labour Market Reform Act of 2011, for example, expanded the list of grounds for dismissal and gave companies greater freedom to ignore sectoral collective agreements (Banyuls Llopis and Recio, 2012: 211). Another reform in 2011, explicitly aimed at promoting youth employment, included the extension of training contracts up to the age of 30, allowing employers to exceed the two-year limit of temporary contracts and to renew them indefinitely (Banyuls Llopis and Recio, 2012: 211). The conservative government continued along this path after 2012. The Decree-Law 3/ 2012, for example, extended the powers of employers to change working conditions without consulting with workers' representatives and to ignore collective bargaining agreements (Sánchez, 2012: 13). In addition, it allowed them to set up temporary contracts with a compulsory one-year probation period, during which the employee could be dismissed at any time for any reason without compensation. The law also allowed for greater flexibility in the area of apprenticeships and training by extending those contracts to up to three years, thereby forcing young people to remain on training wage rates for even longer (Sánchez, 2012: 13). And also in subsequent reforms (for example, Royal Decree-Laws 4/2013, 8/2014 and 16/2014), flexibility and temporary employment were seen as key tools for combating youth unemployment, which, according to Campos (2018: 55), 'have led to a rapid devaluation of the costs of youth labour … [as] young people's right to employment stability has been sacrificed and contractual arrangements have been created that worsen their working conditions'.

So both the economic crisis and the policies to contain it contributed to a situation of structural precarity for young people in Spain. Temporary contracts were one of the most common forms of employment available to them, especially when entering the labour market (García López, 2011). And these contracts were also the first ones to be terminated when the crisis hit the country. Yet, as many scholars point out, these problems were neither new nor unique to the 2008 economic crisis (see López Gómez and López Lara, 2012; Campos, 2018). Rather, they were the continuation or intensification of a trend that had already begun in the 1980s, but was less visible in the 2000s due to the boom in construction and tourism. While during Spain's transition to democracy (1975–1982), labour market regulation was strong, with policies protecting permanent employment and strengthening dismissal protection, by the 1990s flexibilization and deregulation were taking hold, additionally reinforced by the country's accession to the European Union. As a result, the Spanish labour market witnessed Europe's strongest fragmentation into groups of people with stable, permanent and often full-time employment, on the one hand, and those with precarious and often atypical working contracts, on the other hand (López Gómez and López Lara, 2012: 17). Already, then, young people were particularly exposed to temporary employment. In 2004, about seven out of ten young people aged between 15 and 24 had a temporary contract, leaving those looking for their first job in a particularly precarious situation in terms of social protection and employment (López Gómez and López Lara, 2012: 18; France, 2016: 204). The 2008 crisis thus acted like an accelerator and further exacerbated existing structural and intergenerational inequalities from previous decades. All of this was reflected in the rates of poverty and social exclusion, which, even in 2017, affected almost 40 per cent of young people aged between 16 and

29 (Consejo de la Juventud de España, 2017: 16). As a result, some young people saw emigration as a way out. Between 2011 and 2014, the Spanish Youth Council recorded well over 100,000 cases a year of young people deciding to leave Spain (Consejo de la Juventud de España, 2013a, 2014, 2015).[5] Another option on which many pinned their hopes was (further) education and training.

Education and training as a way out? The unfulfilled promise

The accumulation of cultural capital was one of the key ways in which many lower middle-class families, which emerged in the 1980s (that is, during the transition period from Francoism to a parliamentary monarchy), tried to gain a place in the new social order. Social mobility was tied to the meritocratic strategy of educational accumulation and led, among other things, to universities experiencing extensive popularization (López Calle, 2019: 355). Yet, for a long time, the general level of education in Spain was relatively low compared with other countries. With the boom in tourism and real estate around the turn of the millennium, many young people were able to access jobs without necessarily investing in upper secondary or tertiary education. This resulted in Spain having one of the lowest figures of young people in post-16 education within Europe and among Organisation for Economic Co-operation and Development (OECD) countries (France, 2016: 188). However, while scoring relatively low in international terms, the level of education within the country had risen steadily since the transition to democracy and the current generation of young people is described as being the most educated in Spanish history (Moreno Mínguez et al, 2012: 121, 144; Pineda-Herrero et al, 2016). In particular, there has been a significant increase in the number of high school (*bachillerato*) and university graduates, with women in particular achieving higher levels of education (Moreno Mínguez et al, 2012: 119–21). When the crisis hit in 2008, the idea of education and training as an investment with a view to future employment became particularly prominent and many pinned their hopes on it as a way out of unemployment and precarious work (García López, 2011: 15; Colectivo Ioé, 2013: 41f; France, 2016: 188). As a result, the number of young people signing up for vocational education and training had increased from 8 per cent at the end of the 2000s to 28 per cent by 2011, and in 2012 twice as many young people aged between 25 and 34 had completed upper secondary education compared to previous generations (France, 2016: 188–90). Even in 2017, almost ten years after the onset of the crisis, the number of young people under the age of 30 entering university or investing in post-compulsory secondary education continued to rise, reaching a level of 57.1 per cent (Consejo de la Juventud de España, 2017: 3). However, while educational performance was high, the number of young people dropping out of education and training was equally high, placing Spain among the lowest in terms of drop-out rates in Europe at the beginning of the crisis (Moreno Mínguez et al, 2012: 124). Against this background, Moreno Mínguez et al (2012: 144) note that the experiences of young people in the labour market – both those with high levels and low levels of qualifications – were characterized by a structural mismatch between their level of education and the opportunities available to them to find work (see also Herrera Cuesta, 2018). They write that 'both the over-qualification of the most highly educated and the under-qualification of the least educated (that is, young people at the two educational extremes) illustrate this negative lack of matching between training and labour market penetration, which highlights the social vulnerability of this group' (Herrera Cuesta, 2018: 144, author's translation). This mismatch is central to the narratives of the young people in this book, and the perception of education as an unfulfilled promise runs like a thread through their accounts.

For the young people with a high level of education, the mismatch occurred primarily in the form of overqualification. They struggled to capitalize on their studies to find employment in line with their qualifications (Acosta-Ballesteros et al, 2018). In 2017, for instance, almost half of the young people aged between 16 and 29 who had completed higher education were in jobs that required lower qualifications than those they had obtained. And even among the 30–34 year olds, around 40 per cent were still affected by overqualification (Consejo de la Juventud de España, 2017: 10). While even prior to the crisis this trend had made Spain the leader in overqualification within the European Union, after 2008 overeducation turned into a professional trap for many young people (García López, 2011: 8).

For the young people with low levels of education, the mismatch took the form of underqualification. Due to few job opportunities and increasing demands, many entered into a dynamic of accepting precarious jobs with alternating periods of unemployment (Moreno Mínguez et al, 2012: 144). This mismatch was also reflected in the number of young people who were in situations referred to as NEET[6] (not in education, employment or training) (van de Velde, 2016, 2019). Four years after the onset of the crisis, one in five people aged between 16 and 24 and one in three of those aged between 25 and 29 fell into this category (Sánchez, 2012: 11). Especially for young people from less affluent families, the return to further education and training was restricted due to financial limitations. Cebolla-Boado et al (2014: 85, author's translation) therefore argue that crises and subsequent recessions 'not only lead to greater social inequality in the short term by reinforcing the weight of socioeconomic background on the educational attainment of less advantaged students, but may also have an effect on the life chances of individuals in the medium and long term'.

Thus, education and training in Spain had developed in opposite directions in recent years, as a progressive expansion, on the one hand, and a gradual devaluation, on the other hand. 'The traditional equation', as Llopis Goig and Tejerina (2016: 436, author's translation) argue, 'that associates education with affluence – and the opposite: less education with more precariousness – seems to be undergoing profound transformations.' Although education, especially tertiary education, continued to reduce the likelihood of unemployment even after the crisis (Sánchez, 2012: 10; Consejo de la Juventud de España, 2017: 14) and had a positive effect on wages, this was much less the case than it had been for previous generations (Pique et al, 2017: 746). In post-crisis Spain, a higher level of education did not automatically guarantee an easier entry into working life, a longer average duration of contracts (Pique et al, 2017: 741) or protection against financial precariousness altogether (Llopis Goig and Tejerina, 2016: 437). In general, the transition from education into employment took longer and involved entering the labour market through jobs that required a lower level of education than that obtained. Education and training were therefore not necessarily a secure way out of unemployment and precarious work, as we will also see in this book. However, it remained an investment to which many young people turned in order to deal with the long-term impact of the economic crisis.

The structure of the book

This chapter has introduced the general topic of this book. Based on the experiences of young people in post-crisis Spain, we will look at how they have experienced and interpreted the upheavals and ongoing crisis. The focus is on emotions as a link between the structural changes and the young people's experiences. It is assumed that change translates into emotions on an individual and collective level, which can as such be read as indicators of a society in transition.

Chapter 1 introduces the theoretical framework of the book which combines the sociology of emotions with 1) Bourdieu's theory of practice and 2) Goffman's interactional theory in order to see emotions as linking structural conditions to the agency of individuals. The former makes it possible to analyse the changed environment in post-crisis Spain with the metaphor of the game in which the field and its rules have changed, while the young people's ways of seeing and moving in this game have not (yet). Key to understanding the resulting experiences and emotions is the concept of hysteresis that will help us to understand the mismatch between the changed environment and the young people's ways of being and doing. In considering how the young people then interpreted and dealt with emotions of hysteresis, I will use Goffman's notions of frames (1974) and stages (1959), and will combine them with Hochschild's concept of emotion work (1979). They are helpful in showing how people try to explain their experiences of mismatch and use emotion work to adjust. The fact that this does not happen for everyone in the same way and is always dependent on social categories will be captured by the idea of emotions as resources and boundaries. Within a changed and changing environment, emotions can become a (temporary) resource when they help the young people's (re)positioning and their sense of 'placing' (Bourdieu, 2020: 339). At the same time, emotions can turn into boundaries when they are used to mark (symbolic) difference and (re)produce distinction.

Part I delves into the lived experience of hysteresis, that is, feelings of mismatch between the young people's expectations of how their (working) life should be and their actual opportunities on a crisis-ridden labour market. This mismatch was a central structural condition for young people in post-crisis Spain and, as this part demonstrates, translated into a very particular set of emotions: emotions of hysteresis. Chapter 2 starts by highlighting the devaluation of young people's educational capital in the aftermath of the economic crisis and the sense of loss this produced. Young people found that their acquired educational titles did not lead to the expected conversion into economic capital, entitlements and recognition. They felt stuck. Being stuck, as the chapter then shows, assumes different forms and is presented as four types of impasse: being stuck in the provisional job, being stuck between temporary part-time jobs, being stuck in training loops and being stuck to the normative idea of standard employment. Central to both hysteresis and situations of impasse, as we will see in Chapter 3, was the fact that their circumstances produced a very specific 'structure of feeling' (Williams, 1977). Financial hardship produced anxiety over how to cover basic needs without financial dependence from parents. Lost promises about education paying off translated into uncertainty about young people's chances to find work. Many felt they were losing recognition and status, and feared being declassed, which caused frustration and resentment. Finally, lost future prospects produced uncertainty and anxiety as young people did not know what decisions to make about an unknown future. What we will see in this chapter is that change was an embodied experience and the young people's emotional responses were expressions of a way of being and doing that had difficulties fitting into and adapting to the changed circumstances after the crisis.

Part II examines how young people made sense of their emotions of hysteresis and dealt with them in everyday life. Disappointed expectations and crumbling future prospects led the young people to question existing explanatory frameworks and partly replace them with new ones. Key to this process was what I refer to as emotive-cognitive reframing, which entailed cognitive, emotive and bodily forms of emotion work and existed in two forms: individualistic and systemic. Chapter 4 shows that if they resorted to individualistic patterns of explanation, the young people associated uncertainty, anxiety or frustration with their character, biographical events or difficulties in dealing with these emotions. They believed that it was possible to overcome their impasse with their own resources and individual efforts. Emotive-cognitive reframing here meant adapting one's own ideas, expectations and feelings to the changed circumstances. When the young people resorted to systemic frames, as Chapter 5 illustrates, they explained their experiences with the changed circumstances and considered their situation to be a product of economic and political developments. Here, emotive-cognitive reframing had a different function: it was about acknowledging that they felt uncertain, anxious or frustrated and that this was perfectly acceptable. Therefore, they tried not to direct these emotions inwards and against themselves, but outwards and towards the social causes. Frames of systemic failure thus opened up more possibilities for validating frustration and anger (also) with others, resulting in collective spaces for emotion work. These spaces were important as they gave them the opportunity to develop an awareness of shared experiences through encounters with others.

Part III continues with the role of emotions for negotiating place and being placed. It illustrates how young people sometimes drew on particular emotions to maintain or improve their social position, which was (more) difficult under the conditions of change and crisis. This, as Chapter 6 demonstrates, was done for instance by drawing on notions of emotional fulfilment for some types of (worthy) work. Jobs which the young people wanted to do but could not live off were tied to imaginations and idealizations or emotional rewards, joy and fulfilment. At the same time, class habitus was defended by disdain and contempt for the work which they had to do in order to make ends meet. The creation of emotional hierarchies was an important mechanism here, in particular for middle-class youths, through which the job matching their habitus was bound up with emotional fulfilment and the one that did not with frustration. Chapter 7 then shows how referring to anger enabled some of the young people to reject the sense of powerlessness that resulted both from their situations of impasse and their precarious working environments. Anger thus served as a source of empowerment and a mobilizing force for individual or collective action. Yet whether anger helped the young people to communicate where they wished to stand or whether they experienced it as a boundary depended on 1) intersections of class, race and gender, and 2) on whether the anger was supported by a collective or whether it was experienced as an individual emotion that could not be expressed openly or could not be afforded at all.

The conclusion summarizes the main empirical findings and discusses the wider implications. It elaborates on emotions and emotion work of hysteresis and argue that making emotions the object of analysis strengthens Bourdieu's argument that habitus and hysteresis are the interface between individual agency and social structures. In this part I go on to discuss that while we can understand hysteresis in this study as a generation-specific experience, it was structured by emotional stratification along the lines of age, gender, race and social class. I conclude by asking how these insights into hysteresis and emotions can feed into the topic of social change more broadly and beyond the particular case study of young people in post-crisis Spain, highlighting how emotions can be barriers to and catalysts for social change.

1

Emotions, Structure and Agency

In this chapter I introduce the theoretical framework of this book which combines different strands of sociological thinking to explore the link between emotions, structural conditions and individual agency. My understanding of emotions focuses on their social aspects. I therefore see them as emerging *between* people and located in social relationships, but at the same time experienced and processed *in* people (physiologically, cognitively and emotionally) (Burkitt, 2014). Emotions are constitutive of social life; they structure and are structured by the social environment and interactions between people (and objects) (Gordon, 1990; von Scheve, 2009). They are embedded in cultural systems that influence how emotions are conceptualized. As Barbalet (1998: 25–6) argues, we can therefore understand emotions as carriers of social structures and cultural norms that link the individual and society. This understanding of emotions as a social phenomenon forms the basis of this book and combines the social-structural and cultural perspective. While even discrete emotions are shaped, labelled and regulated through culture and its norms and values (Hochschild, 1979), there are, however, general social processes generated through (changing) social structures that are able to elicit certain emotions. Changing relationships in power or social status, for instance, influence how people feel (Kemper, 1978). How these emotions are then named, expressed or recognized is mediated through the cultural context (Wierzbicka, 1999). Finally, bodies, to borrow Skeggs' words (1997: 82), 'are the physical sites' of emotions where social structures and cultural conventions 'come together and are em-bodied and practised'.

Change and emotions

To understand the relationship between (far-reaching) changes and their influence on the emotions of individuals, I draw on Bourdieu's theory of practice and expand on its emotional dimension using concepts developed by Berlant (2011) and Kemper (1978).

A 'feel for the game': habitus, field and change

In the course of his academic career, Bourdieu developed a number of explanatory concepts through which he tried to explain the connection between the individual and society. Using the metaphor of 'the game' to explain the social world (Bourdieu, 2020: 25), he assumed that the various (social) spaces within a society function like playing fields in which people interact according to certain rules and position themselves as best they can. For Bourdieu, fields such as the university, the church, the labour market and the family are to be understood as sites of struggle which are organized around certain interests and where symbolic capital needs to be accumulated (Reed-Danahay, 2005: 11). The structures of the field in which the game takes place are not to be considered as given, but rather as 'the direct result of the successful strategies deployed by field participants in their struggles to use their accumulated capital (*habitus*) to occupy desirable positions within the field' (Hardy 2014, 138, emphasis in original). In order to navigate through the field in the best way possible, the players try to develop a 'feel for the game'. Having a feel for the game means being familiar with the way the game is played and being knowledgeable about its rules and constraints. This, according to Bourdieu, is done through the habitus, which he defined as incorporated historical knowledge that structures thoughts and feelings and guides our actions. It is a system of 'dispositions that are permanent life styles resulting from learning, training and incorporation' (Bourdieu, 2020: 26).

Returning to the metaphor of the game, for Bourdieu (2020: 83–4), 'the essence of a game is to produce the kind of habitus that does not call the game into question and to attract players so profoundly adapted to the game that they never ask questions of the game'. This is achieved through an emotional investment, 'the desire to play, rather than be neutral and remain outside in a state of tranquility and indifference' (Bourdieu, 2020: 85). What he called 'illusio' (Bourdieu, 2020: 83–5) was the belief in and the acceptance of the game and the value of playing it. Investing in social games was therefore for Bourdieu an inherently emotional act and illusio, the very reason why, besides economic and other needs, people keep playing and believing in social games (Bourdieu, 2020: 85).

However, not everyone is able to participate in the game in the same way. It is especially effective for those who can move around the field of play most easily, those who 'feel free in the game because ... [they] understand its needs ... and create its reality' (Bourdieu, 2020: 79–80). This is the case whenever people fit into the environment, into their social position, with their dispositions. Moving through the social field then becomes a self-evident process or, as Bourdieu described it, 'it seemed to go according to plan' (Bourdieu, 2020: 79). In the 'feel for the game' metaphor, the relationship between habitus and field becomes particularly clear, as both need to be in harmony in order for an individual to follow and participate in the game without any problems.

However, the feel for the game is not necessarily something stable and can change. Often, when entering a new field, one must reorient oneself and get a feel for the rules that apply there. People may also feel the need to make adjustments in the same field, namely when it is affected by important upheavals or changes. In such a case, the rules of the field generally change and, with them, the 'structure of possibility' (Bourdieu, 2020: 128) for the individual players. This happens during social transformations, such as those described by Bourdieu (1977) for the Kabyle society in Algeria in the 1960s. But it also applies to situations such as the economic crisis of 2008 in Spain, which brought about far-reaching changes in various fields.

Linking structural change and subjective experience: hysteresis

To link the subjective experience with changes in social structure, Bourdieu used the concept of *hysteresis* (Bourdieu, 1979, 1990, 2000).[1] He adopted this term from the field of natural science, where it had been used in experiments on magnetism to describe 'a *mismatch* between two elements which were previously coordinated, and, second, the possibility of change which is permanent and irreversible' (Hardy, 2010: 133, emphasis in original).

In Bourdieu's use of hysteresis, the mismatch occurs between the habitus of an individual and the social structures around it:[2]

> When the conditions of existence undergo a radical transformation in the space of a generation, the social agents produced by these radically transformed conditions can find themselves out of phase with the objective conditions that come to solicit their profoundly incorporated dispositions. Thus the agents can persist in generating behaviour that was adapted to a different state of affairs and now ends up acting against the grain. (Hardy, 2010: 128–9)

Especially 'when a field undergoes a major crisis and its regularities (even its rules) are profoundly changed', then, Bourdieu argues (2000: 160), 'dispositions are out of line with the field and with the "collective expectations" which are constitutive of its normality'. In such a case, expectations of what is possible are not fulfilled as they no longer correspond to the options available or to the 'structure of possibility' (Bourdieu, 2020: 128) of a particular field. This relationship between expectation and opportunity, according to Bourdieu (2020: 128), is central to our experience of the social world and the way we move therein. It is often part of the everyday process of learning and ageing, in which we compare the ideal situation with reality and in this way develop realistic assessments of our possibilities (Bourdieu, 2020: 134–5).

Yet in times of crisis and major upheavals, such as those experienced by the young people from 2008 onwards, negotiating the relationship between expectations and opportunities may not be as smooth, as the discrepancy between them becomes all too apparent.

Despite the changes, as Bourdieu (2013: 238, author's translation) shows in *Distinction*, 'categories of perception and evaluation are still being applied ... that corresponded to an earlier state of the objective chances of assessment'. This also illustrates the temporal component of hysteresis which Hardy (2014: 128) describes as a 'time lag'. Time is needed to obtain a new feel for the game and adjust the 'fragmented habitus' (Silva, 2016) to the changed conditions of the field. This is because the habitus has a certain inertia, as Bourdieu (2000: 160) argues, and if such changes occur particularly quickly or violently, then adjusting to them might be particularly difficult and time-consuming. Depending on the combinations of capital that are now seen as valuable, some people are able to adapt to the changing conditions more rapidly, while others might have more difficulties in keeping up with the new expectations. For the latter, the time lag of hysteresis is felt particularly strongly or, as Hardy (2014: 135) puts it, 'these people "are stuck" and are aware that this is so'.

While hysteresis is produced at a structural level, it is experienced on a personal level, giving rise to certain forms of emotional responses. In post-crisis Spain the objective and structural condition of hysteresis unfolded against the backdrop of increased scarcity of employment opportunities and job security, where educational goods have progressively lost value and did not necessarily guarantee entry into or progress within the labour market (Moreno Mínguez et al, 2012: 144). I see hysteresis here as a mismatch between incorporated expectations, values and assumptions regarding the young people's opportunities in moving into and through the labour market by means of their accumulated educational capital and the opportunities actually available to them. As a result, many young people found themselves in situations of impasse. That is where hysteresis becomes a subjectively experienced condition. It is the moment where (changing) structural conditions translate as feelings in the young people's everyday life. Hysteresis then feels like being stuck or put on hold.

Trying to adjust and the time in between: the impasse

To describe this time during which the young people felt stuck, I adopt Berlant's concept of the *impasse*. In her book entitled *Cruel Optimism* (2011), she uses this concept to illustrate how people circulate in precariousness. Drawing on readings of film, art and media, she traces the emotional dynamics of the various socioeconomic transformations since the 1980s in the US and Europe, and looks at the ways in which people have been adjusting to them. Arguing that social reality and hence change is first of all felt before it is understood and processed, she sees the impasse as a notion that best captures how people perceive and are able to deal with their everyday life under conditions of increasing precarity. In a general sense, Berlant defines an impasse as:

> a space of time lived without a narrative genre. Adaption to it usually involves a gesture or undramatic action that points to and revises an unresolved situation. ... The impasse is a *cul-de-sac* ... [in which] one keeps moving, but one moves paradoxically in the *same space*. An impasse is a holding station that doesn't hold securely but opens out into anxiety, that dogpaddling around a space whose contours remain obscure. An impasse is decompositional – in the unbound temporality of the stretch of time, it marks a delay that demands activity. The activity can produce impacts and events, but one does not know where they are leading. (Berlant, 2011: 199, emphasis in original)

An impasse is hence a situation initially considered to be temporary or transitional, but which might turn into a long-term condition. It is a situation many people usually pass through in order to get ahead and move on, but this time the movement – the passage – is hindered and delayed indefinitely. According to Berlant, an impasse thus implies movement, in the sense that individuals are moving in order to get closer to someone or something. I would add here that it is not about constant movement, but about certain moments when movements are more likely to happen, such as moving into the labour market or moving out of the parents' home.

An impasse also involves an emotional attachment – an object, idea or person that attracts people in the first place and sets them in motion. This object of motivation and movement is what Berlant (2011: 2) calls the 'good-life fantasies'. These are aspirations, norms and promises of a past to which, she argues, people remain attached, but which no longer seem to be accessible to the majority (if they ever were). These 'means by which people hoard idealizing theories and tableaux about how they and the world "add up to something"' include for her 'particularly upward mobility, job security, political and social equality, and lively, durable intimacy' (Berlant, 2011: 2–3). For her, these fantasies are closely linked to the political promise of social justice and meritocracy, which was made in the aftermath of the Second World War, but which finds ever fewer conditions that allow it to be fulfilled.

Berlant's idea of good-life fantasies as well as her definition of the impasse are wide-ranging and refer to all aspects of everyday life. While she sees the overall political, economic and affective conditions of our present as an impasse, my use of the term will be more limited. For the purposes of this book, I define the impasse as that 'space of time' (Berlant, 2011: 199) in which the hysteresis unfolds and has not (yet) been adjusted to. These are the situations in which young people try to acquire a feel for the game and adjust to the changed conditions or structures of the labour market. The period of time during which they do not manage to do this or manage to do this only to a limited extent then becomes an impasse for them.

Emotional responses to hysteresis and impasse

A range of different feelings such as frustration, anger or a sense of unfairness can emerge when people feel that their place or sense of self is out of line with the particular field they are in. Bourdieu (2000: 160) speaks here about 'a destabilized habitus, torn by contradiction and internal division, generating suffering'. While he points to the emotional consequences of hysteresis, he does not elaborate on them in a more systematic way. This is why I want to bring in Kemper's *A Social Interactional Theory of Emotions* (1978) to help explaining more precisely how emotions are related to changes in structures and individuals' positions within them.[3]

Kemper (2001: 59) was convinced that looking at 'social structural conditions [helps] to explain why specific emotions are either prevalent or likely to arise as the structural conditions either change or continue as before'. He sees emotions as relational, produced and reproduced in interactions and therefore constituted on the basis of power and status (Kemper, 1978: vii). The allocation and interpretation of power and status lead to different emotional responses, which he calls the 'structural emotions' (Kemper, 1978: 50). Depending on our opportunities to acquire and interpret power or status, such emotions emerge when we gain or lose one or both of them. According to his model, we feel guilty when we perceive our amount of power as excessive, secure when we think it is adequate and anxious when it seems insufficient. The same applies to status. We feel ashamed when we perceive our status to be excessive. If we believe that we are entitled to this exact amount, we tend to feel a sense of happiness. Yet, if we experience a loss of it, feelings of depression may arise (Kemper, 1978: 50–70). This classification of the different emotional responses can be broken down much further, depending on whether we attribute the gain or loss of power and status to ourselves, to another person or to a third party. Moreover, it is not only our own status and power allocations that trigger feelings in us, but also those of others (Kemper, 1978: 70).

Kemper also suggests that emotions emerge when we predict changes in status and power relations and anticipate their consequences for us. Expressed in the form of optimism or pessimism, these 'anticipatory emotions' (Kemper, 1978: 72ff) can then be either confirmed or refuted by the 'consequent emotions' that arise from the actual outcome of the changes. In this case, we then feel satisfaction or disappointment (Kemper, 1978: 75).

Still, for all these emotions to occur, Kemper believes that more is needed than the mere existence of differences in power and status relations. For people to actually feel anxious, happy or angry, they must in fact perceive and interpret the changes in distribution of power and status (Kemper, 1981: 337). Yet, when it comes to the question of how people arrive at these interpretations, his explanations remain rather vague.

At this point, let us therefore return to Bourdieu's reflections on the feel for the game. Bourdieu's habitus can explain how and why we interpret certain circumstances in the way we do, since it is the habitus that informs us of what we consider attainable and appropriate for ourselves. Providing us with 'a sense of orientation' and 'a feel for "placing"' (Bourdieu, 2020: 339), the habitus guides our perceptions of whether the position of power/status we inhabit is in line with what we were able to expect. This applies both to what we expect in the present and to what we consider possible for us in the future. A person's confidence or lack thereof, as shaped by past experiences and present circumstances (Kemper, 1978: 72–3), is also expressed in the habitus, which in Bourdieu's view (1990: 5, cited in Reed-Danahay, 2005: 106) is 'nothing but this experience (in its most usual sense) which immediately reveals a hope or an ambition as reasonable or unreasonable, a particular commodity as accessible or inaccessible, a particular action as suitable or unsuitable'. If notions of past entitlements and future prospects become out of balance as a result of far-reaching (structural) changes, such as those that occurred during the 2008 economic crisis, then loss of power and loss of status are both anticipated and experienced in real terms. This explains why in situations of hysteresis – that is, the mismatch between habitus and field – 'negatively' toned feelings of anxiety and depression are (more) likely to arise.

Dealing with emotions: frames and stages

Emotional responses to change do not remain in a vacuum; they are interpreted and dealt with. To analyse how the young people made sense of their experiences in post-crisis Spain, I draw on Goffman's work on *frames* (1974) and *stages* (1959), and Hochschild's (1979) elaboration of these concepts.

Organising and interpreting emotions: frames

In his frame analysis (1974: 10), Goffman assumes that our 'definitions of a situation are built up in accordance with principles of organization which govern events – at least social ones – and our subjective involvement in them'. In his view, experiences are organized by means of frames, which help to classify and give meaning to what we experience and feel. Starting with the question 'What is it that's going on here?' (Goffman, 1974: 8), the individual '"uses" … the frame as a more or less complex *general* (meta-) instruction for understanding' (Willems, 1997: 35, emphasis in original, author's translation). Like a picture frame, the frames define to some extent what is possible or appropriate in a given situation and thus function both as an orientation guide and an indicator of boundaries (Goffman, 1974: 345).

Goffman (1974: 21ff) rejects both the idea that there is only one suitable definition for every situation and the idea that individuals construct the appropriate definition as they wish. Instead, he believes that there is a primary reality that we organize with the help of primary frameworks.[4] In addition, there are a multitude of other frames, some of which are based on or are adjacent to each other. In that sense:

> it is not just that different people might have different definitions of the same situation, but that each participant can be in several complex layers of situational definition at the same time. (The fact that these layers have a structure in relation to one another is one of Goffman's reasons for arguing that they are not simply created by the observer). (Collins, 1988: 58)

Frames help us organize and provide information not only about experience but also about emotions (Hochschild, 1979). They thus provide a set of ideas and expectations as to which feelings are appropriate in a given situation. Hochschild (2003: 97) calls these the feeling rules and describes them as 'social guidelines that direct how we want to try to feel'. They come with certain 'rights and duties [that] set out the proprieties as to the *extent* (one can feel "too" angry or "not angry enough"), the *direction* (one can feel sad when one should feel happy), and the *duration* of a feeling, given the situation against which it is set' (Hochschild, 2003: 97, emphasis in original). To give a concrete example, this means that 'if I interpret a dismissal as a capitalist injustice, the feeling rule associated with this frame says it is legitimate, even expected of me, to feel anger and rage over the dismissal. But if I understand the dismissal as a personal failure, shame, frustration and self-hate follow as legitimate feelings' (Flam, 2002: 131, author's translation).

In other words, when we move between multiple and at times 'quickly changing frames' during the course of the day, as Goffman (1974: 563) argues, we organize and interpret both our experiences and feelings with their help. Bergman Blix and Wettergren (2018) have conceptualized this entwinement of cognitive and emotional processes with their notion of the *emotive-cognitive (judicial) frame*. Developed within a case study on emotions in court, they use the term to demonstrate how legal professionals in their practices, performances and decisions are informed by this frame, which regards emotion and (judicial) objectivity to be opposites. The belief about their work and behaviour being rational structures the judges' and prosecutors' self-perception and language and silences, at the same time, the many different ways in which background emotions and habituated emotion management are essential for and inextricably linked to carrying out cognitive judgements (Bergman Blix and Wettergren, 2018: 163).

So while frames help us constitute and structure cognitive and emotive experiences, framing is the practice by which we use them. It refers to the way in which people apply the frames in everyday life (Willems, 1997: 46f) – a practice, according to Wettergren (2019: 34, emphasis in original), that 'is not merely a process of *learning to feel* but simultaneously *learning to think* in particular ways (and the reverse)'. When carrying out framing, the individual does not always have to be aware of the frames as such. In most cases, behaviour and feelings are adapted to the respective situation in an unconscious and habituated way (Bergman Blix, 2015), as much of this knowledge is internalized through experience, repetition and routine in the process of socialization (Scheer, 2012; Bergman Blix and Wettergren, 2018: 19). It is embodied in the individual's habitus which informs the process of framing. This, however, works only as long as events in everyday life fit with the way(s) they are interpreted. As Bergman Blix and Wettergren (2018: 22) point out, frames 'are taken for granted as long as the interaction that takes place fits with our interpretations' (see also Goffman, 1974: 250). If this is not (or is no longer) the case, people may try to adjust their behaviour and emotions to make them fit again. In doing so, we often engage in what Hochschild (2003: 94) calls *emotion work*, whereby we try 'to change in degree or quality an emotion' by either evoking or suppressing it. So, when we carry out emotion management and work on our deviant emotions (Thoits, 1990), we usually try to change our framing as well. This cognitive technique[5] (Hochschild, 2003: 96) aims to redefine the way we interpret the situation and to give new meaning to our ideas, roles or actions (Flam, 2002: 130).

I would argue that times of upheaval or change – like an economic crisis – can constitute such moments where frames are challenged or even lose their power of interpretation, as they no longer allow people to adequately understand or explain experiences and feelings. In this context, Goffman (1974: 439) speaks of the 'vulnerability of framed experience', which becomes particularly visible when we find 'that no particular frame is immediately applicable, or the frame that … [we] thought was applicable no longer seems to be, or … [we] cannot bind … [ourselves] within the frame that does apparently apply' (Goffman, 1974: 378f, 439).

These frames can then be replaced by alternatives such as those offered, for example, by social movements, religious groups and youth organizations. Flam (2005: 19) has described this process as 'emotional re-framing', whereby actors 're-interpret specific aspects of social reality [and] call for new, obligatory emotions and feeling rules'. For the social movements to which she refers in her text, it means that both the situation and the emotions are redefined. An attempt is made to deconstruct emotions such as fear or shame, anger is re-appropriated and blame is redirected. In this way, social movements try to 'detach individuals from the established institutions, organizations, and cognitive and normative patterns' (Flam, 2005: 31) to get them to participate in and remain part of social mobilization (see also Benford and Snow, 2000; Goodwin et al, 2001; Jasper, 2014).

Taking the cue from Bergman Blix and Wettergren's emotive-cognitive frame and Flam's emotional reframing, I will combine both concepts and will speak of emotive-cognitive reframing when the young people worked both on their way of thinking and feeling to deal with or adjust to hysteresis and situations of impasse. This process implies questioning or even dropping norms and feelings rules – including the sense of rights and duties associated with them – and assuming new or different ones.

Working on and expressing emotions: stages

To think of the spaces in which the young people (re)framed and dealt with their experiences and emotions, it is helpful to use Goffman's stage metaphor (1952; 1959). Goffman used this in his early works to illustrate how, in everyday life, individuals adjust their appearance and self-image for the respective stages in a way which is similar to a theatre play. The front stage was the 'space in which the performance takes place' (2012 [1959]: 100, author's translation), while the backstage provided the space for objects, behaviour, beliefs and feelings that have to be hidden or suppressed on the front stage (Goffman, 2012: 104). In its purest form, the backstage is of individual nature and equivalent to what Goffman (2010: 31) refers to as *personal space*, the 'temporary, situational preserve into whose center the individual moves' and in which the intrusion of others is not desired. As opposed to the backstage as personal space, Goffman also describes situations of collective backstages. He talks, for instance, about a kitchen in the back of a restaurant where waiters can complain about guests or where hierarchies between employee and employer are less strictly followed (Goffman, 2012: 107–9, 112). In both cases, the backstage functions for Goffman (2012: 105–6) as a place of retreat or buffer zone for successfully maintaining the performance on the front stage. Even though Goffman himself hardly considered emotions in his explanations, his backstage can be understood as a space in which emotions that would not be suitable for the performance on the front stage can emerge or be displayed.

Hochschild (1983) later translates this subdivision into real and alienated emotions, whereby the latter are staged and manipulated, usually for a commercial purpose, while the former include the original emotional expressions, those that are not permeated by commodifying logics. Although this distinction is problematic and has been criticized time and again (see, for example, Bogner and Wouters, 1990; Flam, 2002: 203; Tracy, 2005; Neckel, 2013), it nevertheless highlights an important aspect. In some spaces, feeling rules can be perceived as having a particularly strong presence, thus allowing people less freedom to distance themselves from, relax or even escape from such rules. These can be sites relating to work or family, but also entire systems of government (see, for example, Scott, 1990; Yang, 2000). The backstage can thus fulfil the important function of a spatially and temporally confined free space with its own discourse, rules of behaviour and emotions which need to be made invisible in the presence of those in power or the 'order-giving classes' (Collins, 1990: 35).

On that basis, I understand the backstage as a space where feelings, which are not allowed on display on the front stage due to feeling rules or people's positions of power and status, can be made visible. It is thus a place where it is easier to express certain emotions because the feeling rules relevant to the respective situation are temporarily less present or can be momentarily circumvented or revoked. This does not mean that there is a space with and without norms. Both stages are mutually dependent on and in relation to each other; without a front stage, there is no backstage. However, the backstage can be a space that makes it possible to temporarily bypass, ignore or escape the (feeling) rules since relations of power and/or status are not at stake. What makes a space a backstage is therefore linked to issues of power and (social) control, and not necessarily to the question of being in private or public space. The home might be a place where one can let off steam, but it might also be a place where this is unthinkable, for instance, to spare the other household members worries or not to endanger one's own status position (see Blokland et al, 2020).

Yet, additionally and in contrast to Goffman, I do not automatically see the backstage as antithesis or opposite of a person's visible emotions on the front stage. Instead, it might be more fruitful to think of them as a continuum where it is more a matter of supplementing the experiences and emotions that have emerged on the front stage rather than consciously refuting them. Thus, the backstage is not the space of the authentic emotional self in the sense of Hochschild's initial considerations. Rather, it is one part of the self which, according to Collins (1988: 50), is continuously constructed by each and every situation independently of where we are. Emotions on the front stage can therefore be considered to be just as 'real' and constitutive of identity as those on the backstage. Following Tracy (2005: 175), 'emotions and identity are more productively understood as neither real nor fake, but constructed and constrained through various discourses of power'. What follows from this is the fact that which emotions can be made visible on the front stage and which on the backstage varies. This also means that the backstage is dependent on various social factors. Goffman (2012: 113) himself describes how access to the backstage is influenced by positions of class and gender. As an example, he mentions the possibility of separating front and backstage. More affluent social groups, he illustrates, can afford apartments in which there are clearly separated retreats such as bedrooms or bathrooms, a luxury usually denied to poorer social classes. How gender influences the use of the backstage is later highlighted by Hochschild and Machung (1989) in a particularly striking way when they describe how men are more likely than women to use the home as a relaxing backstage. This is because, after finishing their paid work, many women have to take on a second shift in the form of housework and childcare.

This illustrates that not everyone has the same opportunities to express or use emotions and that the same space can be backstage for some, but not for others. In that sense, it links to Bourdieu's habitus as embodiment of positions of class, gender and so on, which, it can be argued, is therefore equally shaping perception of and access to front and backstage. For the young people in this book, this meant that which spaces and activities were seen as backstage was not only a choice of personality, but was also influenced by social position.

In this book, then, I will use Goffman's metaphor of backstage as inspiration to speak of the various spaces the young people used to deal with, express and share their feelings of anxiety, uncertainty and frustration. These were physical spaces into which the young people withdrew to think, let off steam or cry. I will refer to them as *individual* backstages throughout this book. In some cases, they were the personal spaces described by Goffman (2010: 31). Spatially or physically separated, for example, by a bathroom door or a car, the young people were on their own when it came to expressing feelings out of sight. In other cases, they were not necessarily alone. Here, the making of a backstage was not always bound to a specific place, but rather was produced through certain (emotional) practices. Writing a diary has been for some of the young people a way to express their anxieties, frustration or anger, while others found their backstage when moving through space by walking, swimming or taking the bus, and still others consulted experts or care professionals.

The latter shows that apart from physical spaces, there were also social spaces where young people could make visible and address emotions they could not express elsewhere. Here it was important that they were not alone with their experiences and feelings, but could interpret and manage them with and through others. In contrast to the individual backstages, it was not about the individual(istic) process of expressing and working on emotions, but about a collective process that made experiences of empathy and solidarity possible. These social spaces were not always backstages in the stricter sense. Among the people who belonged to them – for instance, fellow unionists or colleagues in a co-working space – there were different social positions and power relations, and thus the need for performances. The separation of front stage and backstage was hence not as clear-cut here. Still, in relation to other places (for example, for some the family and for others the workplace), these social spaces could turn into a backstage-like environment where it was possible to express and share feelings of uncertainty, anxiety and frustration in a way in which it was not possible to do elsewhere. Throughout this book, I will therefore refer to this form of collective backstages as collective spaces for emotion work.

Positioning: emotions as resources and boundaries

The previous section has shown that the way in which people interpret their emotions and the spaces they use to express and deal with them is influenced by relations of power and differences in social positions. Hysteresis, as the dislocation of habitus in times of change, had an impact on the positioning of the young people in post-crisis Spain. It affected their sense of 'placing' (Bourdieu, 2020: 339), the sense of where they stood, relative to others. Now, positioning and repositioning always takes place in relation to other people and in this respect is also a 'game of distinction' (Addison, 2016: 201). In this game, I would argue, distinction is not only produced through bodies, appearance, work practices and leisure activities; it can also be produced through the reference to emotions. Here, emotions can function both as resources and as boundaries. The question therefore arises as to how, in hysteresis and situations of impasse, emotions might or might not become helpful to the young people's (re)positioning and their sense of 'placing' (Bourdieu, 2020: 339) in the face of major change.

Emotions as resources

To consider how emotions might become resources, we could think of them as a form of capital or good, just as Illouz (1997, 2006) does. In her work, she argues that emotional competence has advanced into a new form of social competence, which, particularly in the labour market, can be translated into social or economic advantages such as professional access or promotion opportunities (2015: 97ff). She argues that the idea of emotional intelligence (Goleman, 1995) and the personality tests that are based on it can serve here as primary examples, as they reward a certain 'emotional style' (Illouz, 2015: 98) that best converts emotions into market advantages.[6] Illouz (1997: 55) considers this to be the rise of a new form of habitus, especially of the new middle classes, in which 'their selfhood, their emotional and symbolic style are made forms of competence and resources'. This idea is later reflected in Boltanski's and Chiapello's work on *The New Spirit of Capitalism* (1999) in which they argue that social esteem and social advantages are increasingly being given to those who 'interpret work as the development of their personality … show an authentic self in professional life and make use of all their mental abilities for this purpose' (Neckel, 2005: 422, author's translation).

In a similar vein, Neckel (2005: 427) argues that in flexible capitalism, emotions become a resource, especially for those who manage to use them proactively, that is, who no longer simply deal with their emotions reactively and control them in an 'appropriate' way, but who deliberately evoke them from the ground up. The underlying idea is always to optimize the self and one's emotional experiences while experiencing emotions authentically. Resourcefulness thus arises for those who are believed to experience the socially desirable emotions independently and sincerely and who are able to use them in a purposeful way when competing for social and economic advantages.

For both Illouz and Neckel, the (strategic) use of emotions seems to involve a market logic that permeates almost every aspect of social and economic life from which individuals can hardly escape. This understanding considers emotions as a form of social leverage which, when made profitable, can help in getting ahead. Yet this logic of investment and profit does not always need to be pursued in order for emotions to function as a resource, as scholarships on social movements, (Black) feminism or queer studies show.

In her essay *The Uses of Anger*, Lorde (2007 [1984]) describes how anger can become an important resource for survival and connectedness. Based on her own experiences as a lesbian woman of colour, she illustrates how she came to see anger as a response to racism and a major source of empowerment when she writes: 'I have used it for illumination, laughter, protection, fire in places where there was no light, no food, no sisters, no quarter' (Lorde, 2007: 133). In so doing, Lorde (2007: 127) points out that silenced and ignored anger as well as fear of anger are useless because anger will become a resource only when people acknowledge and express it. Then, she argues, it can be translated into action, which can challenge discriminatory structures. Moreover, anger enables people to connect and create alliances. 'It is in this painful process of this translation [of anger into action]', she writes, 'that we identify who are our allies with whom we have grave differences, and who are our genuine enemies' (Lorde, 2007: 127). Anger can therefore become a collectively unifying resource through which individuals are moved and mobilized.

Similar arguments are put forward by Ahmed (2004) when she describes how grief is appropriated within the queer community in order to negotiate their positioning in the social space. Using the example of activism around AIDS, she shows how their public display of loss has been used to claim a rightful place within the mainstream discourse in which they are often ignored. According to Ahmed, the fact that mourning for queer lives is often not awarded the same status within society manifests itself in many ways: 'for example, when gay or lesbian mourners are not recognised as mourners in hospitals, by families, in law courts' (2004: 155). Activists and representatives of queer communities thus used the public display of grief to draw attention to these forms of marginalization and to demand acknowledgement of their own grief.[7]

Emotions can thus also function as a resource for challenging and (to some extent) breaking free from patterns of power and dominance. As the examples of Lorde's anger and Ahmed's grief illustrate, emotions can become a resource for the respective individuals or social groups at a certain point in time in order for them to make their concerns heard or identities visible. Yet, their emotions do not necessarily have to be recognized and legitimized by the social majority or the dominant group. Black female anger, for instance, might continue to be seen as threatening or inappropriate and may not help these women in turning their anger into other forms of (profitable) capital; however, it can still be resourceful for them if it helps to mobilize energy and encourage people to publicly address issues of racism and sexism.

For the purposes of this book, I therefore do not intend to see emotions (exclusively) as embodied emotional capital or competence, but (also) as a temporary resource that could help the young people to negotiate their social position when being in certain places and around certain people. They drew on emotions in specific situations (for instance, on anxiety to make their suffering visible) or used them for mobilization purposes (for instance, anger in making a stand against rising precarity). As such, they communicated where the young people wished to stand. They served as, what Clark (1990) defines as *place claims*. Yet it is important to bear in mind, as Blokland et al (2016: 13) point out, that in people's attempts to make (place) claims, some of their practices may produce resourceful sites for some, leaving others marginalized and reducing their space of manoeuvre. With regard to emotions, this would mean that if emotions become a resource for some, others may be excluded from this possibility. Thus, emotions can also act as boundaries and allow practices of symbolic boundary drawing.

Emotions as boundaries

Boundaries, as Lamont and Molnár (2002) have shown, can be symbolic and social in nature. Symbolic boundaries, they argue, 'are conceptual distinctions made by social actors to categorize objects, people, practices, and even time and space' (Lamont and Molnár, 2002: 168). These distinctions can include moral classifications such as normal versus deviant, appropriate versus inappropriate, authentic versus inauthentic, or rational versus emotional. With their help, dominant social groups are able to legitimize their own ways of being and doing, and exercise what Bourdieu and Passeron (1970) coined *symbolic violence*. In this way, they can 'impose a specific meaning as legitimate while concealing the power relations that are the basis of its force … translating symbolic distinction into closure' (Lamont and Molnár, 2002: 172). According to Bourdieu (2020: 145), this form of boundary drawing arises through invisible actions and leads to violence, but is not recognized and suffered as such, since it is unclear who the agent of the violence is and of what the act of violence consists. When symbolic boundaries enjoy general acceptance, they can result in institutionalized social differences (Lamont and Molnár, 2002: 168). These social boundaries such as class, gender or race are 'manifested in unequal access to and unequal distribution of resources (material and nonmaterial) and social opportunities' (Lamont and Molnár, 2002: 168) and can translate into various forms of segregation and exclusion.

With regard to emotions, boundaries, as Lamont and Molnár (2002: 168) write, can both be the object of feeling and generate feeling. By drawing boundaries between inner and outer groups, for example, feelings of belonging, commonality and group membership can arise. However, emotions themselves can, I argue, also be used to draw boundaries. Here I adopt Ahmed's line of thinking (2004, 2010), which shows in great detail that emotions can contribute to creating, maintaining and reinforcing boundaries. She demonstrates how emotions can be involved in separating individuals and social groups from each other and marking them as different (see also Margies, 2022). In this way, boundaries are formed when people or objects become associated with certain emotions. This 'stickiness' (Ahmed, 2004: 15, 89ff), as she calls it, involves the construction of one group in contrast to another. This 'other' is assigned certain attributes which make them 'fearsome', 'hateful' or 'loveable'. When people (or objects) get stuck together, boundaries are drawn between those who/which get bound up with a particular emotion and those who/which do not. She shows, for instance, how fear draws boundaries between those who feel it and those who supposedly cause it. Individuals or certain groups such as refugees or Black people are constructed as fearsome and associated with potential danger. This experienced vulnerability can lead to real (spatial) constraints such as the restriction of one's own mobility by avoiding public places or dark streets. It can also restrict the mobility of others by closing borders or imposing visa restrictions for certain countries (Ahmed, 2010: 69). In distinguishing between who is considered a danger in this context and who is allowed to feel fear, we also decide who can be considered a 'legitimate object of emotion' (Ahmed, 2010: 191). Being seen as the legitimate object of emotion then comes with the entitlement to be affected in a certain way.

Emotion might then be understood by some as a form of property that is only available to certain people.

In a similar way, Pernau (2014) shows how emotions can be used to construct difference and hierarchize people. She illustrates how the division between 'civilized' and 'barbaric' feelings was produced as an effective narrative to justify colonial superiority in the 18th and 19th centuries. Pernau (2014: 231, 233) points out that a certain way of dealing with emotions – in this case, their moderate expression and the control of passions – was ascribed to the idea of civility and civilization. As a result, emotions have been used to draw both societal and racial boundaries in which people and states have been hierarchized (Pernau, 2014: 231, 247, 251ff).

These distinctions based on emotions also have a direct impact on the value(s) attributed to people. 'This affective differentiation', Ahmed argues, 'is the basis of an essentially moral economy in which moral distinctions of worth are also social distinctions of value' (Ahmed, 2010: 34; see also Skeggs, 2004, 2014). The construction of emotional women and rational men is a prime example of the way in which emotional hierarchies go hand in hand with the value of personhood (Federici, 1975; Heller, 1979; Walkerdine, 1988; Jónasdóttir, 1991; Lupton, 1998; Shields, 2002). In this gendered form of boundary drawing, femininity is ascribed to emotionality. Yet, being emotional does not necessarily imply being affected by all types of emotions. As Mayer (2009) points out, women are more often considered emotional, whereas men are more often regarded as angry or aggressive. She concludes that 'to be "emotional" does not mean having many or intense emotions, just as to be "rational" does not mean having many (or only) thoughts' (Mayer, 2009: 115). It is more about constructing a certain form of being emotional, which is used as a means to demarcate and devalue. A reference to being emotional, then, was not only a way of attributing female characteristics to someone, but also a way of devaluing a certain behaviour or action. This social construction of emotional difference as characteristics inscribed in female bodies thus served to naturalize existing power relations and economic inequalities. Referring to emotions as a way of marking (symbolic) difference or distinction can hence contribute to the maintenance of institutionalized social differences – in other words, social boundaries of class, gender, race or territorial inequalities. Symbolic boundary drawing with and through emotions may therefore contribute to the way in which people can participate in the struggles for desirable positions.

Conclusion

The overall theoretical framework developed throughout this chapter now enables us to see the stories of the young people in this study as experiences of embodied change in which their emotions can tell us something about the (changing) structural conditions in which they were embedded. Bourdieu's concept of hysteresis will help us understand why the young people talked about being stuck, not able to navigate within the labour market as they expected or hoped for, and what types of emotions resulted from this structural condition. With Goffman's frame analysis and Hochschild's emotion approach, we will see that dealing with change meant for the young people, first of all, making sense of what was going on by drawing on common frames of explanation or looking for new ones. This process of understanding and dealing involved not only cognitive but also emotion work. Finally, emotions played an important role in the young people's (re)positioning and their sense of 'placing' (Bourdieu, 2020: 339) in the face of change and under conditions of job scarcity, structural precarity and the devaluation of educational titles. Conceptualizing emotions as resources and boundaries will allow us to see how emotions were used to communicate where the young people wished to stand, for whom this was possible and for whom it was not.

PART I

Feeling Hysteresis

2

Feeling Stuck: The Impasse

This chapter examines how the young people perceived the structural mismatch between level of education and possibilities to find work in their everyday life – a central structural condition for young people in post-crisis Spain. The first section discusses how they imagined the customary way of getting into and ahead within the labour market by means of educational capital. I will demonstrate how the young people described the 'feel for the game' or knowledge of how this transition was supposed to go as something that had been guiding their actions and had been communicated to them throughout their socialization process by their families and the wider society. It was based on the belief that educational capital was crucial for maintaining or improving one's social position and was linked to ideas of meritocracy. The second section then illustrates how this general structural condition, in which converting educational capital into positions or advantages within the labour market was increasingly difficult, produced four types of impasse and perceptions of feeling stuck.

The devaluation of education and a sense of loss

'We see our parents as a point of reference, and my parents are doctors and have always told me "Well, you study, do the career because that's it", no? You finish your degree, you get a job, end of story.' (Joaquín, 26)

'The idea they have here in Spain is that you get prepared first and then you work when you are 30, that is more or less the idea they have ... first get ready, finish the ESO, finish the postgraduate course, finish the university degree and then you work.' (Jorge, 26)

In the minds of the young people I interviewed, gaining access to the labour market was linked to education and to accruing educational qualifications and certificates. Their narratives revealed how they felt people ought to gain employment or opportunities to move up the career ladder. As we can see in Joaquín's and Jorge's statements, they had a good understanding or 'practical knowledge' (Bourdieu, 2020: 80) of how this transition would go. After completing secondary education (*educación secundaria obligatoria* (ESO)) and thereby obtaining the general compulsory level of schooling, the 'right' thing to do, in their opinion, was to continue with education either by opting for vocational training (*formación profesional*) or by obtaining the high school leavers' baccalaureate certificate (*bachillerato*) followed by a university degree. Their words also reflect how following this educational path was seen not only as necessary but also as sufficient. They believed that by following the logic of capital accumulation, social reproduction and social mobility would follow. This discourse was either transmitted as (embodied) historical knowledge through the family. This is evident in Joaquín's case, where his historical knowledge guided his choice to study – a choice which seemed to be 'instinctive' and reveals a certain familiarity with the idea that social positions could be reproduced by accruing cultural capital. Jorge's case shows how the discourse of education could also be introduced by other institutions than the family, for instance, by the state (the school, the job centre, etc.), where it was about learning what the 'right' way of gaining access to the labour market meant or should imply.

Joaquín and Jorge reproduced the discourse of education, but their words also reveal that they somehow did not feel included in it. The 'traditional equation that associates education and affluence – and the opposite: less education with more precariousness' (Llopis Goig and Tejerina, 2016: 436, author's translation) embedded in this discourse did not reflect the experiences the young people in my study made:

'The truth is that it is important to have a good education and preparation, but the truth is that it doesn't guarantee you anything; the way things are these days, it doesn't guarantee you anything either because as you will know better than I do, now you are preparing, for example, for a career, for which you have to do a doctorate or a master's degree, and the master's degree is already basic, if you don't have the master's degree you have nothing.' (Mateo, 29)

'I mean, my flatmate, who speaks seven languages, should really be earning … Come on, and with a degree and with courses, with a lot of training, with a lot of languages … And nothing. And nothing, I mean, working in a hotel, I mean, it's not…' (Gaia, 24)

Felipe: Because of the situation we've had to live through, in a way, I'm always worried … I mean, my generation, the people around me, we've completed a degree, we've trained as much as we could, we've done a master's degree, we've done a hundred billion courses with the hope or the instinctive feeling that we would do something that, in the end, is obviously work, but that would make us feel valued and that we would enjoy as much as possible. Then, when I finished my degree, the world was infinitely hostile (laughs) and of course, at the beginning, when I finished my degree, in fact, I went on a sabbatical for a year to London to make a living, to work in a Starbucks or wherever I could, thinking 'Yeah, I'm going to conquer the world'. I had finished my degree when I was 21 because I was born in November and my degree lasted four years instead of five. I mean, I finished super early, like, I thought companies were going to kill each other over me (laughs).

Nina: (laughs) And they didn't?

Felipe: They didn't do that at all (laughs). They literally didn't do that at all. And as I said, it was very hostile … so I was getting more and more worried about the world of work, more than I had expected. So yes, I consider myself an ambitious person and I would like to at least receive in the future what I deserve.

It became apparent in the discussions that the young people all felt that something had changed for their generation. They talked about how they and people in their social environment had invested in education, often extensively, but now had the impression that much of their effort was not paying off. They no longer felt that the fact that they had obtained a university degree, acquired several language skills or done extra training would guarantee them access to the world of work. Although they were convinced that they had an understanding of what was needed to enter and get ahead in the labour market, they felt that this no longer matched the circumstances in post-crisis Spain. Throughout their socialization process, Mateo, Gaia and Felipe incorporated the idea that social reproduction and social mobility could be achieved by investing in education and accumulating cultural capital. This embodied and habituated knowledge shaped and influenced their choices. As Felipe noted, it was an 'instinctive feeling' that made him (and his generation) train as much as they could and take 'a hundred billion courses'.

The habitus also orients future expectations and our sense of entitlement. Gaia, for instance, assumed that someone as highly qualified as her flatmate would have no real difficulty finding a job that matched his level of education, both in terms of content and salary. Similarly, Felipe expected to find a professional world in which potential employers would be desperate to recruit him and which would enable him to obtain social recognition. He had invested a lot, had left his village to study in Madrid and had demonstrated an ambitious and proactive attitude, expecting that his efforts would pay off and that he would 'at least receive in the future what I deserve'. Felipe's statement reveals a strong sense of disappointment that emerged when his expectation in the form of a proud feeling that companies would be competing over him turned into bewilderment to such an extent that he actually felt hostility ('the world was infinitely hostile') (see also Kemper, 1978: 75). López Calle (2012: 184) notes that this 'meritocratic system imposed by the labour market as the central institution for integration and regulation of social relations implies ... [the expectation] that those who are more qualified; those who are less demanding; and those who work more, get better jobs'. This included the belief that work allowed people to earn a living and, in the long run, to become independent from the parental home or state institutions. However, these collective expectations were unfulfilled because they no longer corresponded to the options and circumstances that the young people faced in the aftermath of the crisis.

Even though prior to the crisis not all young people had the same opportunities to enter the labour market, and access to education and cultural capital was dependent on social categories of class, gender and race (see, for example, Bernardi and Requena Díez de Revenga, 2010), all of the interviewees reported that something had changed in the way in which the labour market worked for them. In particular, the older ones talked about how they felt that the familiarity with which they were able to navigate the labour market prior to the crisis appeared to be lost, at least in part:

> 'I remember 15 years ago, my friends who had professions more or less ... people who were doctors, who were lawyers ... never had any problems in terms of work and these days everyone has problems. I have a friend who is a doctor, for example, and the contracts have become very precarious, so they have to constantly renew them and they never have the security of knowing that they are going to be able to stay ... And many are like me, accepting jobs lasting two months, six months, or combining jobs.' (Dario, 35)

Dario's words reveal how he and people of his age felt that what was once a matter of course for them was no longer possible today. While at the beginning of their professional career they had no problems practising in their field, especially with higher educational qualifications, and were guaranteed certain material security, after the Great Recession, there was very little of this left. The 'feel for the game' (Bourdieu, 2020: 78) – that is, the feeling of how one will be able to move within the field in the present as well as in the future based on past experiences and habituated knowledge – was being increasingly replaced by the feeling of being out of place.

The impression that young people and their ways of being and doing were no longer in line with the game and its rules was not only a vague feeling, but was also directly related to changes at the social level. Although (higher) education reduced the risk of becoming unemployed, it did not automatically mean protection against precariousness (Sánchez, 2012: 10; Llopis Goig and Tejerina, 2016: 437; Consejo de la Juventud de España, 2017: 14). The transition from education to employment generally took longer and for many it meant getting into the labour market through jobs that required a lower level of education than the one they had attained. Trajectories similar to those of Natalia and Belén could therefore be identified in the vast majority of the interviews:

'I've been a receptionist, call centre agent, clothing designer, community manager, everything (laughs), shop assistant at El Corte Inglés.' (Natalia, 30)

'I started working when I was 18, wrapping gifts in a perfume shop, I had a temporary contract ... Then I became a promoter ... For example, at Carrefour I was promoting chocolates, I was promoting razor blades ... Well, anything that could be promoted, I went on weekends to promote it in the shopping malls (laughs). Then I started working taking care of children ... well, the usual thing, without a contract, without anything, being paid in black [under the table] and earning a pittance per hour. Then I found work at an agricultural company; I had to make all the PowerPoint presentations and Excel spreadsheets for all the pea seeds they sold, the sunflower seeds they sold ... Anyway, a super-precarious contract, all paid in black and all wrong. And then I found a job, a job with a contract that seemed like a very good job. It was at a children's leisure centre, a ball park ... I worked there for three years, and in November they fired me .... And now, nothing, I'm taking care of some children ... in an illegal way too, charging €8 an hour until I find something else.' (Belén, 26)

While prior to the crisis, casual and short-term work had primarily been an everyday reality for students and young people with low levels of education and training, in its aftermath the most common jobs available to young people from the middle and working classes with relatively high levels of training like Natalia and Belén were also characterized by atypical employment contracts and precarious working conditions and required lower qualifications than applicants typically had. Overqualification, as we saw in Chapter 1, was one side of the structural mismatch between the level of education and the possibilities to enter the labour market that characterized young people's experiences in post-crisis Spain. It could have a considerable impact on their professional career and could well turn into a form of trap (Acosta-Ballesteros et al, 2018). As the examples of Natalia and Belén show, young people who had an educational mismatch in their first job were far more likely to end up in positions where they were again overqualified in subsequent jobs (Acosta-Ballesteros et al, 2018: 135). The exchange value of education and its potential for being converted into gainful employment and economic capital had thus decreased significantly. While ever higher levels of education had to be achieved and demonstrated in order for candidates to keep pace, the value of their qualifications simultaneously fell.

The situation where people experienced that their investments in education were worth far less than they had assumed was accompanied by a sense of loss. This included, first and foremost, material loss. As we have seen in the Introduction, high levels of youth unemployment and structural precariousness caused social exclusion and poverty among young people to remain at high levels until well after 2008 (Consejo de la Juventud de España, 2017: 16). Even for those who were in work, employment did not necessarily mean financial independence. The structural precariousness that affected young people regardless of their level of education further intensified after 2008 and led, among other things, to a significant reduction in the average salary for those under 35 (Pineda Herrero et al, 2016: 152–3; Pique et al, 2017: 744). Spain thus ranked fourth in the European Union in terms of highest number of workers at risk of social exclusion (López Calle, 2019: 356).

The experience of material loss was therefore particularly painful for those young people who had to give up possessions and freedoms that they had already acquired. This was especially true for working-class young people, as López Calle (2019: 355–6) notes, who, for example, had bought cars and apartments on credit by starting work early and now had to hand them over to the banks. But it also affected young people of all social classes who had already left their parents' homes and had to return to them or find accommodation elsewhere. This was the case for Dario, who, after being dismissed as an independent contractor working for the local authority, was not entitled to unemployment benefit and was forced to give up his apartment. In order to avoid returning to his parents who lived in a region in the south of Spain where up to 66 per cent of young people were unemployed, he stayed with a friend while he spent a whole year searching for a job and helped out in his grocery store in return:

'I actually spent a whole year out of work. In addition, I didn't receive any benefits in Malaga as self-employed people were not entitled to unemployment benefit. The only thing I had was the money I had saved, so that year was quite difficult for me ... Well, I ... (laughs), I stayed at [my friend's] house. He offered me everything and I helped out in the store and stuff, but I didn't ... I didn't really work.' (Dario, 35)

In addition to experiencing material loss, the young people also talked about cases of immaterial loss. These included the loss of promises, entitlements and future prospects. Such experiences of immaterial loss are characteristic of hysteresis as, in the time in which habitus and field diverge, 'old' categories of perception and evaluation continue to serve as guides, even though they have at least temporarily lost value or validity (Bourdieu, 2013: 238). The preceding quotations from young people already make this very clear. They witnessed the promise that education and hard work would bring them employment and success being broken before their very eyes. The idea that education enables people to maintain or improve their social position and the notion that work allows people to gain financial independence from institutions such as the family or the state turned out to be a farce for many of them. The promises of upward mobility and job security instead turned out to be what Berlant (2011: 2) describes as 'good-life fantasies' – those promises and assurances of the past that people were attracted by and pinned their hopes on and that were fundamental for them in investing in game playing. Yet following the Great Recession of 2008, these fantasies, she argues, have dissolved and are increasingly out of reach for a large part of the population (Berlant, 2011: 3). López Calle (2019: 354, author's translation) argues that for Spain, this includes 'the failure of the project of forming a developed middle-class country and the very failure of the country as a project', which saw itself as a global economic player after joining the European Union and the G-8 states.

The loss of promises also included the loss of entitlements that had been taken for granted. Central to this was the desire for the recognition to which one ought to be entitled based on one's achievements, education and social position, as the discussion with Felipe has already shown ('we would do something that, in the end, is obviously work, but that would make us feel valued and that we would enjoy as much as possible'). Many expected work that required substantial investment in education to be a source of social recognition and to enable the construction of a personal identity. With work being one of the central elements of social recognition in contemporary society (Holtgrewe et al, 2000; Sennett, 2003, 2008), its existence or loss can have a major impact on a person's sense of alienation and lack of acknowledgement or on the likelihood of them feeling appreciated. The feeling of loss therefore emerged as a result of the normative expectation of experiencing recognition through work that was taken for granted but was not fulfilled or only partially fulfilled, as the discussions with Nuria and Vidal illustrate:

'There are two frustrations: one is what Natalia is saying, that it is difficult, they make us tread a difficult path and a lot of the time they do not value us or pay us what they actually should.' (Nuria, 28)

'I was making €900 a month … It was enough for me to make ends meet but that's it, not much more, and I spent a lot of my savings, I said: "Hey, this can't go on. I need a job where I feel better paid"; because I felt valued but I just lacked the remuneration corresponding to something that could have future prospects.' (Vidal, 25)

These excerpts show that not only was work perceived as being increasingly precarious, but so too were the chances for recognition. One way in which Nuria and Vidal measured this was their level of income. For them, it reflected both the appreciation of their professional field and the appreciation of their performance at work and of them as a person. Yet as wages declined considerably over the course of the Great Recession, it had become more difficult to use money as a symbol of recognition (Zelizer, 1994; Honneth, 2013: 23).

Finally, many young people reported a sense of loss of future prospects. As can be seen in Vidal's statement, this was often linked to the loss of financial esteem. The concern expressed by the majority was that, despite all their efforts and investments in education, they would continue to be dependent on family or state support in the future and would have little chance of being able to leave the parental home:

'I would like to become independent in the short term, but of course, if I had been asked five or six years ago "How do you see yourself in five years' time?", I would have said "independent", so I can't say "in 10 years' time I see myself as being independent", because maybe it'll be 10 years, maybe it'll be 15 years or maybe I'll be living with my parents all my life (laughs). I can't know, the future is very uncertain right now. I could tell you how I'd like to see myself, that I'd like to see myself be independent in about five years' time.' (Belén, 26)

'Let's see, I'm fine at my parents' house, but I'd like to live alone again, you know? But the way things are in Madrid right now, I couldn't, you know? So how can I do it? Even with a salary … Where am I going to live? It's kind of like a feeling of complete uncertainty, complete and utter uncertainty.' (Alberta, 27)

Their aspirations for the future, which Belén and Alberta had linked to entering the world of work and advancing in it, seemed to be beyond their reach. Instead of a sense of confidence about their personal and professional development, it was 'complete and utter uncertainty' that determined their outlook for the near and distant future, about which they felt unable to make any assumptions. While Crespo and Serrano (2001) show that in 2001 some young people regarded job instability as providing personal freedom allowing them to be mobile, this form of discourse was almost completely absent among the young people in my study. Even those who had high levels of professional skills and social support saw little scope for treating instability as a personal advantage, as the existence of a ready supply of short-term employment, which made it possible to move between jobs and cities in 2001, had largely disappeared in the wake of the crisis (France, 2016: 204). So what had previously allowed for personal mobility was now instead resembling a dead end.

The four types of impasse

It takes time before the habitus incorporates the changes and is transformed through the new field structures. To master the new rules of the game, practices, attitudes and expectations may need to be adjusted. In order to move into desirable field positions, people first need to grasp what dispositions are now seen as valuable and enable such movement. There is thus always a time lag in conditions of hysteresis (Hardy, 2010: 131). For many of the young people in this book, this time (delay) felt as if their lives were on hold. Not only did they need time to figure out how to cope with the changed conditions, they also found that initial attempts to adjust by accumulating even more educational capital did not actually improve their situation. The period in which the hysteresis unfolded became an impasse for many of them (Berlant, 2011). In my study, four different types of impasse emerged that were linked to their situation on the labour market and that made them feel stuck.

Being stuck in the provisional job

The impasse of being stuck in a provisional job occurred when young people stayed (or had to stay) in employment in which they only wanted to be temporarily. They expected this job to last a short period of time either as a transitory solution or as a bridge to (re-)entry. The former was the case when, for example, someone was initially unable to find employment in the area in which they had completed their training and, in order to secure a livelihood, accepted a job in another field. Typically, this job required fewer or lower qualifications than the person had actually obtained. This was also the case for the bridge to (re-)entry. This was either a job that the young people considered an initial short-term post en route to the labour market (for example, part-time jobs during studies or seasonal work in the summer) or a job that did not necessarily correspond to the person's own qualifications, but allowed them to re-enter working life after a period of unemployment or following maternity leave. What both situations had in common was the expectation that it was for a short time until a job matching the person's own qualifications and habitus was found. While people continued to look for suitable employment in the beginning, over time they realized that it was much more difficult than they had initially imagined. What was initially considered to be only provisional turned out to be more of a constant. After a few years of searching without success, most young people resigned themselves to the fact that they would not find anything and stopped looking.

This was the case for Mateo (29). At the age of 17, he started working for a subcontractor of the state railway company in a temporary post as a ticket office assistant. While completing high school and later his vocational training course in image production (in which he obtained the advanced technical college entrance qualification), he spent his weekends and holidays advising customers, selling tickets and taking care of any issues that arose: "I am sort of like the person in charge of the station." What started as a source of additional income turned into a professional dead end over the next ten years:

'It started out as an adventure, as it does for many people I guess: "Well, I'm going to earn a tiny bit of money" and meanwhile you continue your training because you want to work in your field one day. Well, you keep saying to yourself "this is temporary, this is temporary" but in the end you stay because of how the work situation is here.' (Mateo, 29)

By that time, Mateo had already largely abandoned the idea of working in his field. Not only was he not "lucky enough to be in the right place at the right time", but his internships at a television company had made him realize that he was always welcome as an unpaid intern, but that there were no actual professional job opportunities, not even if he took further (private and expensive) training courses. Finding a job in the midst of the economic crisis was difficult, and working conditions elsewhere were usually fairly "similar or even worse". The fear of being worse off after a job change – that is, with significantly more work but a much lower salary – led Mateo to stay at the railway company. So he kept an eye out within the company and applied for jobs that would offer him some future prospects: a salary of more than €500 a month and ideally working hours that did not constantly fall on weekends and holidays. Adopting a proactive approach, he spoke with his superiors, inquired about possibilities to contact the Human Resources department and submitted applications again and again. He was stopped in his tracks when he was referred to the company's internal policy, which clearly stated that any requests to move must be addressed to an employee's direct line manager, who will then forward it to the next level until it finally reaches the office responsible, which will then get in touch. No one has ever gotten back to him since then.

At the same time, Mateo saw numerous new employees 'passing by'. In order to revive the economy at the peak of the economic crisis, the government implemented a series of economic incentives, including tax reliefs and recruitment subsidies. These enabled companies, for example, to have the state finance their part of social security contributions whenever they hired young people who had been unemployed for a certain amount of time (Gamberoni et al, 2016). What had been introduced as a potential solution to the crisis with good intentions led some companies to undertake some rather 'interesting' practices: contracts were awarded only temporarily, and employees were asked to register as unemployed for a while to then be hired again. These were all practices that made companies eligible for state subsidies. At the railway company, as Mateo and his colleagues saw, job vacancies did not necessarily lead the company to first look internally for suitable or interested candidates, but rather to give preference to new recruits: "The bunch of employees who work on weekends – moreover, many of them young people – don't even get a chance." The feeling of being passed over crept in. Despite their experience and training, Mateo and his colleagues did not feel that they were being taken into account and hence felt overlooked.

A field of tension opened up. On the one hand, for Mateo, education, experience and length of service were resources that were supposed to help him get ahead. The belief in this entitlement was nurtured for years by the discourse of family and school institutions that praised education as the key to advancement and prosperity. On the other hand, he had increasingly experienced that this assumption did not pay off. This raised doubts for him as to whether all the effort he had put into his education was really worth it:

> 'So you ask yourself: "Did I study all those years for this?" It's depressing, it's depressing … It [the certificate] only serves me to have it … placed there in a frame, on a wall, as decoration … In addition, they always tell you as a child: "Study and you will be better off, you will have a better future." Yes, you might but you also have to be lucky enough to be in the right place at the right time.' (Mateo, 29)

Performance, initiative, education and experience – all of these combined still did not seem to provide a guarantee for getting ahead professionally. For Mateo, the supposedly general assumption that the accumulation of educational capital pays off had lost credibility and validity. The path of invest, wait and harvest (Simone and Schilling, 2015) may perhaps exist, but what made it painful for Mateo was the time spent waiting, the uncertainty of whether there would ever be anything to harvest and whether (further) investing was therefore worthwhile.

This was also true for Ricardo (21). When I met him, he had been working as a pizza delivery driver for over three years. Like Mateo, he thought of his job as something temporary. Over time, however, it had become a constant.

Like many Latin and South Americans in the 1990s, Ricardo moved to Spain (Madrid) with his parents when he was a child. After finishing school, he did an apprenticeship to become a mechanic. Through a family contact, he got his first job at a small-scale car repair shop on the outskirts of the city. The pay varied depending on the number of jobs that had been booked in. However, the experience, was short-lived; after approximately four months, the repair shop closed. In order to make ends meet, Ricardo took on a number of short-term jobs as a door-to-door salesman and in a call centre. But at the peak of the crisis in 2012 and 2013, he met with the same fate as around 50 per cent of his generation at that time and found himself unemployed. While he first perceived this situation as liberating and described it as his personal "sabbatical period", after a few months he began to feel increasingly "frustrated", "useless" and trapped in a vicious circle:

> 'You're depressed because you don't do anything. So you need to do something. But since you're depressed, you end up doing nothing, you know? It's a spiral, it's – it totally destroys you.' (Ricardo, 21)

He found the mental consequences particularly hard, even more so than the economic and social consequences:

> 'To be in employment is like – ... it's like a spiritual necessity, you know? To do something, to feel fulfilled, even if you're doing something that you haven't been trained in, at least you're doing something, you're busy. And that's what being unemployed is like. More than – much more than the financial issue, which is important, too, it's about how you feel personally, inside. It's very, very difficult. Well, that was my year of unemployment, very fucked up.' (Ricardo, 21)

After completing several training courses at a youth centre in his neighbourhood and submitting a multitude of applications, Ricardo's year of unemployment finally came to an end when the pizza delivery company to which he had submitted his CV called and hired him for one of its recently opened shops. Since then he has learned to ride a motorbike, seen his temporary contract turned into a permanent one and joined the labour union. While he was happy to have a job that got him back into employment and allowed him to be financially and socially independent, he described a constant underlying feeling of frustration. As with Mateo, this stemmed from the impossibility of turning the accumulated educational capital into economic and symbolic capital. He felt that his training as a mechanic was not of great use to him, that the time had been invested in vain and that the acquired knowledge had already evaporated:

> 'I knew something, damn, I had some experience ... but that doesn't even count anymore ... That pisses me off. I often think of it and say to myself: "These two years of studying electromechanics are two years down the drain" because obviously, if I never work in this field, what was it good for? Nothing!' (Ricardo, 21)

Ricardo and Mateo had both taken on jobs to bridge the gap when they could not find employment in the field in which they had trained and wished to work. Their situation thus mirrored an impasse in which, as Berlant (2011: 199, emphasis in original) notes, 'one keeps moving, but one moves paradoxically in the *same space*'.

Being stuck between temporary part-time jobs

Another type of impasse involved young people being trapped in several temporary part-time jobs that they had to accumulate in order to make ends meet. Given that young people entering the labour market after 2008 saw their salaries decrease substantially, one or two jobs were often not enough to cover their basic needs or to maintain the pre-crisis standards to which they had become accustomed. Temporary work contracts were the main way for young people to get into the labour market regardless of their educational level (García López, 2011: 10) and accounted for almost 65 per cent of all new jobs created for young people at the height of the crisis in 2012 (France, 2016: 204).

One of those affected was Begoña (29), who juggled four different jobs at the same time:

Nina: Tell me a bit more about your work. What are you doing to earn a living?

Begoña: Well, right now I have a job at a school where I do workshops in French from Monday to Friday for one hour. Then I work at a secondary school where I do ... five hours a week, which is on Mondays and Wednesdays, I'm providing school support there. Then I work in a shop on weekends, Fridays, Saturdays and Sundays; and then I work in an association where I ... that is, I have not been hired by the association, it's like volunteer work, but it's paid and I also provide school support there.

During the week, Begoña gave fun and light-hearted lessons to primary school students, introducing them to the basics of the French language. At the secondary school, she provided school support. What was actually intended as content support, where pupils could ask questions about material that they had missed or had not understood, often took the form of emotional support. Whether the issues being raised related to the pupils' families or their social environment, Begoña always had an open ear and tried to help them as much as possible in resolving their issues. On weekends she worked in a clothing store, serving customers at the checkout or folding T-shirts. And only recently, as she added later, she took on more work: organizing a trip across Europe for a group from Brazil. Trying to juggle all of her jobs at once required good organization and a clearly structured schedule. She did not have much of a choice, as she said, since she basically needed "all of them in order to live even modestly". Begoña felt trapped in the midst of different jobs. Financially it was extremely difficult to give up one of them. Then again, the organizational and emotional effort she put into doing justice to all the jobs was big and, in her opinion, kept her from devoting herself more intensively to other activities that might lead to a more stable and better-paid job as a teacher.

Even though Begoña could partly work in the field in which she had been trained, her example reveals a pattern that was similar for many interviewees: one or two part-time jobs provided some basic financial stability, but were usually pure income-generating activities, a necessity that allowed them to pay for basic expenses such as food and accommodation. These jobs often had nothing to do with their training and were generally low-skilled jobs that were intended to be only temporary. At the same time, the young people were trying to gain a foothold in the world of work where their skills and interests lay, but in which they were (still) denied (sufficient) material appreciation. This is what Berlant (2011: 199) describes as the movement undertaken while living the impasse whose outcome is not certain and therefore keeps the person in place rather than allowing him or her to move ahead.

Bélen (26) also shared this feeling of constantly moving while at the same time being fixed in time and space. She had done vocational training in pre-primary education and had several temporary jobs as a nanny, a secretary and an employee at an indoor play centre for children. As none of these allowed her to lead a financially independent life or to move out of her parents' home, she pinned her hopes on the further accumulation of educational capital by starting an undergraduate degree in education and taking additional English classes. Her days were therefore brimming with work and study. As a student, she was doing her internship at a school in the mornings and then in the afternoons she was working as a nanny, after which she was going to English lessons and in the early evening she was attending seminars at the university or studying and preparing for her exams. Although officially registered as unemployed, Belén did not feel like she was out of work. On the contrary, she felt as if she was constantly on her feet from morning till night, always in a rush and with no time to stop:

> 'Then of course, I spend all day doing things outside my house, feeling like I'm never standing still. Of course, the only thing is that at the end of the month you don't have enough money to make ends meet, that's the feeling of standstill you get, that's the one (laughs). That's the feeling of being stopped in your tracks, but then you ask yourself: 'Why can't I have an independent life?' Because I still live with my parents and I'm 26 years old. You can't afford anything, you can't afford anything – English classes? A luxury, because you have to pay for them. The transport pass? A luxury, because you have to pay for it … And that's all, counting the euros to make ends meet.' (Bélen, 26)

In Spanish, the word 'parado' means 'unemployed', but also 'stopped' or 'on hold'. In order to describe how her current situation felt, Belén used both meanings of the word, making clear how paradoxical it felt to her. She was not experiencing a situation where life was on pause without work. She could not afford it, as she said, if she wanted to move forward professionally. Despite being in an almost incessantly turning hamster wheel, she still had the feeling that she was being held up because the financial yield was so small that economic independence and a life outside the parental home seemed to be distant dreams. And even her studies were not progressing as she wanted them to.

Since the reform under the Real Decreto-Ley de Medidas Urgentes de Racionalización del Gasto Público (Royal Decree-Law on urgent measures to rationalize public expenditure in the field of education) of 2012, which was supposed to make the university system more efficient in the light of scarce public funds, tuition fees have risen many times. The price for bachelor's degrees increased between 19 and 32 per cent, and between 50 and 75 per cent[1] for master's programmes. In 2015, students in Spain paid, on average, €1,110 a year for a bachelor's degree and €2,020 a year for a master's degree (CCOO Enseñanza, 2016). As Spain was slipping into the group of European countries where studying is the most expensive and state incentives, such as tax deductions, grants and public scholarships were lacking, this often meant an additional heavy burden on the family budget. Situations like that of Belén – that is, working or receiving unemployment benefit while studying – are therefore the rule rather than the exception. For Belén, however, this situation also resulted in a "vicious circle", as she called it. Her part-time jobs left her little time to study, which meant that she did not progress as much as she wanted to. This meant that she might fail exams from time to time. To be better prepared for exams, she would have to work less. However, financially, she could not afford to do this if she wanted to continue her studies. To make matters worse, the reform of the university system mentioned earlier stipulated that if subjects are repeated due to a failure to attend or pass exams, the respective fees increase successively with each further attempt (Jefatura del Estado, 2012). This increases not only financial pressure but also mental pressure, especially on students like Belén who (have to) reconcile study and work. Justifying failing an exam to yourself and to others, especially those who are paying for your studies and your life, thus becomes (even) more frustrating:

> 'I had been working and studying at the same time, I went to an exam but hadn't spent the same amount of time studying as someone who is not working, so instead of getting a 7 or an 8, I failed. I felt angry but also powerless to say: "I failed the exam because I'm working, but I'm working to pay for my degree because I didn't get a scholarship. I'm chasing my own tail. What do I do? Stop working and study more? But how do I pay for my degree? How do I pay for it?" So, above all I felt anger and frustration when I saw that I failed an exam, that's what I found the most difficult thing to accept ... So it's especially the frustration and anger at not being able to pass and having the feeling of saying: "I can't pass because I have to work and I have to work because I have to pay for my studies." A closed, vicious circle, from which you see no way out.' (Belén, 26)

This experience of failure was particularly painful as her situation might be classified as a personal failure – for example, due to a lack of motivation, laziness or incompetence – even if for Belén it was primarily due to external circumstances. She was certain that if she did not have to work and had more time to study, she would not fail.

Being stuck in training loops

In trying to adjust to hysteresis, many young people decided to acquire further educational capital and got back into the education system, as we saw with Belén. This was the case for both higher education and vocational training. Yet the return to further education and training did not always automatically lead to any improvement in their working life and, for some, it actually resulted in them circulating in the very same 'loops'. This type of impasse was particularly prominent among young people who attended continuing education courses under active labour market policies (ALMPs). These courses were mostly held in organizations or centres commissioned by public authorities[2] and included, among other things, the recovery of qualifications and vocational training, labour market (re)integration and professional retraining. While participants could sign up voluntarily, it was usually a job centre employee or social worker who recommended participation. In cases of unemployment, it could constitute a condition for the payment of social benefits. However, as García López (2011) notes, most of the programmes that young people attended were extremely short. In 2010, for example, 50 per cent of the unemployed in training participated in courses that did not exceed 200 hours and often provided only generic knowledge and a low degree of specialization (García López, 2011: 12). Many of my interviews reflected the results: with few opportunities to find long-term employment, young people with low levels of education were repeatedly sent into (short) training loops with the aim of adding a further qualification to their CV and thus increasing their employability.

Paulina (29), for example, after finishing the first stage of secondary education at the age of 16, did an apprenticeship in hotel and catering management. She then took on some short-term contracts at several cafés and bakeries before she embarked on further training to become a nursery school assistant. Even though she very much enjoyed working with children, it was difficult to find anything more stable than a short-term internship at a kindergarten. "So as not to be stuck in the house" during periods of unemployment, she was eager to attend a training course in cleaning on which she was enrolled by the job centre. When I met her, she was trying to get back into the labour market following maternity leave. At the time, she was also attending another training course in the field of commerce. She explained these various pathways as partly arising from her own interests and partly as a result of the job centre's instructions:

'I trained in hotel management, specifically pastry, because I love baking and from that point on, of course I was working. When I left, I was like "What do I do now? What do I like?" Well, children, so I started as a kindergarten assistant; that was then and now? Nothing. They called me from the cleaning course and I said: "Well, I don't think it's that complicated to clean something but ..." and I started the cleaning course and ... and that's because they've been sending me around. Then, another thing I mentioned was hairdressing, but in the end I got in here [training course on customer service]. So that I wouldn't have to be at home, because that's what suffocates you the most; and if they call from a good place, I'll just leave my training and go, but if they don't, [I will continue with the training] so as not to be bored.' (Paulina, 29)

Paulina's statement illustrates numerous loops with a similar pattern: after an apprenticeship or training course, young people usually completed an internship or one-year training phase often organized through the job centre. Yet they were rarely recruited afterwards and instead fell back into unemployment where the next round of activation measures awaited them. For Paulina, these involved a series of training courses in gender stereotypical service areas such as catering, childcare, cleaning and customer service.[3] The continuous movement that does not allow the individual to move forward, which Berlant (2011: 199) ascribes to the impasse, was particularly evident here. For Paulina, it also meant that she repeatedly failed to break through the same barrier that could make longer-term employment more likely, namely the accumulation of training and experience in one and the same field:

Paulina:	It's just that most ask for two years of experience, three years, I don't know, and it's like … Since I'm just starting to learn this, you're going to ask for two years now, but OK.
Nina:	Sure, you have to start somewhere.
Paulina:	Of course, but if they ask for two years of experience, at what point am I going to start?

While the job centre felt that her recurrent unemployment status was due to the lack of qualifications, Paulina's situation was primarily the result of the profound deregulation of the Spanish labour market. The different labour market reforms, which were introduced, among other things, as emergency measures to combat high (youth) unemployment granted employers a whole series of further powers to continue flexibilizing and deregulating employment (see Introduction). These measures also affected the area of apprenticeships and training, for instance, in terms of probation periods or rates of training wages. The risk, as Sánchez (2012: 13) highlights, was 'that the apprenticeship system can lead to a situation in which young people simply provide a cheap form of labour and … remain for years in unskilled jobs with reduced levels of stability and low wages, without being able to obtain any real and certifiable skills or job specialization'. So even though Paulina enjoyed learning about new fields, she hoped to soon be able to leave this cycle of further training to find a job that would allow her "to have a quiet life, without being so worried about being short of money".

Being stuck to the normative idea of standard employment

While the previous types of impasse were primarily caused by the changing rules of the (labour market) game, the following type was mostly a product of normative ideas about work that had hardly changed at all. These ideas were decisively shaped by the standard employment relationship – paid work as part of a stable and secure position – which from the 1970s onwards was regarded as the social norm and deliberately encouraged by Spanish labour law regulations (Prieto et al, 2009: 58–9). Yet, from 1984 onwards and with Spain's accession to the European Union in 1986, employment became increasingly flexibilized. This split the Spanish labour market into stable, permanent and often full-time employment on the one hand and precarious employment, often with atypical working contracts, on the other hand. The latter has particularly affected women, young people and migrants (López Gómez and López Lara, 2012).

Nevertheless, the idea of 'normal' and 'good' work continued to be associated with standard employment, and for my interviewees' parents' generation, this normative framework had an essential guiding function. The numerous references to parental advice or rebukes[4] in the young people's stories illustrate this aspect:

'We say "normal", which many people in our society, like our mothers, assume is what we have to do to make a living, that's what we call "normal".' (Natalia, 30)

'In general, older people have a much harder time understanding this, it's as if they don't understand it because, of course, they were taught that you have to have a permanent, stable job, forever ... And we want a permanent and stable job, what happens is that we try to look for it through the path or projects that motivate us the most.' (Nuria, 28)

'My relatives tell me that this is not a real job, well ... But who has a fucking permanent job? (laughs). I mean, you're asking me to do something serious, but don't take this the wrong way but they just fired my cousin from the bank (laughs), you know ... who has been working at the bank all his life with bloody security.' (Javier, 35)

'My parents taught me that or I always felt that if I did well with my studies, I would have a permanent job, but it's not the case anymore.' (Joaquín, 26)

Most young people themselves associated 'good' and 'ideal' work with a permanent position.[5] These ideas, however, differed from the actual reality of work. As we saw earlier, not permanent but temporary contracts were their most common forms of employment. There was thus a mismatch between the collective imaginary about 'normal' or 'standard' work and the actual situation on the labour market. Particularly for young people, then, the standard employment relationship can be regarded as a type of good-life-fantasy (Berlant, 2011: 2), which motivated them to invest, but was rarely achieved. As Alonso et al (2017: 172) note, young people were aware that 'this "conventional" past is simultaneously idyllic and unattainable'. At the same time, the idea that accumulating educational capital could increase the chances of achieving a permanent position remained prevalent.

The impasse arose when although, according to the normative idea of work, the young people ought to be entitled to standard employment as they had accumulated high amounts of educational capital, they decided against it. Within my sample, this type of impasse was particularly common among young middle-class people who did not opt for paid employment, but for self-employment, for instance, as freelancers or entrepreneurs. While they were pursuing a 'deviant' form of work, they were not able to free themselves easily from the normative ideas of 'standard' and 'good' work. Rather, these ideas 'stuck' (Ahmed, 2014: 16) to them and involved the expectations of their parents or the wider social environment. We can see this well in Vanesa's case, who had founded a language school with some friends, which they ran as a cooperative. Frustrated by the traditional education system on the one hand and the hierarchical organization of companies on the other, the language school was a way for them to organize work in a different way and to provide education based on their vision. However, Vanesa was far from able to live from the start-up alone, which is why she had two other temporary part-time jobs (one of which was as a sales assistant at an optician's), which meant that she often had to work up to 15 hours a day. Yet she talked about how those in her social environment struggled to understand her. Given her educational capital (university education, languages skills and time spent abroad), they did not feel that she needed to expose herself to such a high workload or to the uncertainty and instability of starting her own business, as her following two statements illustrate:

> 'They say: "Well, get a permanent job and cut the crap" and I'm like "Of course, man, and how do you intend that I do that?" When I was doing 15 hours, they said: "Will this get you somewhere?" Right? So I was like "But I have to carry on" (laughs). [They would say] "Find a permanent job, man, from nine to whatever in an office, some papers, man, you have a degree, alright?" They don't understand you ... Because then you have many people who are like "Ah of course with this type of life you lead, what do you expect? Pff. Just get a job – ah, you're fucked. Of course, you should have done this master's degree and you should have put that on and removed your piercings and tattoos. Look at your cousin, neat as a pin, he earns I don't know how many thousands of euros and you don't".' (Vanesa, 33)

'Of course, there is a part of the family that has certain expectations and this situation is – there is a generation – they don't understand this situation, right? "The crisis I don't know, you should be like your cousin who is working at [the largest electric utility company in Spain] who has a permanent position." … It's the same as this [Vanesa's job at the optician's] but more money and better valued but the atmosphere is the same or the structure is the same. It's a pyramid structure where you have to suck up to the boss … Of course, the previous generation doesn't understand it but obviously you are in a super precarious situation. You don't have any fixed income. What they don't realize is that they [other people at the optician's] don't either, you know? (laughs) What they think is that here they do, but come on, I've seen layoffs here, I've seen layoffs here, you know?' (Vanesa, 33)

While at first glance this type of impasse could be dismissed as being only a perceived one, this explanation would be too short-sighted. It was certainly a more privileged type of impasse, but based on an equally precarious footing. Even though the young freelancers and entrepreneurs in my sample presented their work as a conscious choice, their decision was also influenced by the fact that there were hardly any companies in their field of work that offered permanent positions. As Campos (2018: 52) points out, at the beginning of the crisis alone (2009–11), around 10 per cent of the permanent positions in Spain were destroyed. Young people were therefore often more likely to expect poorly paid internships, short-term work contracts or temporary stand-in positions.[6] Moreover, they criticized the illusion often shared by family members or wider society that permanent employment was a cast-iron guarantee of security and stability. Vanesa, for instance, spoke of how people in her social environment who expressed this idea seemed to ignore that even supposedly secure jobs did not necessarily provide protection against dismissal. The massive job destruction between 2007 and 2013 affected the self-employed and those in paid employment to an equal extent (Campos, 2018: 49). In addition, the labour market reforms carried out in the 1990s and the 2000s, but especially during the course of the crisis specifically promoted the deregulation of employment. As a result, 'the permanent contract [in Spain] has ceased to be synonymous with stability as it has lost its basic characteristics of security and therefore of permanency' (Campos, 2018: 40).

Conclusion

This chapter has analysed the ways in which hysteresis unfolded in the everyday life of young people in post-crisis Spain. Getting into and ahead in the labour market was much more difficult than many had hoped, as it had become more difficult to convert degrees, further training or internships into (good) jobs. The promise that education enabled social reproduction and mobility lost its validity for many. We have seen how the young people's habitus were socialized to believe that accumulating educational qualifications would ease their transition into adulthood and into the labour market. It had guided their choices and shaped their expectations of what they deemed possible and entitlements they deemed appropriate. Yet, applying this practical knowledge in post-crisis Spain proved to be difficult as the 'rules of the game' had significantly changed. Opportunities they believed they had or should have had remained unattainable; social reproduction and social mobility by means of cultural capital seemed threatened. This primarily involved the two forms of institutionalized cultural capital and embodied cultural capital (Bourdieu, 1979). As the institutionalized form of cultural capital was devalued, the young people were disillusioned about the formal prospects that they thought their educational qualifications would provide. Many formal expectations, such as which school-leaving certificate they would need to enter a certain sector, how much they thought they would earn and how many jobs they imagined would be available, were violated, provoking disappointment and frustration. Furthermore, the embodied cultural capital that they had incorporated throughout their socialization process and educational path did not match with reality. This concerned, for instance, the (mis)match between habitus and working environment, as we saw in the case of Begoña, as well as perceptions of fairness and ideas of meritocracy that young people like Belén and Mateo considered to be violated. We therefore saw among the young people, on the one hand, permanent worries and feelings of uncertainty that were bound up with the devaluation of education – that is, institutionalized cultural capital – as well as job scarcity and instability; on the other hand, the sense of loss regarding promises, entitlements and prospects, derived from the embodied cultural capital, led to disappointment.

Against this background, I have identified four types of impasse that hysteresis produced. The young people were stuck in jobs that were intended to be temporary, stuck between several part-time temporary jobs, stuck in training loops or stuck to normative ideas of work and the expectations of others. In that way it became clear that hysteresis was produced at a structural level, but was experienced at an individual level, first and foremost as a feeling of being stuck and as a sense of loss.

3

Emotional Responses

The previous chapter has already shown that doubts, worries and dissatisfaction ran through the young people's narratives. Bourdieu (2000: 160) writes that when major changes occur, such as in times of crises, habitus and field drift apart, a person's way of being and doing gets destabilized and suffers from inner conflict and general insecurity. Garfinkel (1963: 236; 1967: 38) also speaks of feelings of confusion, anxiety and indignation that arise when expectations of the normal are not met or satisfied. Therefore, the mismatch between the environment and a person's own possibility to move therein directly influences their emotional experience. For the young people in this book, the mismatch between what they thought they were trained for and felt entitled to and their actual employment situation was expressed through the feeling that they had lost something compared to previous generations. The aim of this chapter is to illustrate that this sense of loss structured their emotions. The material loss contributed, for example, to fears of declassing (Peugny, 2009) and dependency. Lost, unfulfilled promises translated into disappointment and insecurity. Frustration and a sense of unfairness were often linked to the loss of entitlements. And finally, the loss of future prospects led to feelings of uncertainty and anxiety.

Worries, uncertainty and anxiety

Almost all of the young people in my study were very concerned about work. They felt great uncertainty about how to get out of their impasse despite their proactive efforts and further accumulation of educational capital. A central concern here was their own mental and physical limits. If obtaining decent employment meant accumulating more and more educational capital, some feared that they would not be able to keep up, despite having experience and/or a sound education:

'These days, you not only have to have a Montessori diploma, a Waldorf one is even better. It helps if you are bilingual in English, bilingual in

French, bilingual … and it is like this with everything. And of course, I don't have all of them, I'm sorry, but I don't. My head has a limit (laughs) and I don't want to constantly feel like there's always more, and more, and more, you know? And when you already have a level of studies, it's like never enough, you know, they want even more from you … Uff, for me there comes a moment when you're like: "Stop, Begoña, I need, I need to finally get something rather than just have the qualification for it."' (Begoña, 29)

'But well, it's not easy, because on top of that now, in my area, it seems that you have to do a master's degree to work there, and what they want is young people, with language skills … Well, you go to an interview and if you don't have perfect English, even if you have 16 years of experience.' (Ovidio, 35)

After a period of unemployment, Ovidio realized that in order to get back into his field of work – high-end fashion stores – he would need to fulfil higher requirements, but that he was unable to do so. Higher education and language skills seemed to be more valuable than his 16 years of experience as a sales assistant and store manager. Even though he considered himself perfectly capable of fulfilling this role, he knew that he would struggle to compete with applicants who were both younger and better equipped in terms of educational capital. Similarly, Begoña had the impression of having to do more and more to stay in the game, resulting in her stress of feeling unable to keep up.

The other central concern was linked to financial (in)dependence and the fear of (once again) becoming unemployed:

'I quite often mull over the possibility that I could become unemployed now … That's when I would find myself in a very difficult situation. I hope I don't become unemployed… Work is a worry and has been ever since I started working … especially when you come out of a very long period of unemployment … and you've been frustrated because you haven't been working. After that you start working and you constantly have that worried feeling and keep thinking "I'm going to, I'm going to keep the job, I don't want to lose it".' (Ricardo, 21)

'Of course I'm worried! … Without [a job] you can't … Without [a job], it would be very fucked up. To this day, thank God, I've never been unemployed. I almost was once, but I was lucky. But well, without a job it's very worrying. Then, on top of that, the way the cost of living is going up, things are increasing, while your wages aren't, well, it's getting more and more complicated and more and more worrying.' (Mateo, 29)

'I worry a lot and I'm constantly looking at where I can find work, you know. It's a concern that – and I share it in case someone knows of anything.' (Daria, 22)

'There is the uncertainty that you have to live with because maybe you can get used to it and say "Well, I can live with less money. If I have it, I can spend it, and if I don't have that much, I won't spend it". The problem is the uncertainty that maybe all of a sudden you won't have anything at all, so you have to keep your feet in these other jobs that, well, you want to get out of, but it's like the only foothold you have when you suffer from this instability and this uncertainty.' (Nuria, 28)

Job insecurity translated into constant worries that infiltrated young people's personal lives. Like Ricardo and Daria, many had already experienced unemployment, so the fear of being out of work again and suffering financial difficulties was never far from their minds. The reason why Daria and Ricardo in particular had these concerns was because, as under-25s, they were particularly affected by the lack of state welfare programmes available for young people. The drastic cutbacks in the wake of the economic crisis excluded both from schemes such as the Renta Activa de Inserción (a programme designed to provide benefits to the long-term unemployed over the age of 45) and basic income support (Gille and Klammer, 2017: 48–9).

The feeling of uncertainty reinforced the impasse. Ricardo, Nuria and Natalia all talked about how out of fear of unemployment and financial difficulties, they held on to jobs which they actually wanted to leave and which they had always seen as only a temporary solution. Although they could and did get used to having or spending less money, they found it difficult to adapt to the volatile dynamics of their work situation where they never really knew whether there would be any money at all the following month. In part, they experienced what Sennett (1998: 85) describes as the three kinds of uncertainty that people in flexible capitalism experience when they want to change their work situation. First, they cannot be sure whether changing jobs will really improve their situation or whether it will be more like moving sideways. Second, there is the risk that a change may entail a loss in retrospect. However, Sennett says that it is often quite difficult to assess these risks in advance, especially if the rules of the labour market have partly changed, as was the case with the economic crisis. Third, income trends are not always predictable. Sennett (1998: 86) provides statistics from the US in the 1980s, which show that if people changed jobs, their salary was more likely to fall rather than to increase. Many of the young people in this book who were looking for a better job faced the same risk. They suspected that conditions elsewhere were often similar or even worse, and their search was therefore always accompanied by the question: "Damn, what if you change and it gets worse?" (Mateo, 29).

Both the financial concern and the concern about their own physical and mental limits thus created a general uncertainty as to how the 'structure of possibility' (Bourdieu, 2020: 128) would develop and what chances they would have to participate in it. The uncertainty related not only to the present, but also to their expectations for the future. Uncertainty prevailed over whether or how it would be possible to recover and fulfil certain expectations or whether these had to be largely adjusted or dropped forever:

> 'The constant feeling I have every day is one of complete and utter uncertainty ... In my case, as I have this very clear vocation for research ... Will it be possible? And if so, how long will it last? Under what conditions? You have 40,000 questions. And being in this company, I'd tell you the same thing, no? They're firing people too, even if you have a good position, it's not unusual ... Well, then it's complete uncertainty, isn't it? That's something I notice a lot, you know? Not having a clear path and, based on that, not being able to plan for yourself at all. And not even planning, I mean, gosh, I'm 27 years old and wow (laughs), you know? You say "It's still very bad" (in the working sense). And say "Tomorrow and next year I won't be in a better position either. And at 30? Pff, not even" (laughs)... As for feelings, it completely takes over me, so to speak.' (Alberta, 27)

Alberta's words indicate a lot of uncertainty and reveal how it structured her daily feelings and those related to the future. Despite having a full-time job at a communications agency, doing a lot of overtime and working on her doctoral thesis at the weekend, her salary was not enough to leave the family home. She therefore considered her professional and financial situation to be "still very bad" for her age and had little confidence that this would change in the next few years. The lack of predictability and thus the issue of not being able to make plans translated into a feeling of being totally governed by uncertainty. What Alberta described here was found in a number of accounts but was most strongly expressed by young people from the middle class. Looking again at Bourdieu and his concept of habitus may help us understand why.

Orientation towards the future, Bourdieu (2020: 259) argues, is guided by the habitus and based on past and present experiences. The habitus forms what we can deem accessible and appropriate and what we cannot. For the middle classes, Schimank (2015) argues, it implies shaping the future by planning their way of life. He speaks in this context of the planning imperative[1] of the middle classes, which can already be found in Max Weber's 'methodische Lebensführung' (Schimank. 2015: 13):

> [In order to] follow patterns of life that are institutionally predetermined, but leave room for manoeuvre in decision-making ... such as the acquisition of qualifications, financial independence from parents, marriage, parenthood and the educational paths of children ... members of the middle class have always had to deal, to a considerable extent, with their longer-term life plans and with many events in their everyday lives in a decision-making manner. (Schimank, 2015: 9, author's translation).

While for Schimank, planning means rationally weighing up options and sounding out alternatives, from an emotion-sociological perspective, the question as to whether planning is at all possible and worthwhile is based primarily on the feeling of confidence. Confidence, as Barbalet (1998: 89) writes, 'is a feeling of assurance about the future', which we feel in the present and which provides us with a sense of certainty. According to Kemper, it arises, on the one hand, through knowledge of the formal aspects of a situation, that is, the laws, norms or rules; on the other hand, it is influenced by the resources available to us. For Kemper (1978: 73), being well equipped, for example with educational capital, is a basis of confidence. I would add here that confidence also arises from habitualized practices and ways of life that convey familiarity and a sense of predictability. With hysteresis, as we have seen, the habitus is 'destabilized' and 'torn by contradictions and internal division' (Bourdieu, 2000: 160). The necessary requirements for confidence were, to some extent, no longer met: the rules of the game for the labour market, which were believed to be familiar, had changed and the resources available to young people – that is, their educational capital – were in many cases no longer sufficient. Confidence started to crumble. Alberta did not believe that planning was possible and therefore worthwhile. Confidence 'through which a possible future is brought into the present' (Barbalet, 1998: 87) turned into a lack of confidence through which an uncertain future was brought into the present.

When both present and future events are viewed with pessimism, anxiety emerges (Kemper, 1978: 74–5). Anxiety here is often the result of individuals perceiving their own room for manoeuvre as insufficient and therefore feeling as though they have no influence on the future. The aspect of time plays a role too. Many of the young people I spoke to said that they suffered from anxiety because uncertainty and impasse stretched over many years, as we can see in Mateo's account:

> 'It makes you anxious. Anxiety, depression ... You see that the years are going by and your future prospects are not going to materialize. I'm

going to remain stuck where I was 10 years ago, when I was 17 years old. Am I going to be studying all my life? I want to escape. In fact, I want to continue training and studying, but you say to yourself "I can't live my whole life, for example, on €500." You can't live on €500 and you can't imagine being able to live at your own place tomorrow, having a family.' (Mateo, 29)

In Alberta's case, too, anxiety and the fearful anticipation of the future were associated with a persistent lack of power or control over her own life and the fear that she would not gain financial independence:

'What scares me the most is being dependent, even at my age, on my parents, you know? It's awful, it's awful. And you say to yourself "Fuck, I'm working, I'm doing everything at once, how can I still be dependent?" (laughs). That's the most difficult thing to deal with.' (Alberta, 27)

Alberta's difficulties in dealing with this anxiety were caused not only by her lack of room for manoeuvre but also by the moral connotation that (financial) dependence implies. As Fraser and Gordon (1994) indicate, dependency as an ideological concept serves to label and classify individuals and social groups in economic but particularly in moral terms.[2] It is seen as highly individualized since it is not social relations but personality that determines who and when one is considered dependent. This view, they argue, implies the assumption that dependency on the state and the family can be avoided through willingness and hard (self-)work. Nuria, however, emphasized that young people did not lack willingness and indeed continued to invest:

'Let us look at it: we have done a lot of things, we have incredible CVs, we have worked on huge projects and – but, of course, if we look towards the future, they have put so much social pressure on us like: "You won't have any retirement arrangements in place, you don't have any stability, you don't have …" Of course, we are totally conditioned, we feel as if they are kicking us.' (Nuria, 28)

Her interview highlights how the moral connotation of dependence translated into social pressure and reinforced her feelings of uncertainty and anxiety. The message about her future instability, which her social environment seemed to constantly convey to her, was inscribed in her thoughts and feelings. Every memory of her dependence and uncertain situation made Nuria and her co-worker Natalia feel like they were being kicked.

Feelings of uncertainty and anxiety left their mark on the young people's mental health. Many talked about how their health or health-related habits had been influenced and how the situations of impasse in which the interviewees felt stuck caused them "stomach cramps", "many sleepless nights" or "anxiety attacks along with depression and pills":

'After all, work is your life and many bad moments [are] caused by work, and not by work, by – I don't know, by bad family moments … There has been, well, there were a couple of years when I didn't have, well, my hair fell out completely, I had just a little bit of hair left because of the stress and so on, and on top of that it coincided with a job that was back-breaking.' (Antonio, 26)

'Stress, a lot of stress. A lot of grey hair, I get grey hair. And I often feel irritable. Sometimes, even though I have energy, I get up and am in a bad mood and say to myself "I don't feel like doing this, I don't feel like doing that", but you have to do it.' (Alejandra, 25)

'A solution never arrived. Summer passed, September arrived, October … Winter arrived, nobody lifted a finger there, nobody told me anything and it got to the point where all that discomfort I had inside was making me physically ill, I had awful digestion problems. I had a terrible time, I felt very very very bad, very weak, I ate very little, I was very thin, very sad, with very little motivation and all these things.' (Dorotea, 35)

'That's what I ask myself too, where do I get the energy from? In fact, I was working in three different places at once … and on weekends … Then, how do you do it? Well, instead of sleeping eight hours a day, you sleep four … And with the help of Coca-Cola, which is what gives me the caffeine to survive (laughs).' (Belén, 26)

What all four of these interviewees reported here came up in a large number of the interviews: insomnia, sleep deprivation, stress, mood swings and anxiety attacks as well as various forms of physical illness. These examples are consistent with studies that assessed the development of mental health in Spain in recent years and documented a substantial rise in mental health disorders in the aftermath of the economic crisis (Bartoll et al, 2014; Dessy, 2016).[3] According to Roca et al (2013: 1978), who compared data in primary care centres between 2006 and 2010, 'the proportion of patients with mood disorder, anxiety, somatoform, and alcohol-related disorders' increased significantly. They also observed an increased consumption of pharmaceuticals, with tranquilisers and antidepressants topping the list of the most prescribed medications (Gili et al, 2014: 106–7).[4] This is also consistent with the findings of Reibling et al (2017: 51), who observed an increase in depressive feelings in Spain during the economic crisis. According to

Robert et al (2014), young people without employment, with increased working hours, a reduced salary or one that remained stuck in the lower income bracket were particularly exposed to the risk of poor mental health. Moreover, young people whose perception was marked by permanent (job) insecurity suffered more frequently from anxiety, depression, physical complaints, stress and increased self-doubt (Berth et al, 2003: 555).

Worries, uncertainty and anxiety were thus omnipresent. They were feelings of hysteresis as opposed to feelings people have when their habitus is in line with structural conditions (for example, confidence and security). Yet, they represented only one set of feelings. Frustration, resentment and a sense of unfairness were just as frequent.

Frustration, resentment and a sense of unfairness

As already evident from numerous interview excerpts, frustration arose from the disappointment that efforts and investments were not rewarded as they had expected, notably in relation to income and status. Dubet aptly describes the devaluation of educational qualifications and the resulting experience of declassification as a 'powerful machine for producing relative frustration' (2008: 294, author's translation).

Frustration often draws on comparison. The young people compared their expectations with their actual situation, which, for the vast majority of them, was anything but satisfactory. Hysteresis and impasse had created an immense discrepancy here, and it was unclear how they could reduce this. The young people also compared their own situation with others of their generation:

'What I felt most was frustration because they make it so difficult for people like Nuria and me, because I consider us − ... we are the opposite of passive people, we are super-responsible, we have achieved good grades at university, we have done some very good projects, we are very tenacious and we like work to be done well ... Well, then you realize that there are people who have done nothing except follow the path and, moreover, putting in little effort, but who get results ... I'm not saying that it's wrong that they have them, just that we don't have the same opportunities.' (Natalia, 30)

'It's true that I felt a certain, well, to see my former colleagues who did the training with me end up working in something, damn, like mechanics, which was something I did the training for and I had to work in something else. Yes, it's true that it makes you feel like "Damn, why does this have to happen to me?" You know? (laughs). There are friends who easily find work in something else and you're looking for a job and don't find one and have to be satisfied with what you get. It's true that – it's not really a feeling of envy, well, it's true it does make you feel a bit envious, but it's more like: "Damn, why doesn't that happen to me?" You know? (laughs). I don't know, it's strange.' (Ricardo, 21)

'You see people at 26, or 22, or 18, who, fortunately, have found a job, have a house, have their independence. And you see that you're getting older … and you feel like you're stagnating, no matter how many things you do, you feel like you're stagnating, as if you have hit a glass ceiling and aren't able to break through it …

However, for example, my sister-in-law, my boyfriend's sister, did an intermediate degree [vocational training] as a nursing assistant, and is working at a dental clinic … Well, she earns a fortune… I think it's €1,300 a month and, on top of that, she gets commission, so some months she makes €1,800 or €2,000 easily. And she has an intermediate degree, that's what I was telling you before about studying. I'm studying, I have my higher degree [vocational training], and so on and I'm not able to have the purchasing power that you have. Why?' (Belén, 26)

Natalia, Ricardo and Belén viewed their situation in relation to that of other young people in their (immediate) professional, family or social environments and identified a discrepancy that made their own impasse particularly obvious to them. Natalia compared herself to other young people in her professional environment who, in her opinion, were able to obtain social and financial recognition without much effort, something she felt she had been denied. She provided numerous examples, such as a reference to the low level of appreciation and often poor remuneration received by those involved in creative work compared to those working in other areas like marketing. She also referred to the unfair selection criteria of the few private and public funding opportunities for freelancers in the creative and cultural industries, which either supported recent graduates or those with many years of professional experience, leaving her in a 'limbo, totally abandoned in a desert'. Natalia's comparison was thus directed at those who were moving forward despite the economic crisis. What she found frustrating and unfair was that she felt that she was being deprived of the same opportunities that other highly trained young middle-class people seemed to be enjoying while she herself was putting in all the effort and (passionate) commitment she could in order to play the game.

The same happened to Ricardo. He witnessed how his former fellow apprentices successfully managed to become mechanics and how even most of his friends seemed to find jobs much more easily, while his own efforts through various further training courses and job applications were, for a long time, in vain. Like Natalia, he said that he did not begrudge his friends and colleagues their success, but did feel that it was unfair that, with more or less the same starting conditions and level of commitment, the results were so different. His rather rhetorical question "Damn, why doesn't that happen to me?" thus expresses the implied entitlement and, in his eyes, the violated norm of fairness.

Belén's excerpt involves a comparison with those who were deemed not to have prepared or trained enough in order to be successful. She talked about how her sister-in-law had only an intermediate vocational training degree and was, compared to her, much less well equipped with educational capital. Although Belén therefore considered herself more deserving than her sister-in-law, she was not able to 'outpace' her (Kemper, 1978: 227). Seeing her sister-in-law with more financial resources at her disposal than her violated her sense of fairness based on meritocracy and generated a lot of frustration and a strong sense of unfairness.

All three examples show a pattern that ran through many other accounts as well. Frustration and a sense of unfairness arose due to the difference between the movement of (supposedly undeserving) others and the individual's own impasse, despite constant effort and investment in education. It mirrors what Hochschild (2016: 148) describes as 'the experience of being "cut in on"'. She illustrates this experience with the metaphor of the line in which people stand waiting to get closer to the destination:

> You are patiently standing in a long line … you've waited a long time, worked hard, and the line is barely moving… Will we be waiting in line forever? … In fact, is it moving backward? … Look! You see people *cutting line ahead of you*! You're following the rules. They aren't. As they cut in, it feels like you are being moved back … You feel uneasy. It has to be said: the line cutters irritate you. They are violating the rules of fairness. You resent them, and you feel it's right that you do. (Hochschild, 2016: 136–9, emphasis in original)

In Hochschild's case (2016: 139), the people waiting in line are mainly white, elderly, male US Americans and the destination is the American Dream. She describes how the feeling of their standstill or even downward mobility, in contrast to the moving forward of other social groups such as women, people of colour or immigrants, produced increasing frustration but also a rise in nationalism and racism. Yet, she stresses that this 'deep story of the right, the *feel-as-if story*, corresponds to a real structural squeeze' (Hochschild, 2016: 146, emphasis in original). This is also true for the young people in this book who also felt stuck, outpaced and, in a sense, betrayed.

The latter was most evident in the story of Jacobo (30). He was among the young people who were stuck in training loops. When we met, he was taking part in a socioprofessional reintegration programme which included carpentry training and classes on social skills. At that time, he had been unemployed for almost six years and described his situation as bad: "My situation is that of a homeless person, I have no family, it is, I mean, very bad." He relied on this training to end his dependency on the state for welfare benefits[5] and on friends for overnight accommodation. He wanted to rid himself of the strong feelings of shame that he had always had. But finding a job proved to be extremely difficult, as he emphasized repeatedly: "It's just very difficult. And I try to do my best, but just when you lift your head up you fall back down again." The constant rejections of his applications and the lack of respectability generated frustration. This was especially the case when he compared himself to those who were in an equally marginalized position, yet still seemed to pass him by:

'It's rage. Listen, I'm not racist, OK? I want to make that clear, but it's true that where I could be working there are other people who are foreign ... I don't care. Here everyone ekes out a living as well as they can, and they are worth it and valid, but I often make comparisons. I have many years of experience and you don't hire me, but you do hire the other person. Why? The same thing happens with the Community of Madrid, eh, because, for housing, housing as part of *Ivima* [Housing Institute of Madrid], for me they ask for nothing but papers, papers, papers. On the other hand, refugees come and they are given a flat, well, what do you want me to say? Well, it frustrates me, it bothers me, it makes me angry. It makes me angry, not with the people around me, but with the bunch of idiots that we have as politicians, you know, who only look at the people outside and do not look at the people they have inside. At the Plaza Mayor, in an alley, right, there are Spanish families with children sleeping there. That's not, god, that's not normal, not normal. When a South American comes and they give him housing, they give him millions in allowances, you know? And me, to ask *Caritas*, they had to ask me for a fucking report on social exclusion; that's when I get angry, because, damn it, where are Spanish people's rights? There are no rights for Spanish people ... For me to get fucking social housing, nothing but papers, and more papers, and more papers; and refugees come from Syria and they give them apartments. Don't fuck with me, it makes me look like an idiot. It bothers me a lot ... In that ... I am very angry about this situation, because I see myself ... It's not that I'm excluded anymore, it's that they force me to be excluded, they make me feel excluded.' (Jacobo, 30)

Jacobo's words reveal how he felt betrayed from 'above' and outpaced from 'below'. While Jacobo saw the 'migrant other' as in the same existential struggle for work, housing and benefits, he felt that employers and institutions made it easy for them, but hard for him. He therefore stressed that he himself ought to be at least as equally deserving as the 'migrant others' were. His last sentences make it quite clear that he felt overlooked and excluded. At the same time, he talked about being under constant scrutiny, about having to fill out a multitude of documents over and over again, and having to provide evidence of his marginalized and vulnerable position for every application he made. He did not necessarily consider himself as being excluded from society as such. Yet, the way he was treated by arbitrarily being given too much attention at times but not enough attention at other times and the need to constantly prove his respectability made him feel as if he did not belong. He faced what Skeggs (1997: 93) calls the 'double movement of being made to feel invisible and under scrutiny' at the same time: he was either labelled as deficient or felt he did not exist. His comment about how this situation made him look like an idiot then reveals that he did not feel taken seriously, but rather betrayed – betrayed in terms of the mismatch between his own impasse and the movement of (migrant) others into work and housing who, he felt, had it so much easier than him.

What Jacobo and the young people described as frustration, anger and a sense of unfairness can be subsumed under the emotion of resentment. It is the feeling that someone else has unfairly received better treatment or benefits whereby you express indignation about such inequalities (Barbalet, 1998: 68). Resentment, as Barbalet (1998: 137) notes, 'is the emotional apprehension of advantage gained at the expense of what is desirable or acceptable from the perspective of established rights'. At the core of resentment is thus the violation or disregarding of rights that were thought to be socially shared and accepted, and in most cases also taken for granted. The young people felt resentment when they became aware of the mismatch between what they believed to be their right and entitlement and the way they were being treated.

The feeling of resentment was even stronger when the young people felt that the unfair advantage gained by others was at their expense (Barbalet, 1998: 137). We saw this, for instance, in Jacobo's case. His frustration and sense of unfairness were particularly strong when he felt that the preference being given to migrant others by employers resulted in him being ignored and losing out in the job search. We saw the same with Mateo (see Chapter 2). The priority given by his company to hiring external people meant that Mateo and his colleagues were not considered for vacant positions and their chances of promotion and professional development were therefore reduced. In both cases, neither the migrant other nor the external new recruits were the object of Jacobo's or Mateo's resentment, but rather those who helped them to gain this unfair advantage – here the employers – were seen as responsible.

Since resentment is a feeling which relates to inequalities, it is inevitably linked to class (Barbalet,1998: 62ff). As Hochschild (2016: 148) writes, the feeling of being outpaced while other people seem to cut in line up ahead is an expression of an underlying class conflict in which structural asymmetries of power and status generate resentment. But general patterns of class inequalities are not the only source of resentment. Barbalet (1998: 76) emphasizes that resentment exists both between and within classes, which is why movements of ascending and descending prospects of income also need to be taken into consideration. Belén's case makes this particularly clear. She shared the same (lower middle-)class position as her sister-in-law, but felt resentment towards her, which resulted from the unequal amount of financial progress made. While her sister-in-law earned "a fortune", Belén's income was not anywhere near enough for her to even contemplate parental independence, and any non-essential expenditure such as a monthly transport ticket or English courses became a "luxury". Resentment can thus 'develop an emotional pattern congruent with status defensiveness' (Barbalet, 1998: 75) in people who feel left behind by ascending groups. This is particularly the case for those whose economic situation was rather favourable and for those who perceive their (minimal) area of ascent as threatened. This, according to Barbalet (1998: 75), can mean that 'white-collar workers may resent unionized blue-collar workers, and manual workers resent welfare recipients'. Resentment as experienced by Belén and the other young people is therefore also a result of the impossibility of keeping their relative social position away from those considered to be less fortunate, in terms of the distribution of material resources and opportunities, or less deserving.

Apart from worries, uncertainty and anxiety, this section has shown that we need to add frustration, resentment and a sense of unfairness to the picture of how hysteresis was felt by the young people in my study. They too can be seen as (collective) emotions that were embedded in hysteresis and its resulting types of impasse.

Conclusion

This chapter has shown that the structural condition of hysteresis and the resulting types of impasse produced a very specific 'structure of feeling' (Williams, 1977: 128–35): a 'social ... rather than ... "personal" experience' (Williams, 1977: 131) of an ill-adjusted habitus in the midst of a changing field. The young people's impasse not only existed in material form, but also constituted the basis of a particular emotional condition. Hysteresis produced emotions of uncertainty, anxiety, frustration and resentment. We can see the young people's emotions as expressions of a way of being and doing that had difficulties fitting into and adjusting to the changed circumstances after the crisis. Their emotions resulted from the changed structures and corresponded to what Kemper (1978: 43ff) calls the 'structural emotions'. At the same time, they were also a response to how the young people assessed their future and were thus what he refers to as 'anticipatory emotions' (Kemper, 1978: 72ff).

We might think now that the shared feelings have led to a kind of collective awareness, a kind of 'we' feeling of a crisis generation. In fact, the social movements in 2011 and the subsequent years can be seen as a form of collectivization of emotions. Disappointment, frustration and anger made the 'indignados' take their claims to the streets over several months. The shared emotion of indignation served as a source of mobilization and collective action and at the same time openly highlighted the participants' discontent regarding the social, economic and political circumstances at that time. Yet, as I have pointed out in this chapter, the idea that there is one single crisis generation needs to be challenged to a certain extent. Even though feelings of uncertainty, anxiety, frustration and a sense of unfairness were shared by the majority, they were in some cases related to different aspects.

The feeling of uncertainty, for instance, was generally shared by the young people in my study across different social classes. It resulted mostly from job instability as well as unpredictability in terms of material security. The issue of uncertainty was also raised in terms of the loss of the ability to plan one's own life. However, this was mainly the case for those young people whose habitus had been able to incorporate ideas of planning in the past. For Jacobo, for example, it was clear that "it is not you that chooses the job but the job that chooses you". Alberta, on the other hand, believed the opposite, but saw her confidence dwindling, which until then had given her the feeling that planning was possible and worthwhile. Alberta's uncertainty was thus related to the middle-class loss of status, which was reflected in the loss of control – control over one's own way of life to which Jacobo never had access in that way.

Both feelings resulted, among other things, from the lack of social recognition being received which the young people believed was due to their impasse. While for some, such as Nuria and Natalia, it was their way of doing and thinking about work that was not being recognized, for others (such as Jacobo) the lack of recognition concerned their whole way of being and doing, and the impression that they were not passing as respectable. In both cases, the young people felt frustrated and resented those who seemed to have it easier. However, the layers of this lack of recognition that nurtured frustration and a sense of unfairness differed with their social position. Therefore, the claims regarding rights, on which their resentment was based, differed as well. While Jacobo, for example, demanded the right to exist as a respectable person and a fully fledged member of society who was not excluded from access to basic resources, Nuria's and Natalia's claims related to them maintaining their status as members of the middle class. The chapter hence showed that the 'structure of feeling' in post-crisis Spain that emerged with hysteresis and impasse laid the foundations for shared feelings of uncertainty, anxiety, frustration and resentment. Yet, these feelings did not have the same object, direction or scope for everyone; they differed in terms of what was at stake.

As we turn to the following chapter, we will see how the young people dealt with these emotions, how they interpreted and made sense of them. We will pay attention to the more visible forms of mobilising and channelling emotions, such as unions, and to the small, everyday practices of dealing with them.

Interpreting and Dealing with Emotions of Hysteresis

In Part I, I considered how structural change caused by the economic crisis translated into individual as well as collectively shared feelings. The increasing mismatch faced by young people in post-crisis Spain between their level of education and the possibilities to enter the labour market resulted in hysteresis. While hysteresis is produced at the structural level, the young people in my study felt it in their everyday life as a mismatch between expectations and opportunities, and thus as uncertainty, anxiety, frustration and resentment. How did the young people then interpret and deal with these emotions in everyday life?

In Part II, I examine this question drawing on Goffman's (1959, 1974) concepts of *frames* and *stages*, and Hochschild's theory (1979) on *emotion work*. To recap, frames, according to Goffman, help us to organize and understand our lived and felt experiences. They demarcate what is considered appropriate and expected, and define our types of behaviour and feelings. How we interpret an experience therefore has an impact on which feelings we consider legitimate and how we work on them. Our interpretation also affects where – that is, on the front stage or backstage – we express or rather suppress our feelings. The backstage in particular can serve as a space in which feelings can be made visible, which would not be perceived as appropriate on the front stage due to social norms or our social position.

To make sense of their experiences of mismatch and impasse, the young people in my study drew on two patterns of interpretation: individualistic and systemic frames. Their interpretations involved practices of what I identified as emotive-cognitive reframing, a complex and embodied process of emotional and cognitive work in which existing patterns of explanation were questioned and partly replaced by new ones. Chapter 4 then starts with individualistic frames and individual backstages before I move on to systemic frames and collective spaces for emotion work in Chapter 5.

Individualistic Frames and Individual Backstages

Individualistic frames were patterns of interpretations drawn on by the young people when they felt that dealing with their impasse was a personal affair. Feelings of uncertainty, anxiety and frustration were often associated with an individual's character, biographical events or difficulties in dealing with them effectively. Many shared the belief described by López Calle in his article on young people in post-crisis Spain: they thought that it was possible 'to break with this structural situation on the basis of their own resources and individual effort' (López Calle, 2012: 178, author's translation).

What we will see in this chapter is that the young people redefined and reinterpreted parts of the individualistic frames in order to make sense of their impasse and related feelings. This reframing included emotion work which they carried out using different 'deep acting' techniques (Hochschild, 1979: 561) in order to change, appease or suppress their emotions. Physical spaces where the young people could be for themselves were especially important here and turned into their individual backstage where emotion work could be done.

'Cambiar el chip': emotive-cognitive reframing

The mismatch faced by many young people between their expectations and the opportunities available to them was reflected not only in their impasse but also in their attempts to understand and interpret it. For this reason, they questioned some of the available explanatory patterns and, in some cases, adjusted them. This process of emotive-cognitive reframing was most clearly embodied by the phrase 'cambiar el chip'.[1] While this term is generally translated as 'changing one's mindset or way of thinking',[2] I will keep the literal translation of 'changing the chip'. I do so because the way in which the young people referred to it; it included not only cognitive processes but also the working on and changing one's feelings and behaviour. In this sense, it was a truly embodied process or practice which came up in many interviews when young people explained how they dealt with their impasse and related feelings of anxiety and frustration:

Joaquín: That's how it is now and we have to learn to live with it. So, you have to 'change the chip' and say: 'Well, my parents taught me that, or I always felt that if I did well in my studies, I would have a permanent job, but it's not the case more … This is not what I expected but I'm not going to get anywhere if I just do nothing, I'm going to try something else that might work out well for me.'

Nina: How did you manage to 'change the chip'?

Joaquín: How did I change it? Pfff, well I guess it's a process … When it's affecting you in a negative way, you learn to detect it and to say 'No! I don't want this, and as scary as change is, and as much anxiety as it may cause, I'm going to change it because it's not what I want, nor is it making me feel good'.

'So, by "changing the chip" … of course it's not easy, of course it's not easy … Do you feel like it? Not at all, but you have no choice. If you want to get ahead, you have no other choice.' (Belén, 26)

'Changing the chip' involved putting aside 'old' ideas of social mobility and social reproduction and facing up to the 'new' rules of the game. It also included the belief that it was better to get used to the changes in post-crisis Spain and that there was usually no other choice if one wished to continue playing. While the young people did not necessarily see 'changing the chip' as a matter of discretion, they framed it as something that was in their own hands. Joaquín, for instance, stressed the need to create the space in order to be able to 'change the chip'. It was an active decision, not a passive reaction, as evidenced by the words "I'm not going to get anywhere if I just do nothing". Joaquin's description also illustrates the way in which emotions played a role in this. On the one hand, they served as a signal indicating that it was "affecting [him] in a negative way", that it did not make him feel good. They were hence a trigger to reassess his situation and then to re-align if necessary. On the other hand, his statement implied that certain emotions also needed to be reassessed. Fear and anxiety should not gain the upper hand, preventing him from 'changing the chip'. His words also indicate that this form of dealing with fear and anxiety was primarily an individual act. This way of understanding the impasse was shared by many other young people, as the following two quotes by Romeo and Jacobo demonstrate:

'Whenever I have a personal or professional problem, I have learned to manage it on my own.' (Romeo, 25)

'Me. Only I can help me … It's very easy to ask for help from others, but it doesn't teach you anything. You teach yourself, I think, don't you? Yes, I think that from the many times that you fall, you get up by yourself, you know?' (Jacobo, 30)

Romeo's and Jacobo's words highlight how they regarded the impasse and the related feelings as something they had to deal with by themselves. Although both described moments in which they shared emotions with others, they saw the responsibility of dealing with them as an individual act. As Thoits (1985: 237) writes, this belief can emerge when people experience stressful or painful circumstances over a longer period of time and then tend to interpret their (emotional) reactions to them as evidence of their own deviation and consequently (individual) responsibility. While the young people did not necessarily consider themselves to be deviant, as they were generally aware of the bigger picture in post-crisis Spain, they still believed that dealing with their impasse and feelings was their personal problem.

The reframing practices which will now be discussed in more detail, and which all fall under the umbrella term of 'changing the chip', were thus not only particularly relevant for the way in which the young people reinterpreted their impasse and related feelings, but were also understood as primarily individualistic practices.

"I was lucky"

One form of emotive-cognitive reframing was when young people defined their own situation as fortunate compared to that of others. In doing so, they usually put parts of their impasse and precarious working conditions into perspective. As Dubet (2008: 256, author's translation) writes, 'the mechanism of comparison is … reversible; it increases frustrations but can also reduce them depending on the comparison criteria used'. The choice of comparative points of reference was hence key to this form of 'changing the chip'. The narratives of Anam, Vidal and Antonio, all three of whom were stuck in short-term employment loops, illustrate how the reframing was carried out:

'In other words, I think I was lucky, given the timing, because we ended up in the worst moment to find work, because we were in the midst of a crisis. So, I was lucky because I found it quickly, but at that time it wasn't so easy.' (Anam, 29)

'I have been very lucky, I have had many opportunities, that is, I mean, precarious opportunities, but good opportunities, so to speak, to develop in what I have been trained in.' (Vidal, 25)

'Personally, I think I was lucky in terms of what I decided to learn although the jobs are not well paid and so on … I was lucky to find them compared to other sectors. My work in installations [as a mechanic], where I can change jobs more easily, is not the same as that of someone who studies … who has opted for a degree and studies history, for example. Of course, in their situation, if you find a job, you can't go taking another one every year.' (Antonio, 26)

To help them understand their situation, they changed the reference points of comparison. For Vidal, what was more important was that he had opportunities at all, even if they were all precarious. A good opportunity was not one with decent working conditions, but one which allowed him to work in a field in which he had been trained. The same was true for Antonio. He considered his situation to be fortunate as it was still possible to change jobs in his sector, even though these jobs were generally poorly paid. He framed the sequencing of short-term employment, actually a feature of structural precariousness, as an advantage, providing the possibility to switch at any time. He underlined this advantage by comparing it with higher education. While the latter used to provide greater opportunities (remuneration, promotion, development and stability, etc.), its image increasingly crumbled over the course of the crisis. Therefore, as Antonio's example shows, reframing included comparisons with social groups that went beyond an individual's own reference group (Merton, 1968: 335ff). In some cases, this made the young people perceive their situation as privileged despite their impasse:

'I'm lucky enough to be able to rely on my parents for a few months … And, besides, I have internalized this, I know that's the way it is, otherwise I would surely be considering something totally different in life, no? … I'm a privileged person in that sense, you know? I'm very aware of it … For example … well, people who since the age of 16 … or, for example, an ex-partner of mine who began to work and help out at their uncle's restaurant at the age of 12. That was the way it was – to make a living for yourself as soon as possible because nobody is going to support you in those moments or because you have to contribute to the house, to the family household. I think these people are the ones who – I think that in that sense I'm privileged, right? I'm very clear about that.' (Alberta, 27)

Despite having a full-time job, Alberta could not afford to live independently and had to move back into the family home. This form of impasse caused her a great deal of uncertainty that structured her daily feelings and those related to the future. Yet comparing herself with other young people who also had financial difficulties but did not have the same family safety net made her perceive her situation as less helpless. Qualifying their own impasse was thus a form of anxiety and frustration management whereby the young people tried to turn their disappointment into satisfaction and their worries into confidence.

In the previous examples, the young people focused on thoughts and action when reframing their situation. Emotions changed rather implicitly. Yet, at other times, their focus was more explicitly on emotions and on how to change or work on them. Mateo, for example, described how he deliberately tried to work through his frustration at being stuck for years in what was initially meant to be only a temporary job by focusing on any improvements, however small they might be:

> 'I try to say to myself: "Man, look on the bright side. What do you have?" You look back and say: "Well, what have you gained?" I, for example, have been [at the company for] ten years, well, I'm already in a better situation, financially I'm doing better, I'm no longer earning €500 working weekends ... You start to see certain things, and it might not have been easy but you get better little by little, and with regard to things that you didn't used to think about before, well, you say "It might well be that I can start to think about them now albeit with great difficulty, because the way the standard of living is now it is like that, but, well, if you can keep on going, these are small successes".' (Mateo, 29)

Mateo reminded himself of the little changes, such as his slightly higher income. Using this interpretation, financial recognition became a 'small success' rather than a matter of course as his professional experience increased. He used both deep acting techniques (Hochschild, 1979) in the process: on the one hand, he worked on his feelings as he tried to minimize his frustration; on the other hand, he worked on ideas and images that went along with these feelings or could trigger them (Hochschild, 1979: 562), such as the expectations as to how long it should take to get ahead professionally and financially.

Mateo's reframing was embedded in and supported by public discourse which suggested that the situation in the labour market did not allow young people to make higher demands or criticize their working conditions. Moreover, the substantial imbalance between low supply and high demand for jobs reduced people's opportunities to negotiate for or demand better employment terms, as it was easy for employers to replace those who were not satisfied. In light of high youth unemployment and general hardship throughout the country, demands were framed as a sign of a lack of gratitude and hence thought of as shameful, as Monica's account illustrates:

> 'The government has made you believe that the salary you have is good, but it isn't good, of course it's not, it's very bad ... I mean, it seems that you can't work in what you want to because there's no work, which means you have to work in what's there, with the salary on offer and under the conditions on offer and you have to keep your mouth shut. But sometimes it becomes a little difficult, you're frustrated because you say to yourself: "I want to play the flute" (laughs) but you can't ... So they kind of make you believe that, you know? In other words, "feel grateful because ...".' (Monica, 28)

Monica's quote illustrates the normative shift that occurred in terms of what was capable of causing shame. The shaming she identified, as done by the government, was seen as a sign that society required people to adjust to the changed circumstances. Against this background, framing one's situation as fortunate in comparison to that of others was thus a form of internalizing the framing and feeling rules (Hochschild, 1979: 563ff), which implied that it was appropriate, given the situation in post-crisis Spain, to keep expectations and demands in check and to be grateful in some way for having a job.

Living from day to day

Another form of emotive-cognitive reframing concerned future planning. Many of the young people lost confidence about their possibilities to make future plans. To counteract the uncertainty and anxiety caused by the difficulty of carrying out the habitualized practice of planning, especially among the middle class, many of the young people tried to focus less on the long term and more on living in the moment. Framing it this way became one of the young people's forms of anxiety and uncertainty management. By concentrating on the present, they tried to put these feelings aside and distance themselves from them:

> 'A hope for the future, which for me is not so much thinking about the long term, but living more from day to day, and the long term will come at a time when I see that I can ... That is, not everything has to be so planned. Well, living according to the accidents you've had. Are you having an unexpected baby? Well, you have to change your life. Well, and suddenly I think it's time to get married. No, the time to get married is when you decide, never – ... there are people who

get married at 40, do you have to get married now at 27? Is there a law that says "No, you have to get married at 27" or something like that? Therefore, a life plan that is very much focused on the here and now.' (Vidal, 25)

'It is to live more, to live more in the present and to live more from day to day, no? I think that before, what you did was, well, if you were in high school, you were thinking that you were going to study at university, while you were at university you were thinking about what you were going to do at work tomorrow, when you are at work you are thinking about buying a house and getting a mortgage, eh, then children, you know? It's like, instead of living your life right now, you're always living what your life will be in five years' time, you know? So, I think that's good, isn't it? I mean, to think about the future and what you're going to do or what you want to be, but you have to focus on − … I think you have to focus on the day to day … bring the focus to the present but of course, otherwise it [the uncertainty] wears you down, I mean if you start thinking, if I start thinking now and say: "Let's see, at 35, it will be the same, I'll be out of work, eh, I don't know", you know?' (Joaquín, 26)

Vidal's and Joaquín's statements show how long-term planning for the future was perceived as something that did not fit their current circumstances. It was seen as a framework which, in their view, used to imply linear and clearly defined stages in time, but which no longer matched. They believed that their lives should take place in the present and not in a potential future that they perceived as unpredictable, as their expectations remained unfulfilled. For Vidal in particular, planning was not so much about drawing up a plan in advance as adapting to the circumstances, "according to the accidents you've had". Even more than Joaquín, he questioned certain norms often associated with planning the future, such as getting married at a certain age. However, he was keen to point out that he himself would decide when the time was right. This cognitive-normative reframing was accompanied by emotional reframing (Flam, 2005: 19). As Joaquín openly pointed out, defining this day-to-day life as the focus of his attention helped him to manage his feelings of anxiety and uncertainty. In order for him not to become anxious, they had to be repressed and pushed aside. Not dealing explicitly with the future should make this possible:

'I've learned not to make plans because, if you're going to try to plan … where we're going to be and when we're going to be together and if we're going to be in the same city and what we're going to do, it stresses me out … So I've learned that the best way not to get stressed out is not to think about it. It's something I've learned because of my personal situation and, having noticed that by adopting this mentality my personal situation has been getting better, I now apply it to everything else, which is ... not to stress out myself.' (Emilia, 25)

Intentionally not drawing up any plans was therefore an attempt to worry less and to limit the space for feelings of anxiety. It also meant minimizing expectations and hence protecting oneself from possible disappointment. Adopting the new 'mentality' required Emilia to reassess the situation. In this context, Hochschild (1979: 562) speaks of a 'recodification' or 'reclassification of a situation into what are previously established mental categories of situations'. With this form of deep acting (Hochschild, 1979: 561), Emilia had revised her approach to the future, also with the aim of changing the feelings connected with it. Having initially applied this 'mentality' only to the area of social relationships, the (positive) results she experienced, whereby her anxiety was reduced, led her to extend it to all other areas of her life.

Reframing aspects of work

Since the different types of impasse were linked to the young people's situation in relation to the labour market, much of the emotive-cognitive reframing concerned aspects of work. Among other things, the types of impasse involved being stuck in jobs which were intended to be temporary, positions for which they were overqualified or, as the following example shows, in parallel (temporary) part-time jobs.

In the examples of Belén and Begoña (see Chapter 2) we saw that, contrary to their expectations (as well as those of their immediate social environment), their institutionalized cultural capital did not enable them to earn a living in the field in which they were trained. Instead, they were dependent on carrying out temporary and part-time jobs that did not match with their ways of being and doing. To give meaning to this situation, they reframed the different jobs as a welcome change from a monotonous routine:

'I try to see the positive side of having this ... you know, like this ... I don't know if it's a chaotic life, but like, err ... variety, or ... something, you know? Every day, actually, new things happen to you ... So I'm really happy to have the variety and so on because, you know, not being in the same place all day, it brings me some peace of mind ... Ultimately, I really like the fact that there is variety in my life. I think that maybe if I had a job where every day I was doing the same thing and so on, I don't know if I would run out of – ... I mean, not if it was in a school (laughs); but the monotony, the idea of something monotonous. I don't know if … I don't know, I see the jobs of my friends and so on and deep down I see that it's not what I want.' (Begoña, 29)

Begoña's statement illustrates how she put a label and a positive spin on her work situation. The fact that she opted to describe it more as variety than as a chaotic life had a decisive influence on how she saw and felt about her situation. The term 'variety' allowed her to see the impasse in a more positive light. Thoits (1985: 235) calls this process the cognitive change of an (emotional) label. An existing description of a situation is replaced by a more appropriate label with the aim of transforming non-normative feelings into normative ones. For Begoña, this meant that she could frame her fragmented working days, the different parallel and temporary jobs as well as the different (emotional) demands on her as a variety of experiences, which protected her from monotony. At the same time, she equated continuity (the full-time jobs of her friends) with monotony and portrayed it as something less desirable to her ("it's not what I want").

Begoña's statement also reveals how framing has an influence on which emotions are considered appropriate in a given context. Framing her situation as variety meant being satisfied with it ("I'm really happy to have the variety"). Defining variety as something positive also implied that feeling resentment towards friends with full-time jobs was neither necessary nor helpful. Instead, by equating continuity with monotony, it was possible to underpin the joy of having variety.

Another form of reframing aspects of work was when the young people defined jobs for which they were overqualified as enriching or informative experiences. The educational mismatch due to jobs requiring lower qualifications than those that people held had caused disappointment and frustration, especially among young people who had completed higher education. This was partly due to the devaluation of institutionalized cultural capital, that is, the opportunities to convert their educational qualifications into 'suitable' positions in the labour market. On the other hand, the issue also arose from the devaluation of embodied cultural capital, that is, expectations of how a person's own habitus should fit in with the working position and working environment. Defining a job for which a person was overqualified and in which they felt out of place as an enriching experience was thus a form of frustration management, a way of dealing with the disappointment and frustration concerning their devalued institutionalized and embodied cultural capital.

Natalia, for instance, had a number of jobs that required lower qualifications than those she had acquired. In the following excerpt she talked about how being in these positions had made her become aware of other social realities of which she would otherwise not have had any knowledge:

'In the end, you also get to know other realities depending on the job you're in … I've worked as a receptionist or as a call centre agent and you get to know other social realities that also connect you to the world, because you live in a circle of freelancers, designers, sociologists, people who see life in a different way, and you end up isolating yourself from the reality of the majority, because it is the reality of the majority; so, it's also good to work with a lady who has a grandson and children whose concern is her home. It also helps you to understand that yours is not a big deal, that you can't be all the time … In other words, there are bigger concerns than yours …

You realize that nobody likes it – in other words, you're not the only one who doesn't like that job, people who do it every day don't like it either, they would prefer to do something else, but they're happy because their objective is to earn money to maintain their house and support their family. And that's enough for them. And there's a lot to learn there too, because, maybe, you have to realize that you're not always going to love your job and that it doesn't matter.' (Natalia, 30)

Natalia's statement shows how she presented the idea of working in environments where neither her institutionalized nor her embodied cultural capital 'fitted in' as enriching, allowing her to step out of her own bubble and gain an insight into the "reality of the majority". The comparison with this social reality in which she identified other standards of evaluation ("whose concern is her home") led her to qualify her own dissatisfaction ("there are bigger concerns than yours"). Natalia framed it as a learning experience which showed her that basing an identity on and seeking self-fulfilment through work was not a priority for everyone, and might not even be possible for her either. The statement "you have to realize that you're not always going to love your job" can therefore be understood as an instruction as to how to feel when applying this frame. Disappointment and frustration were to be minimized or reduced. It was not so much a matter of changing or replacing frustration with an emotion with positive connotations, but above all of reducing the intensity of the emotion.[3]

However, this form of emotive-cognitive reframing in which the person's own impasse was redefined as an enriching experience was not accessible to all of the young people in my study. Natalia, in this example, benefited from the 'framing *potentials*' described by Willems (1997: 215, emphasis in original, author's translation) which emerge depending on a person's social position. This concept implies that certain frames can be 'as habitus – only dominated and mediated by certain groups' (Willems, 1997: 215, author's translation). This was similar to the way in which Begoña framed her parallel part-time jobs as providing a variety of experiences. Giving meaning to her situation in this way was compatible with her way of being and doing. 'What it comes down to in practice', as Willems (1997: 214, author's translation) argues, 'is that social meaning (frame) becomes "appropriate" to the situation through "appropriate" subjectivity (habitus).'

A final form of reframing in relation to work was the young people's attempts to (re)define provisional jobs in which they were stuck solely as activities for generating income. To deal with the disappointment and frustration that arose from having no way out in spite of having educational qualifications and putting in plenty of effort, some of the young people tried to reduce their emotional attachment and to drop their expectations of achieving social recognition or personal development through (this) work. Mateo, for instance, described how he suffered from being stuck in his provisional job for over ten years, in which he mainly worked at weekends. He talked about how he attempted to deal with his feelings of anxiety and frustration by trying to change them. Music proved to be helpful here. When friends of his were looking for a keyboardist, they convinced him to join their band. Joint rehearsals and performances became a new source of joy and self-esteem:

'And the weekends went from being an ordeal for me of working every weekend to being a job, but nothing more. When I left work I went to play, I went to rehearse. It became liberating, I already saw my weekends in a different light, as if to say: "Well, I work for a while, I take a little nap and I go to the rehearsal and I'm with some friends playing and having a good time." Later I got some experience, not much, we played I think three concerts or so, but well, to have the experience of playing in front of people, we felt like we had done something different and it's something I'm going to take with me. At least I said to myself: "Those are the little things."' (Mateo, 29)

Mateo's words show that redefining his work made him turn his suffering around and see it as a job that was nothing more than a means of earning an income. By depriving his work of its meaning and potential for social recognition, he was able to distance himself from it emotionally. At the same time, he shifted the source and field of satisfaction and the sense of moving forward or towards something from work to leisure. Music, playing in a band with friends and performing in front of an audience became the focus of his attention and repressed, at least temporarily, thoughts and feelings about his impasse at work. He perceived this process as "liberating" and talked about how he could see the change that the emotive–cognitive reframing had brought about for him ("I already saw my weekends in a different light").

All of these forms of emotive-cognitive reframing described in this section were forms of individual emotion management through which the young people tried to deal with their fragmented habitus (Silva, 2016) and the contradictions between what they perceived as expectations and entitlements, and what opportunities were available to them in post-crisis Spain. I have shown how they shifted their reference points and expectations as society changed around them. While this section focused on how the young people dealt with hysteresis and impasse cognitively as well as emotionally, the following section explores the bodily techniques that the young people applied and the spaces that they used in the process.

Individual backstages and bodily techniques

For Goffman (2012: 104–5), backstages are places where people can prepare for their performances on the front stage, but also where they can relax and deviate from their representations and roles. They are a kind of buffer zone by means of which one tries to 'buffer oneself against the deterministic claims by which one is surrounded' (Goffman, 2012: 106, author's translation). The backstage can be an isolated physical space, but it does not necessarily have to be; it can also be found in the anonymity of public space. For the young people in this book, individual backstages were places where they diluted, reduced or tried to detach themselves from their feelings of anxiety and frustration. For this purpose, they used bodily techniques whereby they worked on their feelings not so much through thoughts as through (working on) their body. This meant that alongside cognitive and expressive techniques, the third technique of emotion work described by Hochschild (1979: 562) came into play, in which emotions were to be influenced by changing somatic or other bodily sensations.

Using the bathroom

The bathroom is, in classic Goffmanian terms, a backstage (Goffman, 2012: 111). It was mentioned on several occasions in the interviews as a refuge to which some of the young people could withdraw. As a physically separated space which is thus protected from the eyes of the audience, the bathroom became a space of physical and emotional intimacy for them. Daria, for example, spoke of how she used the bathroom in the evening to soothe and relax her mind and body. To do so, she used certain rituals. In the beginning it was a warm footbath or a shower, but when that was no longer enough, she took a hot bath and listened to music:

Nina: And when you have these moments of anxiety or worries, what do you normally do then? Do you have a place or an activity that helps you to deal with it?

Daria: Well, it could be the bathroom. I do the typical thing of having a hot bath, listening to music and relaxing, you know? Right now I do it at night because I come home at night, I'm stressed out and everything and very, very tired and a little bath is perfect for clearing my head (laughs).

Nina: How did you find out that this is something that helps you?

Daria: I started to do it, look, I started to do that thing with my exhausted feet of needing the warmth of the water. The shower was not enough (laughs), you know? To relax … I think that there's something therapeutic about it (laughs). Yes, yes, it feels good, with music … I'm not saying that it's music to sleep to, no, any kind of music helps (laughs) … and the bathroom is a very private space. When you're in the bathroom, it's your space (laughs) it's a part of the home where you have privacy.

Thoits (1990: 193) describes these relaxation techniques as *emotion-focused strategies* by means of which we try to influence our physiological functioning in order to influence our general emotional state. Daria had to cross Madrid several times a week from the northern edge of the city to its southern tip in order to participate in further training at a youth centre, hoping to free herself from her impasse of constant training loops. Against this background, the bathroom was a therapeutic place for her and somewhere she could carry out emotion management. By targeting physiological or bodily sensations, Daria tried to alter her feelings of stress and fatigue, and ultimately deal with her constant worries and feelings of uncertainty.

Daria's statement also highlights the importance of controlling the backstage. The bathroom provided her with a private and intimate space which she did not seem to have elsewhere. It was a secure personal space and what Young (2005) calls 'a room of one's own'. In this context, her words 'it's your space' illustrate her sovereignty over the space in which she could allow herself (a certain) freedom of choice in terms of her behaviour and feelings. Goffman (2012: 106–11) himself points out the difficulty of controlling the backstage using various examples. Whether in professional or personal settings, having control over the backstage can prove difficult if there is no place that is at least temporarily protected from the eyes and ears of others. The bathroom, with its clear function as a physically separated retreat, is therefore an important backstage. This was especially the case for those young people in my study who were still living or were back living with their parents and also had children themselves, as illustrated by the following example:

'When I'm with my family, I go to the bathroom; and when I'm there, I don't know, I've had an argument with someone and … Well, when

I'm with my family, I mean when the whole family is there at a family gathering, and they've said something that has upset me, I go to the bathroom … And, until I get over it and my eyes are normal, I don't go out (laughs). No matter how much they bang on the door, I don't go out.' (Paulina, 29)

It is apparent from Paulina's account that the bathroom served as a place of escape where she could air her emotions privately. Here she could let her tears run free without being seen by her parents and her son. It was not only the spatial separation that allowed her to control this backstage but also the possibility to lock the room. This enabled her to maintain the state of privacy and intimacy for as long as she felt necessary, regardless of "how much they bang on the door". The time she needed for herself on the backstage also depended on how long it took before she felt ready again for any presentation or interaction on the front stage. Goffman (2012: 112, author's translation) describes the transition from one stage to another as an important point at which 'role characters are put on or taken off'. As we can clearly see in Paulina's case, this transition typically included emotion work. The traces of her emotional expression had to become invisible before she felt able to leave the bathroom again. To ensure this, she used a combination of surface and deep acting (Hochschild, 1979) by means of which she tried to return to a 'normal state' both externally ("my eyes are normal") and internally ("until I get over it").

Moving in space

While the bathroom was a clearly defined backstage, the following backstages were rather diffuse, sometimes situated in public and other times in private spaces.

Many of the young people I interviewed mentioned how they used moving their body in and across space as a way of dealing with their emotions, that is, reflecting upon them or simply disconnecting. They talked about walking in public spaces and parks, walking at home from one room to another, and taking the bus or underground. This is not surprising since, according to Scheer (2016: 30, author's translation), 'mobilizing emotional practices often occur when moving and manipulating one's own body'.

Many of the young people therefore moved their body to clear their mind and escape from burdening thoughts and feelings for a short time. They often did not have a defined destination, and simply drifted around and let time pass without having to use it in a productive or profitable way. This formed a temporary contrast to their work and daily routine, which were often rigorously timed for many of them. Romeo, for example, talked about how he took the bus without wanting to go to a particular destination. If he felt that a situation was particularly oppressive or his thoughts were spinning in circles too much, moving through the city helped him to put some distance between himself and his thoughts and feelings:

'I really like getting on the bus, listening to music … Not on the underground, on the bus to see the city and escape, I see things and I don't think about anything and my stress levels go down. So, I do that, I travel as far as I can and then I come back … I don't go to a specific place, I get off when I want to, and then I start walking and later I go back. So, I don't go to a specific place, because when you go to a specific place, you end up thinking about the place … so I say to myself: "Look, I'm not going anywhere specific. I'll go by bus and, when I feel like it, I'll get off". Or sometimes I don't get off and I go straight back to the same point. There are times when I get off, I take the bus here in Atocha and in Paseo de la Castellana, well, I get off, I walk for a while, I come back and then I take another bus that I know will drop me close … It works for me because I see, well, the behaviour of people: one person is running, another is in the car overwhelmed, another doesn't know what … I mean, we all have our problems and, after all, we have to go on living, we have to get on with the day to day. Tomorrow the night will also come, then, either you disconnect or … I always say: "Either you swallow it and go through it and free yourself and take advantage of the day, or you're going to be thinking about it, your day is going to end, you're not going to get anything clear and you'll have wasted a beautiful day and won't have done the things you could have done."' (Romeo, 25)

Romeo's statement reveals how taking the bus became a backstage for him that allowed him to escape and disconnect. The movement of the bus and the ever-changing cityscape in front of his eyes were as important as the lack of a clear destination. This combination helped Romeo distract himself and feel less stressed. The opportunity to gain momentary insights into other people's lives ("one person is running, another is in the car overwhelmed") were equally helpful. These brief glimpses helped him to (re-)evaluate his situation and feelings as they not only distracted him from his own situation, but also enabled him to relate to the world. Rosa (2016) refers to this relationship to the world as *resonance* and thereby describes not so much a state of feeling as a constellation of relationships, a relationship to the world and oneself therein. This form of relating to the world made Romeo put his own situation into perspective and conclude that "we all have our problems and, after all, we have to go on living".

For Teresa too, moving through public space was a kind of backstage which helped her to deal with the impasse and her feelings of uncertainty and anxiety. Like many of the young people in this book, she particularly enjoyed walking in the park:

Teresa: I usually go to a park, you know, in a way to feel, you know, to clear my mind and feel good about myself. Or sometimes I stay in my room. It's just that in my room I don't … No, I almost never stay [inside] when I'm like that, I like to go out, yes.

Nina: And how did you discover that parks help you during these moments?

Teresa: Because … I don't know, I see more people, I don't feel alone, I like the atmosphere, I don't know, the kids playing, well, all of it is entertaining and I like it.

The lively atmosphere, the presence of other people and the sight of children playing distracted Teresa and made her feel less lonely. She emphasized that staying inside, for instance in her room, did not have the same effect on her emotional state as the open and sociable atmosphere of the park. Moving outside corresponds to what Schmitz (1990: 115–27) describes as a dynamic between confinement and vastness of bodily space, whereby an individual can move from 'a perceptible confinement (for example, in fear) … [into] vastness (for example, in relief)' (Gugutzer, 2013: 308, author's translation). The atmospheres of the respective locations play an important role in this. The social, convivial atmosphere of the park in which Teresa strolled resulted in her being physically affected (Schmitz, 1993) and contributed to changing her emotional state. She thus felt less insecure or alone and instead good about herself.

Teresa's example also illustrates another point, namely the extent to which moving acted as an antithesis to the impasse. While the young people often felt fixed in time and space on the front stage, on the backstage the feeling of being stuck was counteracted by movement. This could involve their own movement or the act of observing and immersing themselves in spaces in which (a lot of) movement was created by others.

Ricardo also got his body moving when he needed to reflect on work-related issues. While he preferred to stay inside, he used to move within the apartment:

'I like to walk (laughs), especially when I think. When I think, I like to walk, so while I think, I walk from my room to the living room, from the living room to the kitchen, from the kitchen to the living room (laughs) … not only when I feel irritated, but also when I think "Fuck, I have to do this and that. Let's see how I can do this" … My mother saw me once and … she often asks me: "What are you looking for?", and I respond by saying: "Nothing, nothing. I'm not looking for anything" (laughs). And yes, I'm walking. I don't know why, I simply start walking (laughs). So when I think, when I start reflecting on things, I walk and walk ... And then, well, little by little, it goes away ... Yes, it helps me, well yes ... I mean, it doesn't help me because it doesn't help me at all, but at least I'm walking, you know (laughs)?' (Ricardo, 21)

Moving this way, as Ricardo explained, was not something he did on purpose, not a sophisticated strategy with a specific function or aim. Reflecting, as the last sentence shows, did not usually help him to solve his situation of impasse, but moving felt at least better than being stuck. Like him, many of the other interviewees did not expect the act of moving to solve or improve their situation. It was not intended to replace or compensate for anything and did not serve to work on or improve the self. Drawing on Berlant, this practice could be understood as 'neither identical to making it or oneself *better* nor a mimetic response to the structural conditions of a collective failure to thrive, nor just a mini-vacation from being responsible – such activity is also directed toward making a less-bad experience. It's a relief, a reprieve, not a repair' (Berlant, 2011: 117, emphasis in original).

Ricardo's remark "And then, well, little by little, it goes away" also shows that it was not only about moving himself as a contrast to the felt impasse but also about using certain practices and spaces to make the feelings move on. We can also see this in Begoña's case. She talked about how her diary was an important backstage for her, which she used to become aware of her feelings and to try to deal with them. However, it made a difference to her whether she wrote at home or outdoors:

'I have a diary that is super-important to me because I come back to it a lot; and I draw. In other words, I have both a notebook and – because sometimes, like when I don't get the emotion out in a written form, I try to paint it; and that's how I get things clear, as I know what it is that I'm thinking ...

I write at home but more in parks. At home you're closed, you know? Your emotion is totally submerged, you know? You're much more in the grey ... In a park, well, you write, you expose it, but you see, that is, you feel ... When I write there's a freedom, there's something that connects you with nature, right? Something which I, for example, don't have at home. Inside the house there's noise, and when I go out and write outside, it's like the feeling, you know, you accept it and it moves on.' (Begoña, 29)

The spatial limitation of the apartment also seemed to curtail her emotion, preventing it from emerging. Writing outside, in contrast, achieved the opposite effect, whereby it gave her and her feelings more room to move and to move on.

Consulting experts

The young people's emotion work was not always done in complete isolation. Sometimes it was done with the support of experts. As a final form of backstage in this chapter, I will therefore examine cases where the techniques of emotive-cognitive reframing and bodily reframing were embedded in a professional setting or guided by care professionals.

Let us first look at the former, that is, the backstage where the young people received professional support in 'changing the chip'. The experiences of hysteresis led many young people to feel confused about what was going on. This ambiguity of how they should interpret their situations of impasse translated into uncertainty. Goffman writes in this regard that when there is uncertainty about how to frame a situation, people are more likely to turn to experts that help in 'clearing up an ambiguity of frame' (1993: 303, author's translation). Some of my interviewees mentioned that they had consulted professionals for advice and support in dealing with the impasse and related feelings. Usually these were doctors, therapists, personal coaches or psychologists, whereby the latter in particular offered a backstage where the young people could give space to their framing-related insecurities and deviant emotions. Willems (1997: 369, author's translation) therefore writes that 'therapy can function as a kind of overall existential "backstage" … as a place "behind the scenes" where otherwise socially placeless subjects, affects and various irrational behaviours find a legitimate "stage"'.

For Javier, the backstage provided by his psychologist was an important place that helped him in the process of understanding and (re)interpreting:

'I think that seeing a psychologist is one of the most wonderful things that can happen to you, a good psychologist fixes a lot of shit that … Come on, day to day, uh, super-dumb stuff that you can turn into a drama if you're not paying attention and all of a sudden it's like "Oh, no! OK, I'm just pissed off … Why am I so pissed off?" First of all, it helps you to detect things, no? I'm pissed off – and maybe many times I didn't even realize it. "Where does this come from? Let's see … Ah, fuck, I'm frustrated, I thought I was going to leave work early today or that I've been arguing with my mother again, I don't know." So, for me personally, the psychologist has helped me to understand and, from that understanding, to be more coherent … So, of course, understanding those emotions, well, it allows you to pinpoint things … Then I have to understand why I'm sad, accept it and, from there, see how I react on the basis of that understanding.' (Javier, 35)

Javier's account provides an insight first into how framing-related insecurities occurred and influenced his everyday life and, second, into how he could address and learn to understand them within the therapeutic sessions. The psychologist provided a backstage for him where the reframing could be discussed and practised under guidance. This guidance included, among other things, a reflective approach to emotions and a structured process for understanding and classifying them. Against this background, Javier described how he tried to use emotions as clues to understand himself in the context of uncertainty and the resulting behaviour towards himself and others.

For Javier, this form of emotional reflexivity[4] (Holmes, 2010) was a prerequisite to "see how I react" and "to be more coherent". Holmes (2015: 61) points out that 'especially when facing new situations or ways of living where an emotional habitus is little help and feeling rules are unformed or unclear', people draw on and reflect on emotions to navigate their path. With the help of the psychologist, Javier established a clear procedure for this, which included the reflexive practices of detecting, understanding and accepting emotions. Yet, it also shows how it was much less the framework than the person that needed to be understood and changed if necessary.

A backstage provided by a psychologist could also be a place where forms of re-evaluation could be proposed and then prepared, as we see in Mateo's case:

'Well, talking about it, for example, with the psychologist. The psychologist told me: "Look at things that you like, get motivated by other things, use the weekdays, apart from looking for work, to do things that satisfy you. I don't know, do you like music, for example? Then start playing music. Do you like movies? Then go to the cinema. These things fill your time." And well, yes, it helps you and yes, you take note of it and you let go of all the weight you have inside you by talking about it.' (Mateo, 29)

Mateo's psychologist was trying to help him in finding a framework of understanding to apply in his situation of work-related impasse and, once found, how to go about putting it into practice. In proposing this re-evaluation, his psychologist advised him to shift his focus of attention and to obtain motivation and self-esteem from areas other than work. The psychologist suggested, for example, that a substitute in the form of a leisure activity ought to be found that could take over this function. Earlier on, we saw Mateo trying to implement this proposal. By focusing on music and playing in a band, he re-evaluated the importance of work to no longer see it as something that could generate recognition and self-esteem, but only as a way of ensuring an income. While emotion work is often described as burdensome or even alienating (Hochschild, 1983), Mateo's example shows how it can also have a 'liberating' effect. This reflects what Mills and

Kleinman (1988: 1019) already argued in 1988, that 'emotion work can be experienced as liberating when it is part of the process of leaving a bad situation'. This is where backstages with experts can assume a guiding or support function.

This was similar in the case of bodily techniques. We can see this clearly in the example of yoga, a form of bodily reframing with the help of experts. Some of the young people, particularly women, talked about how yoga practice turned into a backstage for them that helped them to deal with their emotions:

'Well yoga, the space itself induced in me strong feelings of serenity, peace and self-empowerment, you know, the idea that I'm there for myself. We close the door of the classroom and it's just us, and it's about what I have inside and I don't give a damn about what's outside. So I found a very good space to work on my feelings, especially on the negative ones.' (Dorotea, 35)

'Yoga helped me a lot, that is, a lot, a lot. The sensation of feeling yourself, of, you know, like … I don't know, of being in your body, of getting to know yourself, right? Of knowing all the things it generates in you.' (Begoña, 29)

'Well, I try to go running if I have more energy, if I have less, I go to yoga. In fact, all these are activities that I have done with only one objective, which is to disconnect and release stress, that is to say, that is the objective, not another one (laughs).' (Alberta, 27)

Similarly to the use of the bathroom, emotion-focused strategies (Thoits, 1990: 193) were adopted on the backstage of yoga practice. Here, however, the emotion management was carried out with the help of support provided within a professional setting whereby relaxation and meditation techniques aimed at deliberately manipulating how the person's physiological sensations were introduced and practised. The focus was on concentrating on the individual's own body and blocking out all external influences and thoughts. We can see this aspect of focusing inwards and 'freeing yourself', especially in Dorotea's and Begoña's accounts: "We close the door of the classroom and it's just us." They spoke of how disconnecting from the outside world helped them gain greater awareness of their own bodies and needs. The "feelings of serenity, peace and self-empowerment", as described by Dorotea, reflect the therapeutic and beneficial effects that yoga produces, according to neurological and psychological studies. Research suggests that it helps to reduce people's stress, anxiety and depression, and can improve their mood and wellbeing (Streeter et al, 2010; Froeliger et al, 2012; Li and Goldsmith,

2012; Gard et al, 2014; Telles et al, 2019). Even with work-related stress, according to Hartfiel et al (2011), practising yoga can have a positive effect on people's self-confidence and energy levels, and may make them more resilient to stress.

From a sociological perspective, it can, of course, be argued that yoga's beneficial potential for emotion regulation sees the body as yet another instrument for self-optimization, entirely in the service of the entrepreneurial project of the self (Bröckling, 2007; Villa, 2008). For Rosa (2016), for example, *resonance oases* – that is, places like the bathroom or the yoga studio into which people flee when they feel alienated from the world and themselves – are associated with a certain purposiveness. Rosa argues that when people frequent these sites to try and gain (back) access to their emotional resonance, they also do so with the aim of using their increased wellbeing in the competition for resources and positions. He therefore writes that:

> even where late-modern actors go to the resonance oases of nature or religion or to the concert hall … they do so (also) in the knowledge – and certainly on the basis of experience – that in doing so they will increase their chances of success in the competitive struggle of capitalist society, in which not only jobs and money, but also privileges and positions, friends and partners, status and recognition are fought for. (Rosa, 2016: 623, author's translation)

In this view, the calculating and co-opted individual is quite prominent and leaves little room for other explanations. Yet, from a sociology of emotion perspective, we could also argue that people who frequent resonance oases in order to increase their wellbeing do not necessarily do so with the aim of competing for resources and positions, but rather to strive for emotional energy (Collins, 1990).[5] It might well be that an increased level of emotional energy is helpful in competing for resources and positions, but this can also happen as a byproduct and does not necessarily include a person's conscious decision in the first place. For Dorotea, Begoña and Alberta, the main motive to practise yoga was to disconnect from "what's outside" and to relieve stress and pressure related to the competitive struggle over educational qualifications, employment and social recognition. In that sense, yoga practice and movements in space, as described earlier in this chapter, were similar in terms of the way in which the young people used these two bodily techniques to momentarily disconnect.

Still, this does not mean that everyone used or had access to both techniques in the same way. Practising yoga was related to a certain middle-class habitus. This was also the case for the other expert variants of bodily techniques and 'changing the chip' (such as therapy and coaching). Habitus and thus dimensions and intersections of class, race and gender influenced their emotion management techniques and the way in which they were approved as such (by institutions, insurance companies and medical professionals, etc.). Though public health insurance covered the costs of therapy, especially in cases of anxiety and depression, the waiting lists were often quite long due to increased demand (especially in Madrid), and regular sessions over a longer period of time were rarely possible, which meant that the use of private services was often the only alternative (Sánchez Becerril, 2019). Furthermore, the practice of reflecting on emotions, in particular, but also certain activities, such as yoga, are habitualized practices of the middle class (see, for example, Alter, 2011; Illouz, 2015) and therefore financially or symbolically often less accessible to others than were the other forms of individual backstages described earlier.

Conclusion

In this chapter, I have demonstrated how the young people explained and dealt with their emotions of uncertainty, anxiety and frustration. Using Goffman's concepts of frames and stages (1959, 1974) and Hochschild's notion of emotion work (1979), I have illustrated the young people's search for (new) patterns of explanation and coping strategies, which were necessary due to their experiences of hysteresis and impasse. The mismatch faced by many young people between their expectations and the opportunities available to them led them to question existing explanatory frameworks and partly replace them with new ones. Key to this process was emotive-cognitive reframing, as illustrated by the recurring expression 'changing the chip'. 'Changing the chip' encompassed the three forms of emotion work identified by Hochschild (1979: 562) – namely, cognitive, emotive and bodily – and helped the young people to deal with their fragmented habitus (Silva, 2016) and the contradictions between what they perceived as expectations and entitlements, and the opportunities available to them in post-crisis Spain. 'Changing the chip' thus involved the young people shifting reference points and expectations.

Yet, the forms of emotive-cognitive reframing to which they resorted depended on whether they understood and framed their experiences and emotions as either individualistic or systemic. If they resorted to individualistic patterns of explanation, as I have demonstrated in this chapter, the shift took place at the individual level. 'Changing the chip' thus meant adapting one's ideas and expectations to the changed circumstances. To this end, they changed practices of social comparison (for example, qualifying one's own impasse), reconsidered their relationship to time (for example, concentrating on the present instead of long-term planning) or modified their understanding of the meaning and function of work (for example, seeing work as a mere income-generating activity rather than one for social recognition or self-fulfilment). Consequently, emotion work helped them primarily to adapt by suppressing or changing (deviant) emotions such as uncertainty, anxiety and frustration. When, for example, Begoña and Natalia framed their positions for which they were overqualified and their several temporary jobs as enriching experiences, and Alberta framed her impasse as relatively privileged compared to that of other young people, they were all engaging in a form of anxiety and frustration management with the aim of turning their disappointment into satisfaction and their worries into confidence.

Individual backstages supported the emotive-cognitive reframing process of qualifying the impasse and of adapting and suppressing emotions at an individual level. They provided room for carrying out emotion (work) and offered a space in which the young people could rehearse, get to know or create frames. Additionally, they were particularly important for emotion work through bodily techniques, which served to dilute feelings and provide a sense of calm. In this way, individual backstages helped people to disconnect and (temporarily) escape from experiences of impasse.

It would be tempting now to equate individualistic frames and individual backstages with the perfect internalization of neoliberal subjectivity. There is no doubt that public discourse in Spain, especially against the background of austerity measures, was strongly influenced by the narrative of individual accountability (see Alonso et al, 2016). Yet, individualistic framing and coping were not always just about feeding into the idea of neoliberal self-responsibility; they could also be an attempt to grasp meaning beyond the common frames that did not fit anymore. Diluting, disconnecting or escaping through individual(istic) reframing and emotion work therefore both constituted an attempt to cope with loss of meaning and to protect oneself in order to create distance from the feelings as well as the circumstances to which the feelings were directed. Nevertheless, López Calle rightly observes that 'the palliative effect that this type of interventions occasionally achieves at individual level – which reinforces their public acceptance and promotion – on the one hand does not resolve the structural origin of these problems – which will therefore continue to increase – and on the other hand, and because of this, indirectly contributes to the concealment of their ultimate causes' (2012: 187, author's translation).

5

Systemic Frames and Collective Spaces for Emotion Work

After having looked at individualistic frames and individual backstages in Chapter 4, the focus in this chapter is on systemic frames and collective spaces for emotion work. Systemic frames were patterns of interpretation that the young people used when they felt that the impasse in which they were stuck was structurally conditioned. In this case, they explained their feelings of uncertainty, anxiety and frustration as a consequence of their political, economic and social context over which they felt they had only little or no influence as an individual. Here too, their (re)interpretation of impasse and feelings involved emotion work. Yet, this consisted primarily of turning emotions inside out and redirecting them from the individual towards external actors and structural conditions. Collective spaces for emotion work played an important role here: on the one hand, they provided a space in which the young people could carry out emotive-cognitive reframing collectively; on the other hand, they provided the 'right' or legitimate space and time to express and share (deviant) emotions.

While this chapter does not include as much data as the previous one, it does provide indications that are worth emphasizing, especially in present times where we see many (youth-led) protest movements emerging globally. Analysing the seeds of emerging critical consciousness and counter-emotions among young people in my data can begin to offer an understanding of how emotions generated by hysteresis may turn into collective claims for system change.

From personal to systemic failure

When the young people related their impasse and feelings to the changing structural conditions, they generally viewed their situation as a product of economic and political developments rather than something for which they were personally accountable. Consequently, they viewed their situation as being beyond their personal control and affecting most of their generation. There was a common perception of intergenerational inequalities, which only increased with the onset of the economic crisis. Even though some of the young people had seen their parents lose their jobs or struggle financially, there was a general consensus that it was particularly hard for the young generation to enter the labour market and relatively common for them to be given exploitative working conditions. The economic and political model, which was not only perceived as disadvantageous for (the majority of) the young generation but was also generally questioned, was referred to as one of the reasons for their sense of unfairness and feelings of frustration. While accusations of corruption, nepotism and a lack of trust in national politics and the world of global finance were a common thread running through many of the young people's accounts, there was also a general awareness that this was not entirely a question of morality, but also something inherent in the system and the way in which politics and the economy were organized:

'Most of the time what I say is "It's not your problem, it's a problem of your generation".' (Alberta, 27)

'We are the most educated generation with the least work. Well, no generation will ever live the way our parents did. I don't know, that's how it is, we have to change the way we understand work, because it's never going to be the way it was.' (Nuria, 28)

'Logically, many people see that living like this is not viable. Who wants to live like this for the rest of your life? I don't know. Well, yes, you live, you live well … You have – well let's say, the city gives you that security, it gives you the security that you're going to be able – as long as you're working like that – you're going to be able to live well or badly … It gives you the security of living your 10 hours a day working Monday to Friday, and even Saturdays, 10 hours a day to be able to earn your living.' (Antonio, 26)

The mismatch between expectations and opportunities that shaped their individual experiences was seen as an outcome of a more general mismatch whereby the way in which work was once understood and the expectations that emerged from this understanding seemed mostly at odds with the reality of post-crisis Spain. For Nuria, this mismatch was best expressed through the contradiction of being "the most educated generation with the least work". Antonio was also critical of the fact that following the current rules of the labour market might still allow people to make a living, but they were "paying" with exploitative working conditions which he felt were hardly "viable".

This awareness of shared precariousness and shared emotions also led to the idea that dealing with it was a collective process. They did not believe that they could cope with the situation through individual reframing alone and felt that a collective effort was also needed. This demand for a change in framing at a societal level was expressed, among other things, by the use of the pronoun 'we'. In demanding "we have to change the way we understand work", Nuria emphasized that it was not up to her to find a new definition of work for herself, but that the concept of work had to be reconsidered and adapted within society as a whole.

From blaming oneself to blaming the system

Re-evaluating the impasse and related feelings by drawing on systemic frames included emotion work. As we will see in this section, this work consisted mainly of validating and redirecting (deviant) emotions. Let us first look at the redirecting of emotions. This type of emotion work involved redirecting emotions, which were originally addressed to oneself, to the outside. In this process, Flam (2005: 20) argues that 'subversive counter-emotions' are generated, which often lead to a 'disaffection from the system'. Feelings of shame and guilt play a central role here, as these are usually directed at the individual and its deviations from the norm, and thus have a demobilizing effect.

Alonso et al (2016) observed such a process when they conducted the same study in 2010, at the beginning of the economic crisis, and again in 2014. They examined how people in Spain interpreted their own socioeconomic situation and that of others, and examined who people felt was responsible for the emergence and management of the crisis. In 2010, the blame was primarily assigned to the inappropriate behaviour of the population. Using the common shaming sentence that some have lived beyond their means, both economic and political actors as well as social groups of the middle and upper classes developed a discourse that placed the blame on the working class and on all those who could not cope with their debts or who contributed to the emergence of these debts by relying on public money and social welfare (Alonso et al, 2016: 376). This moralist finger pointing seeped into the self-disciplinary discourses of the middle and lower classes. In this way, allegedly excessive consumption and lavish lifestyles were questioned in a self-critical manner and ways of getting out of the crisis were located in the personal sphere by changing one's own behaviour and way of thinking (Alonso et al, 2016: 358ff). Four years later, in 2014, the authors observed that with ongoing socioeconomic repercussions for large parts of the Spanish society, the once-dominant discourse of morality had increasingly given way to an awareness of precariousness. Although the authors do not go so far as to mention an emerging collective identity around this precarious condition, they do see that the awareness of precariousness and the related fears of (not) being able to improve or maintain one's social position are perceived as a form of shared condition (Alonso et al, 2016: 361f). This change in perception was possible, as in addition to personal responsibilities, people increasingly saw structural inequalities as causes of their socioeconomic situation. The power of banks, corruption and inability of politics as well as the economic system as such, based on ever more growth and consumption, were now cited as the causes of the ongoing crisis and the growing impoverishment of numerous population groups (Alonso et al , 2016: 359, 363). This shift from blaming individual misconduct to blaming structural conditions was also reflected in the young people's narratives in this book:

'The TV doesn't tell you this, the TV tells you figures and tells you that there are people who don't study and that there are people who don't work, so we seem to be the ones to blame. So, it's like: is it the individual's fault or society's fault? Well, more that of society, of those who run society. So, for me it's a worrying issue at the moment. In other words, we are in a crisis and, although everything seems to be going phenomenally well, this continues to be a crisis, especially for those of us who are poor, … and even more so for us young people.' (Amelia, 23)

'Well, understanding that it's a problem of … above all, what I've told you, that it's a problem of our generation, that it's not a problem of my own, that it's not that I'm not worth it in some way, right? A little bit of convincing yourself that, it's not convincing yourself, it's about getting things straight in your head, that it's not really you who's doing it wrong, that it's the labour system that's wrong, it's an overall issue.' (Alberta, 27)

Amelia's and Alberta's statements clearly demonstrate how resorting to systemic patterns of explanation rather than individualistic ones led them to reject guilt and shame. For Amelia, these emotions were caused, among other things, by the way in which the media reported on young people in the labour market, which gave her the impression that she was personally responsible for her impasse. But she rejected this guilt and redirected it, along with the shame it entailed, towards society and in particular "those who run society". In the same vein, Alberta explained her situation in terms of structural conditions ("it's the labour system that's wrong, it's an overall issue") and therefore rejected the possible feelings of shame. In both cases, we can thus observe what Flam (2005: 30) calls the switch 'from being ashamed to shaming out'. Shaming is used to remind people of their position within a group or society and serves to maintain social order (Kemper, 1981; Neckel,

1991); however, it is 'only effective when the individuals at which ... [it is] directed share norms with those applying these sanctions' (Flam, 2005: 23). If this is not the case, and shaming, as happened with Alberta and Amelia, is not accepted but rather redirected, it can have a liberating or even activating effect instead of a demobilizing one (see also Gould, 2002).

Validating frustration and anger

We may see why this is the case by looking at Kemper's early work (1978). Kemper argues that people who feel that they can negotiate less status or power than they think they deserve, and blame themselves for this, usually feel shame. Conversely, people who are convinced that the blame lies not with themselves but with outside forces are more likely to feel anger.[1] So, if the young people used systemic patterns of explanation to make sense of their impasse, they were able to suppress demobilizing feelings such as shame and guilt, making room for feelings such as indignation and anger. This process of emotive-cognitive reframing involved what I would refer to as validation work. This is required in order to validate the perception and displaying of anger. In line with Thoits (1985: 239) and Skeggs (1997: 85), I specifically speak of validation here and not legitimization.[2] The latter requires sufficient symbolic capital to present feelings not only as understandable and appropriate, but also as normative, and for the majority of the young people in this book, this was not the case.

Jesus and Vidal both expressed frustration and anger about their impasse, but made it very clear that they considered these feelings to be appropriate:

> 'It's an appropriate feeling and a sense of injustice, of course, because it's not fair for anyone to have to feel like this. It's a feeling appropriate to the circumstances in which we live. In other words, it's a consequence of the system in which we live, wage labour and capitalism. That's how it is.' (Jesus, 34)

> 'Man, of course, because it's normal to be indignant about such situations, especially the way things are today. I mean, that's what I'm telling you, this feeling is indeed widespread. No one says: "Ah, well, I'm fine with it." No, everyone says: "It's a bloody disgrace."' (Vidal, 25)

Jesus' and Vidal's accounts provide an insight into how the validation work was carried out. First, it was done through linguistic normalization. Jesus and Vidal both used a certain choice of words in their descriptions to underline the normality and appropriateness of their feelings (for example, "it's normal" or "it's an appropriate ... feeling"). In this way, they produced, through language, what we can understand from Misztal (2001) to be situational normalcy. Referring to Heritage (1984), Misztal writes that 'under the condition of change, what was abnormal/deviant becomes the focus of the development of a new accounting framework. As a result of the new normalizing coda of ordering, what was seen as "deviant" in the light of the old framework will be viewed under its new alternative "as appropriate, normal or natural" (Heritage, 1984: 231)' (Misztal, 2015: 54). Second, validation work involved embedding emotions in their context. For Jesus and Vidal, feeling indignant and angry was "appropriate to the circumstances" and "the way things are today". They presented their feelings as a logical consequence of the external circumstances and not of their personal biography or limited abilities. Finally, they validated their emotions by referring to the shared experience. Jesus and Vidal framed their personal impasse as one that was shared by other young people. They were therefore not the only ones in this situation and with these feelings. Consequently, frustration and anger were presented as a collective experience: "that feeling is indeed widespread" and "everyone says: 'It's a bloody disgrace.'" Frustration and anger were thus used as a form of vocabulary with a moral quality, pointing to a moral order which both of them saw as violated. Jesus, for example, referred to values of fairness and justice that he regarded as being breached ("it's not fair for anyone to have to feel like this"), thus making it very clear that he wouldn't feel anger if the situation were more just.

As we have seen with Jesus and Vidal as well as with Amelia and Alberta, they did not validate frustration and anger and redirect shame in a vacuum. In order for them to be able to carry out these forms of systemic emotive-cognitive reframing, a reference to a shared experience and a shared understanding of what was going on were needed. These preconditions could emerge, for instance, in collective spaces for emotion work.

Collective spaces for emotion work

Collective spaces for emotion work were mainly social and often backstage-like spaces where the young people could share their individual emotions with others. Many talked about how this was done with family members and friends, and how this helped to alleviate their feelings of hysteresis and impasse. Some collective spaces for emotion work emerged in the context of the working environment, sometimes spontaneously, sometimes more ritualized and at other times in rather institutionalized settings. It was essential that these social spaces not only provided a space in which the young people could express and share (deviant) emotions (Thoits, 1990), but that they also offered a framework that enabled them to understand and deal with these emotions collectively.

Expressing and sharing deviant emotions

Spaces in which people can share individual experiences and emotions with others are often described in movement studies as an important prerequisite for creating an awareness of one's own situation through comparison with others and thus acquiring an awareness of structural inequalities (Goodwin et al, 2001; Flam and King, 2005; Munson, 2009; Kleres and Wettergren, 2017). Furthermore, they are described as important sites of emotional exchange and social support, assuming that the emotions are validated or accepted by others (Thoits, 1985: 238; Summers-Effler, 2002). For the young people in this book, these spaces were not always necessarily large groups, as in the case of social movements. Spaces for sharing and expressing emotions also emerged in small groups:

> 'Then you have your colleagues, here, OK? Well, it's also very important to be with people who have similar life experiences, who understand you, you know? You can say: "Well, man, this is happening to me", and of course there are probably other people who say: "But, damn, you're in a situation of serious uncertainty" because sure, the problems I have are like – ... They say: "Well, find a permanent job and stop messing around" ... They don't understand you. Here for example, in this space with my colleagues, well yes, you can cry at ease and say: "Fuck, I'm doing terrible", "Yeah, me too". And maybe they'll even suddenly say: "Why don't we set something up?" You know? (laughs) That's already another life, another story. You have to – ... they understand. So, it's important that people around you are not judging you all the time, you know? Because then you have a lot of people who are like: "Oh, of course with the kind of life you lead, what do you expect?" Pff.' (Vanesa, 33)

Vanesa's statement reveals the importance of a collective space for expressing and sharing emotions she could not easily express elsewhere. Here she could openly complain about her situation and let her tears run free without fear of being misunderstood. It helped her to realize that her situation was shared by others, which helped her to understand her impasse and the uncertainty involved. The collective space for emotion work was a space where people shared "similar life experiences", that is, a similar kind of impasse but also similar ways of framing it. This is particularly evident in Vanesa's juxtaposition of the different professional and personal circles in which she was moving. Within her workplace at a co-working space, where experiences of impasse were shared, she felt understood ("they understand"). Here, Vanesa was able to have her deviant emotions validated. Her colleagues not only confirmed that they felt similarly to her, but also confirmed that it was OK to feel this way given her impasse. On the other hand, there were those by whom she felt judged and in front of whom she did not feel she could show her feelings of uncertainty, frustration or anger. The comment "then you have a lot of people who are like: 'Oh, of course with the kind of life you lead, what do you expect?'" shows the feeling rule she perceived in this context, giving her the impression that she did not really have the right to complain about her situation. Among some of her colleagues at the co-working space, there was room for these deviant emotions. Moreover, as Summers-Effler (2002: 50) writes: 'In solidarity, deviant emotions come to represent less of a threat to one's social bonds because the deviant emotions themselves have come to be associated with new sources of solidarity and emotional energy formed in collective identity.' Frustration and anxiety, which Vanesa could not share elsewhere, became a common ground and source of solidarity in her co-working space. By having her deviant emotions validated by others, she felt less deviant herself than reactions from her other professional and social circles made her believe. At the same time, new motivating emotions emerged. Vanesa described how, as a result of exchanges, a form of emotional energy (Collins, 1990) came into being: on the one hand, by mirroring her own experiences and feelings and, on the other hand, when shared experiences and feelings became the basis for something new, like common ideas and projects.

While Vanesa's example is one of a collective space for emotion work that was used rather spontaneously, others were specifically organized to create a common space for (emotional) exchanges. Lara and Roberto, for example, introduced the ritual of sitting together every Monday to talk about everything that had affected them and any feelings that they wished to express. As colleagues setting up their own company they were confronted with normative ideas of 'standard' and 'good' work. They felt being stuck to the ideas, in particular that of standard employment, and felt unable to free themselves as easily from the expectations that these ideas involved, expressed, for instance, by their parents and friends. They had created the Monday ritual to provide a space for regularly airing their feelings of frustration and uncertainty:

'Most Mondays, like today, we have our "Fuck Everything!" session (laughs). On the first day of the week it's all about complaining about the world at large ... The point is that there are days when we work more as partners, but we are friends, so ... In other words, our close space is always there too, which is important.' (Lara, 32)

This quote illustrates how Lara and Roberto created their own collective space where they could display and share their deviant emotions. They used their backstage-like environment to complain about "the world at large", but it was particularly helpful to them in dealing with the way people reacted to their decision to start their own company and people's opinions of what constituted 'real' work. It was a deliberate outlet for their pent-up frustration and anger, as also indicated by the name they chose for it – the "Fuck Everything!" session. This represented an important "close space" in which they acted not only in their role as colleagues but also in their role as friends. The 'result of this conversational ritual', as Collins (1988: 47) writes, was 'to create a little temporary cult, a shared reality consisting of whatever is being talked about'. Lara's and Roberto's Monday session was thus a ritualized practice of 'Miteinanderfühlen' (feeling together) (Scheler, 1923: 9–10). It is one of the four forms of compassion or emotional contagion that Scheler distinguishes between in his work *The Nature of Sympathy*.[3] This form arises when a shared experience of emotions is also oriented towards one and the same object or situation. For Lara and Roberto, the 'Miteinanderfühlen' resulted not only from the experience of the same impasse, but also from the same emotional reactions to it. As we saw with Vanesa, a collective space for emotion work was not only somewhere to share similar emotional experiences, but was also a place where common systemic frames were developed with which the young people tried to organize and explain their experiences and feelings.

Turning emotions inside out

'If deviant emotions are handled within the self', Summers-Effler (2002: 49) argues, then 'there is little opportunity to realize that one's experiences are not necessarily a personal problem or inadequacy. When one experiences solidarity in ritual, one's identity expands, and larger social dynamics can be revealed in the process'. Summers-Effler describes here a form of emotive-cognitive reframing in which the deviant emotions are not directed inwards, against oneself, but instead outwards. One could also say that emotions are turned inside out (Ahmed, 2014: 9). While Ahmed describes (and criticizes) this term as a psychology-based approach, which assumes that we have feelings within ourselves and carry them outwards by expressing them, the way in which I use the idea of turning emotions inside out refers to Summers-Effler's (2002: 51) considerations and is more about carrying the (emotional) conflict from the individual level to a social interaction level. This process makes it possible to recognize personal situations such as impasse and hysteresis as part of a social pattern. For this to happen, a form of opportunity for awareness or collective experience is needed that provides space, inspiration, guidance and support for reframing. Collective spaces for emotion work like those of Vanesa or of Lara and Roberto constituted such spaces and offered them the opportunity to get in touch with systemic frames or to be involved in creating them. The following example involving Mateo shows how this process of turning emotions inside out came about.

Mateo talked about dealing with his feelings of frustration and his anxiety (attacks) by trying to minimize them and by redirecting his attention from work towards more fun activities such as music (see Chapter 4). Both of these emotion work techniques were based on an understanding of keeping the emotional conflict within himself and of dealing with it individually. His individual backstage provided by the psychologist was an important place where he came into contact with this form of emotive-cognitive reframing and could rehearse it (under 'professional' guidance). While this helped him at first, he soon realized that he could neither forget nor easily repress his frustration with and anxiety about the impasse. In a way, he experienced what Thoits (1985: 236) calls 'emotion-work failure', whereby contrary to (emotional) expectations, deviant emotions cannot be reduced or changed in the long run. According to Thoits (1985: 236–8), this is particularly the case when the emotion-producing event persists and when there are no spaces of shared experience, which she subsumes under lack of 'social support':

'It [consulting the psychologist] helps you and yes, you take note of it and you let go of all the weight you have inside you by talking about it with your family and so on, but of course you saw that your situation remained more or less the same. It's a bit frustrating, but on the other hand you say: "I'm just not going to let it beat me". I said, for example: "I'm not going to let them beat me, I'm going to keep fighting". And it got to the point that, the last time they opened a new train station, I remember saying to my colleague in the union: "Look, this [train station] has to be mine, either way. If they're not going to give it to me, I'm ready to report them, with all the consequences. As far as I'm concerned they can dismiss me but I won't be wasting any more of my life, because I'm not willing to do that."' (Mateo, 29)

This quote shows the process of how the emotions were turned inside out. What made Mateo go beyond the individual to deal with his emotions was the contact with a collective (here the union) that opened his eyes to other ways of framing his situation. We also see that this process was triggered by what Munson (2009: 55ff) calls a 'turning point'. Such a turning point is often crucial for people to join a collective or movement, as the decisive event creates a cognitive and emotional availability to rethink the relationship between beliefs and action (Munson, 2009: 56). For Mateo, this turning point was reached when, with the opening of a new train station, a new job was due to be advertised – the type of position for which he had been trying to qualify and apply internally for a long time (see Chapter 2). The idea that he might once again not be considered for the post and might remain stuck in the impasse created the necessary conditions for him to become open and receptive to the union's approaches. He had joined the trade union shortly after entering the labour market, but it was only with his continuing experience of impasse that it took on an increasingly prominent role for him. According to Munson (2009: 47), existing personal contact with a collective – the trade union in Mateo's case – is not necessarily decisive to get people involved, but it is an essential precondition for ensuring that, once people experience a turning point, they do not carry the conflict inwards, but instead outwards to the social interaction level within the collective. Collective spaces for emotion work are thus places that enable room to be made for the social conflict in order for it not to be moved inwards.

If the turning point is the trigger that initiates the process of turning emotions inside out, then Summers-Effler's work (2002) can be used to illustrate how this process continues. She identifies several steps of the emotional dynamics that take place when, through a collective, people no longer interpret their situation in life or their subordinate position using individualistic patterns of explanation but rather systemic ones. To begin with, Summers-Effler (2002: 51) suggests that being in contact with a collective leads to the formation of a collective identity. This enables the individual to see their own situation through a perspective of sharedness and – as we saw earlier on – not to assign shame inwards, but to direct it outwards. A sense of injustice emerges, which can finally lead to critical consciousness. Here, she writes that 'the closer one is to consciously experiencing deviant emotions and understanding that they are shared across a social group with whom one identifies, the closer one is to experiencing critical consciousness' (Summers-Effler, 2002: 51–2). If this critical consciousness can be maintained, it can lead to participation in (subversive) activities. Mateo's account shows how, after the turning point, the emotional dynamic described by Summers-Effler emerged:

'Since I've been a union representative, I've learned a lot of things, things that … above all, about work, things that can be combated, that can be supported, that can be improved … I've been with the guys from the Youth section of the union, and seeing other workplaces and other professional experiences opens doors for you, opens your mind. You see other problems, which are often similar, and the experience is very good, enriching … The desire to improve things, the desire for these things to be turned around, because if we don't do it, no one will, because I don't see [Prime Minister] Rajoy wanting to change Spain, for example. Honestly, I don't see it. I think that he's going to stay the same or worse, that he's going to impose more restrictions, that he's going to privatize everything. So, then, each one of us, from our jobs, tries to give a little bit more, it's the only way (laughs).' (Mateo, 29)

All of the steps described earlier can be found in Mateo's statement. For him, the collective identity had developed through his regular contact with the trade union and his increased involvement. It manifested itself, among other things, in his choice of words such as "if we don't do it" and "each one of us", which emphasized his group membership. Gaining an insight into the life situations of the other group members also allowed him to see the problems they faced as a recurrent pattern. What he described as a "very good" and "enriching" experience that "opens your mind" was the sense of injustice that emerged. That his sense of injustice had also developed into critical consciousness was evident in his awareness of seeing the patterns he had recognized and the deviant emotions associated with them as legitimate reasons to become (politically) active. ("things that can be combated, that can be supported, that can be improved").[4] In order for the act of turning emotions inside out to be followed by participation in activities targeting system change, it was necessary for Mateo to overcome the fear or resignation that may be associated with it. He pitted "the desire to improve things, the desire for these things to be turned around" against the anxiety attacks from which he had suffered and the frustration he felt over his impasse. This was where demobilizing emotions were pushed back and new ones, which Flam (2005: 20) calls 'counter-emotions', emerged.

Generating counter-emotions

Collective spaces for emotion work were thus sites where counter-emotions emerged. Taking social movements as an example, Flam describes them as emotions that are ascribed to movements' own members and those that are directed against their opponents. Besides anger and hate, as well as distrust and contempt, she also counts hope among counter-emotions (Flam, 2005: 20). They activate and mobilize, whereby people are able to overcome their fear, redirect shame or transform resignation into hope. Against this background, counter-emotions provided the foundation for collective action based on shared emotions and systemic framing for the young people in this book. This was the case with looser forms of collective social spaces, as we saw, for example, with Vanesa. In addition to her sharing frustration and despair about hysteresis and impasse, and having a common understanding of these experiences, the exchange with colleagues generated new emotional energy (Collins, 1990). Hope emerged at the moment when the shared situation promised to provide a basis for new ideas and joint projects ("And maybe they'll even suddenly say: 'Why don't we set something up?', You know? (laughs) That's already another life, another story").

The situation was similar with collective spaces that were far more organized or even institutionalized. Mateo's account was one example of this, while another was the following from Antonio. He was also an active union member, but, unlike Mateo, who was in one of Spain's largest trade unions, Antonio had joined a smaller one which describes itself as an anarchosyndicalist labour union:

'For example, it's very easy to share the anger with my colleagues in the union, or with colleagues involved in other activities … I find it very easy to share it with those people, well, with the people who are in activism, because they feel … Well, actually we all feel the same, but they also act that way; but other people, most of the people I know, friends, relatives and so on, they also have that, let's say, I think they have that anger because, pff, you get home angry due to work and you start arguing, and they have that anger, too, but I can't share it that way, not with them, because, with activists we focus the anger on the same objective, but with people … Well, I come here to the park, I talk to my friends, they're mad at the company, they don't stop saying nasty things about it like "Motherfuckers, my boss, son of a …", but then, instead, they don't do anything to change it or – … Then, I say: "Yes, he may be a son of a bitch, but he's going to keep on doing it, it's going to be like that. You better get used to it or something because…" (laughs).' (Antonio, 26)

With the trade union, Antonio had found a collective platform where he could not only share frustration about his impasse but also transform rather paralysing feelings into mobilizing ones of anger and hope. His comment makes it clear why sharing the same feelings alone might not be enough for common action to emerge. He shared the same feelings as his friends of anger about their precarious situations in an economy of temporary, low-skilled and low-paid jobs, and both he and they directed it towards the employers whom they considered responsible. For Antonio, however, the sharing was perceived as easy when not only the feeling but also the actions that resulted from it were shared. There had to be a common direction in which the feelings could be diverted in order to make the collective space work for Antonio and to allow him to share his anger freely. Being able to "focus the anger on the same objective" was therefore decisive for him. The common goal Antonio spoke of here was, as with Mateo, the will to fight for change. While, according to him, his friends dealt with their anger by "enduring every day", "focusing on their [leisure] activities" or "waiting to have the weekends off to be able to enjoy something", he maintained his anger and redirected it to what he perceived to be its cause:

'I try to apply my rage, I try to … That's why I err … Let's say I'm an activist, let's say in this sense, I try to take my anger there [to the union],

I try to apply it in ... At the same time as I'm part of this, of all these jobs and of this system, I try to change it in my way.' (Antonio, 26)

While his friends' anger seemed to turn into resignation, Antonio tried to channel his anger and use it as a mobilizing force in activism. This difference which he identified here can be explained by a combination of Flam's (missing) counter-emotions and Summers-Effler's idea of emotional requirements. The latter implies that (subversive) action is most likely to occur when certain emotional requirements are met. Accordingly, Summers-Effler (2002: 53) writes that 'anger with low emotional energy ... turns into feelings of depression. Alternately, anger with high emotional energy produces ... hope'. And she goes on to say that even people 'who have developed a sense of injustice and critical consciousness may still be overwhelmed with fear, or they may be angry and cynical. Neither of these will lead to resistance action. Hope is required to inspire subversive action' (Summers-Effler, 2002: 53). This is why a space is needed, like a collective space for emotion work, which allows anger to gain the necessary emotional energy and to generate the counter-emotion of hope. After all, aiming for and fighting for change implies a sense of hope that it is worth engaging in protest and subversive action. We can also see this in the following quote from Jesus, who was a member of the same union as Antonio:

'In the long term, I hope that, one day, well, something will explode where we can then implement a different system to the one we are in, because that is what we are fighting for as well. But to be honest, in the short term, I don't see that.' (Jesus, 34)

Even though Jesus did not believe that anything would change in the short term, he still had hope – that is, he expected that, at some point, the effort would pay off and that an opportunity would arise to actively shape the change. Contrary to the practices of being in the present described in Chapter 4, where references to the future were avoided and (long-term) planning was not seen as feasible or useful, Jesus, Vanesa and Mateo sought to influence the future that would bring about change; they engaged in creating the future. Collective spaces for emotion work were thus spaces for sharing and jointly redirecting emotions towards a common goal which was a collective investment in the future.

Moving between the individual/individualistic and the systemic/collective

When talking about individualistic framing and individual backstages on the one hand and systemic framing and collective spaces for emotion work on the other hand, the impression may arise that they behave like opposites. However, such a dichotomy would contradict the young people's stories mentioned so far. In Chapter 4, we saw Mateo trying to deal with his impasse individually by working on his feelings and ideas that went along with them. The individual backstage provided by his psychologist supported these practices. At the same time, we saw him in this chapter as a member of a trade union who realized that others were in a similar situation and, like Antonio and Jesus, channelling his anger into collective action. Then there was Alberta (Chapter 4), who qualified her impasse and thus used individualistic emotive-cognitive reframing to try to change her emotions from disappointment into satisfaction and her worries into confidence. At the same time, she saw her impasse as an outcome of structural conditions and by drawing on systemic patterns of explanation, she rejected the idea of blaming herself for her situation.

These two examples indicate that the process of framing and dealing with emotions was not at all straightforward. On the contrary, the young people were moving between the individual/individualistic and systemic/collective and in their narratives the forms intermingled. Most of the young people who understood their impasse as a personal problem which only they could solve were well aware that the economic crisis had had an impact on the job market and their chances within it. Conversely, drawing on systemic frames and collective spaces for emotion work did not automatically mean that they were no longer receptive to individualistic explanations. As Benedicto et al (2014: 156) point out, these contradictions in narratives and framing are 'a fundamental tool of survival and an instrument of adaptation' which result from the young people's 'sense of lack of control over life trajectories, of constant adaptability and flexibilisation in the face of continuous changes in life'. Moving between the individual/individualistic and the systemic/ collective could happen subconsciously, whereas at other times the young people were quite aware of it, as Jesus' example demonstrates:

> 'Well, I was lucky enough that they took me on ... Fuck, look at the language I'm using, I'm lucky that they gave me a job. I mean, I have already internalized it when they should be the ones feeling lucky that we are going to enrich them, but well ... People tend to say that I'm lucky that I found this job, in which they exploit me.' (Jesus, 34)

While he was speaking, Jesus realized that the way he described the promising situation of being recruited after several years of unemployment was not compatible with his view of how the labour market and society should work, but rather echoed the common rhetoric to which he objected. In a self-reflective manner, he noticed that while he rejected this individualistic framing, he had nevertheless internalized it to a certain extent. Indeed, in Chapter 4 we saw how the expression 'I was lucky' was part of an individualistic emotive-cognitive reframing technique where considering oneself lucky in comparison to others was a form of internalizing the framing and feeling rules (Hochschild, 1979). According to these rules, keeping expectations in check, not making demands and being grateful for having a job was appropriate in post-crisis Spain.

Jesus' example also shows that the process of turning emotions inside out, which was given space and support in collective social spaces, is an ongoing process that is not completed once a person has come into contact with or applied systemic patterns of explanation. This is consistent with Summers-Effler's (2002: 52) observation about 'maintaining critical consciousness'. She emphasizes that this process does not end once critical consciousness is attained. On the contrary, it requires constant cognitive and emotional effort to maintain it, which can be achieved through, among other things, recurrent engagement in collective rituals and action. However, this constant effort concerns the management not only of one's own emotions but also those of others (Thoits, 1996). This was especially the case when the young people moved outside their collective spaces for emotion work where their feelings and/or their framing were no longer necessarily shared. Javier described how he did emotion work both internally and externally:

'Well, it requires that kind of … It requires you to grow thicker skin and adapt your mindset to get rid of certain prejudices that you often have yourself. For instance, many times you might look at yourself and think: "Damn, I'm 35 years old and I still don't have a permanent job." But then you look around and you say: "But who has a fucking permanent job?" (laughs). So, there are two – … You have to look at it two ways, one with yourself and another with your environment.' (Javier, 35)

Here, too, we see how Javier oscillated between individualistic and systemic framing. Through a constant inner dialogue, he reminded himself that he did not have to move the conflict inwards and accept the shame, since his impasse was a widespread one that allowed him to reject shame and guilt. When he said "You have to look at it two ways", he was referring both to work on his own thoughts and feelings and to emotive-cognitive work on those of others. This dual approach was needed because, as Summers-Effler (2002: 52) notes, 'when interacting outside … [collective] circles, their subordinate position remains despite … [people's critical] consciousness'.

Internal conflicts and contradictions could also occur within the collective spaces for emotion work, which then led people to withdraw and turn to other social or physical spaces and sometimes individual backstages. Ricardo's experience provided a good example of this. As an active member of a trade union, which was a central space for collective emotion work for him, his involvement resulted not only in emotional energy and a sense of solidarity but also in new experiences of frustration and stress, for example, due to conflicts with the staff or management. He felt that he could not deal with these kinds of conflict in the same social space – the trade union. This led him to deal with his emotions somewhere else – in the personal space of his own car:

> 'I haven't told anyone this, err (laughs). Err … When I had that moment, those months of being under a lot of pressure, I used to return home by car … Well then, I got home at midnight., 1 am, that was the time I usually clocked off. I, damn, I was under pressure, I remember I left [work] and, whenever I got home, I didn't want to work there ever again. I remember there were a few weeks when I came home, parked and stayed in the car for half an hour. Half an hour and, perhaps of that half an hour, I spent 10 minutes fully crying … In other words, crying … but in order to let off steam, not for anything in particular, you know, but just to let off some steam, and … And after finishing, I spent another 10 to 15 minutes recovering. After that half an hour, I got out [of the car] and went inside, like normal.' (Ricardo, 21)

The car temporarily became an individual backstage for Ricardo where he could let off steam. It offered him spatial separation from the outside world, protecting him from unwanted glances from outsiders, both from his work colleagues and his family. The darkness of the night provided additional shielding. For Ricardo, it was important that no one from either his professional circle or his private circle could see him releasing such feelings, as he explained in the course of the interview:

> 'It was to control things a little bit, what I did was stay in the car before going inside because I didn't want my family to see me all fucked up.' (Ricardo, 21)

He did not want to let off steam by crying in front of others or share it with someone afterwards ("I haven't told anyone this"). It is impossible to say whether this was out of fear of being perceived as weak and emotional or in order to prevent his parents from worrying about him and his work situation, or on account of both. However, what his statement does illustrate is what Goffman (1974) and later Collins (1988) described as moving in and between several frames. While we draw on primary frameworks to make sense of the world around us, we also engage in a complex set of levels and layers of other frames that shape the way we think and act. Against this background, systemic framing may, for instance, make it possible to consider shame as inappropriate and anger as righteous, yet the influence of other frames (such as those of gender and class) may actually render the act of letting off steam or crying impossible when around certain people and in certain places.

Conclusion

This chapter has shown that when young people resorted to systemic frames, the shift took place from the individual level to the societal level. Key to this form of (re)framing was not to carry the social conflict inside, but to move it outwards. Situations of impasse were thus seen neither as self-inflicted nor as something which was to be dealt under the sole responsibility of the individual alone. Consequently, emotion work was not about adapting; instead, it had the function of acknowledging (deviant) emotions of shame or anger and validating them as appropriate. Emotions directed inwards were thus turned outwards and redirected towards people and structures that were considered the cause of experiences of impasse. When Alberta and Mateo explained their situation with the (changed) structural conditions, they engaged in what I refer to as turning emotions inside out, whereby being ashamed turned into shaming others and disappointment with oneself turned into anger with the system.

Space – both physical and social – played a crucial role in the creation and use of systemic frames. Durkheim writes that 'most of our ideas and our tendencies are not developed by ourselves but come to us from without' (1966: 4, cited in Ahmed, 2014: 9). What I have identified as collective spaces for emotion work were, in this sense, spaces on the outside where young people had the opportunity to develop an awareness of shared experiences through encounters with others and thus came into contact with systemic frames or were involved in their creation. They were a space for sharing, expressing and validating deviant emotions which the young people felt were inappropriate elsewhere. While the emotive-cognitive and bodily techniques on the individual backstages were primarily about creating a sense of calm and staying in the present, collective spaces for emotion work provided a context in which reframing and emotion work helped to generate counter-emotions such as hope. This allowed people to (jointly) redirect emotions towards a common goal by means of which collective investment in the future was possible.

As with individualistic frames and individual backstages, it would be tempting now to equate systemic frames and collective spaces for emotion work automatically with mobilization or resistance. Systemic framing enabled the young people to uncover the structural character of the impasse and to pinpoint it as the cause of their emotions. Exchanges in collective spaces for emotion work in which the young people realized that they shared not only similar experiences but also similar emotional reactions to these experiences strengthened their awareness about the structural character of their situation. However, despite this awareness of shared experience, emotions might still be dealt with individually without spilling over into joint intentional actions. This was perhaps most evident in Antonio's narrative about his friends with whom he shared the same experience of being stuck and the related frustrations, but their shared emotions did not mobilize them. Shared emotions, as Salmela (2012: 42ff) aptly notes, can thus have different degrees[5] and therefore not automatically imply joint action.

While we have now seen how the young people in this book interpreted and dealt with their emotions, the next two chapters will explore how emotions were (explicitly) drawn on in order to negotiate a social position that was (more) difficult to maintain or improve in the face of changing conditions in post-crisis Spain.

PART III

(Re)Positioning in the Face of Change

In Part II, I discussed how the young people experienced the changes on the labour market in the aftermath of the crisis and how they dealt with what they felt. So far, I have shown that in their everyday lives, structural change appeared as a mismatch between how the young people expected their (working) life to be and what was actually possible on a precarious labour market in post-crisis Spain. This structural condition of hysteresis was perceived as impasse and translated into feelings of uncertainty, anxiety, frustration and resentment. In order to understand and deal with these emotions, many young people detached from frameworks of interpretation and value systems that they felt were no longer useful in their situation and looked for other niches of individual and collective emotional expression.

Yet, emotions were not only an outcome of structural change; they were also a source of motivation and driving force for action. Part III, then, is a discussion about the role that emotions played in young people's (re)positioning and their sense of 'placing' (Bourdieu, 2020: 339) when faced with changing conditions. Hysteresis had affected this sense of place, the sense of where the young people stood, relative to others. In situations involving fewer job opportunities and limited possibilities to draw on educational capital, emotions, as I will show, served to communicate and negotiate where the young people wished to stand. They functioned as 'place claims' (Clark, 1990: 314) in the process of adjusting to a social position that was challenged or reinforced through hysteresis.[1] I will consider two examples here: one where work was bound up with the idea of being emotionally fulfilling leading to satisfaction and happiness, and another where anger-related emotions were mobilized. As we will see, these ways of drawing on emotions enabled some young people to claim a sense of agency even when they felt stuck in an impasse, whereas others could not. This

121

also meant that the feelings of mismatch between expectations and actual opportunities became more bearable for some, while they were further intensified for others. In examining how the young people used emotions for position taking, my aim is to show that emotions can work both as resources and as boundaries, as a way of marking (symbolic) difference and creating distinction.

6

Emotional Fulfilment and Work

People may mobilize emotions in themselves and others. 'They do so', Clark (1990: 314) explains, 'to shape definitions of situations and of self. Often they want affirmation of their standing … [and] negotiate their place, trying to move (usually up, sometimes down), reminding and counter-reminding each other of their proper place with "emotion-cues".' The emotionally fulfilling work was such an emotion cue, as this chapter will show. In the young people's descriptions, whether they related to their actual job(s) or the idea of their ideal job, they saw work as a pleasant, enjoyable and stimulating activity. For some, this meant having some form of autonomy, while for others, it involved avoiding a monotonous routine and for the majority, it meant that the job is or should be something with which they felt comfortable. Whatever definition the young people ultimately referred to, talking about emotionally fulfilling work involved positioning: emotions such as passion, joy or happiness related the young people to a (work) position they occupied or wished to occupy. We will see that emotionally fulfilling work, as it came across in my material, took three different forms: as habitus defence, as an attempt to detach from good-life fantasies or as reinforcing the impasse.

Emotional fulfilment as habitus defence

Emotional fulfilment as habitus defence featured most prominently in the narratives of middle-class youths who had several (part-time) jobs in order to make ends meet. In most cases, one of these jobs was in an area relating to the individual's educational studies, but did not pay enough for the person to earn a living from it alone. The others were often jobs for which the person was overqualified in terms of their educational background. How emotionally fulfilling work helped to communicate where these young people wished to stand is illustrated by the stories of Begoña (29) and Vanesa (33) (who appeared in Chapter 2). Both wished to work in the field of education in which they had been trained and in which they had an interest, yet they remained financially dependent on having other jobs. Besides teaching in a school, Begoña was also working in a large clothing store. And Vanesa, who could not live off her job as a teacher at the language school which she had founded with friends, drew a second salary as a saleswoman at an optician's. Their impasse therefore consisted of the impossibility of converting their accumulated cultural capital (university education, internships and experience abroad, etc.) into a position on the labour market through which they could make a decent living. Instead, they reported being trapped: if they concentrated more on their preferred field of work, then they would run out of financial resources; if they worked more hours at the clothing store or the optician's, then they would feel as if they were turning their backs on the opportunity to work in the education sector. The mismatch between their imagined pathway into and within the labour market and the actual reality led to feelings of frustration and a sense of insecurity about their possibilities for position taking as young middle-class adults. Even though it was difficult for Begoña and Vanesa to signal and maintain their position as middle class through their work in practical terms, they were able to do so by performing their identities in a certain way in which emotional fulfilment played a crucial role. Both felt passionate for their jobs in education and saw in them their vocation in the Weberian sense (Weber, 1934, 2004):

'The language school [which we founded] is very much like a vocation, I think, because education is a vocation, I like it very much, err, it is your own business, you do what you want, it's like, in this case, you say: "I have an education but I have the education that I want which I treasure".' (Vanesa, 33)

'In fact, I took the job at the store because it allowed me to combine it with the rest [of my jobs], otherwise I wouldn't have taken it, no matter how much I needed it, no matter how much … No, because I know what I need these days and that is to be at a school … I just need it, it fulfils me, it simply fulfils me. I don't know how to explain it to you, but yes, I go to school feeling a lot of joy (laughs); I say: "It's good to be here."' (Begoña, 29)

In both of these quotes, their choice of words illustrates the strong emotions which they associated with their work and the field of education. They saw it as a "treasure" that filled them with joy and that they needed more than money. Emotional necessity was described as more important than financial necessity and was assigned a higher value. Emphasizing the emotional significance of work thus made it possible to disguise the fact that financial stability was often out of reach. Moreover, Begoña and Vanesa were able to frame their work as a conscious decision, as an act of self-determination within a situation involving fewer opportunities and limited choice.

Let us have a closer look at Begoña's case. Whereas she felt generally frustrated about not getting a job in the education system that would allow her to live on alone, she was particularly frustrated about having to take on a job at a clothing store in order to make ends meet:

> 'I find the store a huge frustration because I don't want to work there. I don't want to. And in fact I don't feel at all err … I don't feel comfortable. It's not my kind of place at all. It's … Well, I do it for the money, but not − I mean it's also a contradiction for me because I don't believe in that form of excessive consumption either … So, for me it's frustrating because … I'm here selling or folding T-shirts for a kind of life or society that I don't believe in. I don't think we have to wear a different T-shirt every day.' (Begoña, 29)

Begoña described this job as one that did not fit with her ideas about consumption or general view of the world. As a large mainstream fashion company whose business model was based on ever faster-changing collections and questionable working conditions, to her mind it represented a consumer and throwaway society to which she strongly objected. Her way of being and doing was hence at odds with what the clothing store represented for her. When spending time there and around the other employees, she thus felt out of place and ill at ease:

> 'Yes, I behave differently and in fact, I feel differently too. When I'm in the store I feel much … smaller … like a child, like very subject to everything. They boss you around … first this person and then another one, and another one, and another one … Well, basically you're here and the other person is above you.' (Begoña, 29)

This feeling of unease and the mismatch that covered her like a piece of clothing when she entered the store translated into an inner conflict. She was torn between staying in the job and thus being financially independent from her parents or leaving and freeing herself from an environment that, she felt, did not match her way of being and doing:

> 'It's true that my contract at the store expires soon and I don't know if I'm going to renew it because it wears me out a lot. More than physical fatigue and so on it's the fact of, you know, having studied, having certain expectations and being in a store. I basically get frustrated and I feel like I need to leave it so that something else can come along that makes more sense for me.' (Begoña, 29)

Begoña's statements show that her frustration was linked to what she perceived as status inconsistency. She clearly felt a discrepancy between what she thought she was entitled to, given her dispositions of capital, and her actual situation. These feelings of insecurity about her personal integrity indicate the struggle regarding class difference and the difficulties to produce distinctions through certain ways of being and doing. Begoña associated working in this environment with a certain habitus which she did not consider her own. To protect herself from any feelings of status inconsistency, on the one hand, she attached less importance to the job ("it's a job, it's six hours on weekends and that's it"), framing it purely as a means to an end ("I do it because it brings me money"). On the other hand, she distanced herself emotionally from that field of work by setting herself apart, among other things, from the values that the company conveyed and stood for, its organizational structures and the staff. In this way, Begoña made it clear that she and her colleagues did not have much in common and that they had a completely different view of the world:

'I don't feel ... like I'm on the same wavelength as the rest of my colleagues because, well, despite the fact that they are also educated people but well, it's true that we don't see things in the same way or have the same views of life ... And then, I hear comments, things from my colleagues ... well, that I don't share, and they upset me a lot and make me angry because I don't know how to manage the situation by saying: "What are you saying?" You know? For example, Islamophobia, well, in one of the stores which many Arabs visit, I hear racist comments from my colleagues, but every day ... well, obviously I think that all people are the same.' (Begoña, 29)

Separating herself discoursively and emotionally from that working environment thus became an important practice in ensuring that Begoña maintained distinction. To do so, she also used the linguistic imagery of energy flows. When working at the clothing shop, she primarily felt that she received and gave off "negative energy". She felt this "negative energy increasing" whenever the difference in habitus was most evident to her. Like a physical and mental purification process, Begoña wanted to free herself from these negative energies "in order to find [her] true self".

While Begoña and Vanesa added value to their jobs in the education sector by associating them with emotional fulfilment, this association also created distance in relation to their roles as saleswomen. As Begoña's preceding quote already suggests, their various part-time jobs were located at opposite ends of the scale. Their work in the education sector provided maximum emotional fulfilment, including feelings such as joy, satisfaction, passion and happiness. Their positions as sales assistants at the clothing store and at the optician's were at the other end of the scale and were associated with aversion and frustration. In this way, Begoña and Vanesa set up a form of emotional hierarchy (Illouz, 2015: 11) through which they could assure themselves of their agency and degree of self-determination. They were doing something that was fulfilling and meaningful. Thus, associating their educational work with feelings of fulfilment, passion and joy also served as a source of motivation for them to keep investing in these jobs, even though they did not know if or when this investment would eventually pay off.

The emotional hierarchy also functioned as a way of drawing symbolic boundaries (Lamont and Molnár, 2002) and created distinction between those jobs which, according to Begoña and Vanesa, could lead to fulfilment and joy and those which could not. The former were synonymous with feeling comfortable, while the latter were associated with feeling out of place and ill at ease, as illustrated by Begoña's quotation ("I don't feel comfortable. It's not my kind of place at all"). To feel comfortable thus meant having a job that was in line with their way of being and doing. In creating distance with those jobs deemed to be at odds with their habitus while, at the same time, giving higher value to those they saw fitting their habitus, the emotional hierarchy allowed them to communicate where they wished to stand. The narrative of emotionally fulfilling work thus functioned as a tool to produce distinction (Bourdieu, 1979).

This was particularly evident in the way that Begoña and Vanesa used emotions for position taking in relation to their colleagues at the clothing store and at the optician's. Their accounts illustrate how they assumed that their fellow workers (mostly working-class individuals) were not capable of having the very same feelings that they claimed to have themselves in the field of education:

'For me, they're people like very grey, they're satisfied with, okay, give me a schedule, give me money, you know?' (Vanesa, 33)

'[They] cared more about the iPhone.' (Vanesa, 33)

Begoña and Vanesa assumed that their co-workers were incapable of being passionate about or interested in any activities or matters outside of consumerism ("[They] cared more about the iPhone") and shamed them for it. They denied their colleagues their autonomy by implying that they simply took commands. They thought that their co-workers had a stronger sense of financial satisfaction than emotional satisfaction. While they acknowledged that "certain things are structural", they both emphasized the difference between them and their colleagues that came with different ways of being moved by emotions such as passion or joy.

Another example concerned their ideas of self-identification through work. While Begoña and Vanesa themselves both practised it, they devalued this activity when it was carried out by their working-class colleagues. As Vanesa noted: "Err, then work is also, work becomes something very important [for them] and very defining of who they are, and work, well, they did things that were crazy in my opinion, you know?" While Vanesa herself considered work "an identity process, [something that] provides you with an identity", it seemed exaggerated and inappropriate in the context of the optician's. In this way, she reinforced the emotional hierarchy in which she placed some forms of self-realization and passion higher than others. The emotional hierarchy was thus also a social one in which class distinctions were upheld. Using the emotional hierarchy as habitus defence reveals a fear of declassing, which Alonso et al (2016) found to be a recurring theme among the Spanish middle-class when discussing their experiences of the crisis. The precarization of working (and living) conditions, as Alonso et al (2016: 362–3) argue, made it increasingly difficult to elaborate discourses from a middle-class position and therefore made it seem even more pressing to defend one's status. Even if people were not necessarily personally affected by declassing, the crisis did bring about a general visibility of professional and social decline (in the form of dismissals and forced evictions, etc.) and, as a result, led to an increased awareness of the vulnerability of one's class position (Alonso et al, 2016: 363). Against this background, Begoña and Vanesa were also 'afraid of falling' in a way that made it vital for them to establish differences between themselves and their (working-class) colleagues.

Let us return once again to Vanesa's quote ("Err, then work is also, work becomes something very important [for them] and very defining of who they are, and work, well, they did things that were crazy in my opinion, you know?"). The distinction becomes particularly evident from the fact that she thought certain things her colleagues did were crazy. These "crazy" things included particular working conditions her colleagues accepted, such as rotating shifts or the creation of a WhatsApp group for staff members. The latter enabled them to discuss work-related issues outside of official working hours and when not physically at the optician's. Vanesa deliberately did not join the group and mentioned that she had become aware of her labour rights through her political science studies. She knew what could and could not be asked of her, and being available to respond to inquiries about orders or customers outside of her regular working hours was not part of it. But what Begoña and Vanesa considered inappropriate for their colleagues at the optician's or the clothing store became less of a problem when they carried it out themselves. When it came to the field of education, the reference to emotionally fulfilling work seemed to normalize the idea of activities extending beyond work and encroaching on their free time:

'Well, I don't really feel like disconnecting from school, but I don't want to disconnect, I like it a lot, you know? … And my friends are also heavily involved in education stuff, so if we go out or have a drink, we talk about education (laughs). Yes, but in this moment it is really what I want, that is, I want to soak myself in this.' (Begoña, 29)

Soaking herself in everything that was related to education implied mobilizing time and effort as often as possible. As she framed her work as a vocation and not as a pure income-generating activity, discussing incidents that happened at school with colleagues while having a drink in the evening or accumulating further knowledge on educational topics by consuming cultural goods such as films or books was considered 'normal'. Here, again, the symbolic distinction between different work identities served to uphold the class boundaries.

While the narrative of emotionally fulfilling work helped Begoña and Vanesa to distance themselves from a workplace with which and colleagues with whom they did not feel comfortable, it also enabled them to emphasize where they felt 'their place' was. This enabled them to signal and maintain a middle-class position where this turned out to be far more difficult than expected. Drawing on the narrative of emotionally fulfilling work was particularly helpful when people in their surrounding reminded them of what could be expected of them. They felt that there was a certain idea and corresponding expectations of how job and personality should fit together which they became aware of most when people both in their immediate and wider environment found it difficult to read them correctly and classify them accordingly:

'For example, in other contexts, not at work but in family or other contexts, it's like: "Eh you, where do you work?" "Well, man, I work here, here and here." And of course, it's like: "What kind of person are you? I don't know where to put you." … It's difficult to put you in a box because you're like really hard-working, like a woman in Zara, you're slaving away, but at the same time you're like an artist … and above all you have set up your own company or I mean (laughs) you're like divided in eight, right?' (Vanesa, 33)

In this quote, Vanesa explains how her part-time jobs not fitting her habitus could turn into a risk to signal her social position in a way that other people could 'read' her easily. This example helps to better understand why both Vanesa and Begoña felt that they needed a particularly clear demarcation and the strong reference to passion and fulfilment helped them in emphasizing which field of work they considered was the best match with their way of being and doing. As a result, the (over)emphasis on the field of their vocation and the friends and colleagues who belonged to it became part of a coping and defence mechanism against the feeling of status inconsistency. Emotional fulfilment was thus not only about emphasizing the joy of teaching at the school, but was also a way of doing symbolic boundary work in order to make clear where they saw themselves and where they wanted to be seen by others.

Detaching from the stickiness of good-life fantasies

Along with habitus defence, emotionally fulfilling work also appeared in attempts to break free from conventional ideas about 'proper' and 'good' work. These ideas usually involved standard employment concepts, especially the ideal of a permanent and steady job. While often out of reach, these concepts were still present in the young people's minds, even for those who pursued other forms of work like self-employment. They stuck to them as 'conventional good-life fantasies' (Berlant, 2011: 2) that involved certain expectations of how 'proper' or valuable work should look and feel, as imparted by their parents or institutions. Drawing on the narrative of emotionally fulfilling work helped freeing themselves of this 'stickiness' (Ahmed, 2014: 89).

We can see this in the case of Javier (35). Javier had founded a small collective with some fellow architecture graduates. Disillusioned with the ideas of what makes a proper architect that they were taught at university, they decided to practise architecture differently. However, their decision to become self-employed with their own cultural and town-planning projects was largely met with incomprehension:

'So imagine starting with your family and friends who look at you ... even your university colleagues: "What are you going to do with that? ... Be real professionals, be architects." And your parents, imagine your parents, right? "But, son, when are you going to do something proper?" Right? That is, "When are you going to do something serious?"' (Javier, 35)

Javier found that his way of working was perceived as being (too) different from standard expectations and, consequently, people associated it with feelings of doubts and unfamiliarity. Furthermore, he felt being denied not only the recognition of being a real architect, but also that of doing proper work in general. He had the impression that his work was not valued as highly as that of his former fellow students who pursued the apparently 'normal' path of working in architecture offices drawing a (relatively high) salary. Being denied the recognition of carrying out a proper job made him angry:

'But how can they say "something serious"? ... Is there anything more serious than doing what you love to do and managing to turn it into a source of income? I mean, I can't think of anything more serious than that. What do you want? Do you want me to live a double life? To work as a public official for eight hours and spend the rest of the time trying to be me? Do you know what that is? It's crazy! I mean, eight hours being another person and then eight hours a day getting used to being me again? I mean, my brain would explode.' (Javier, 35)

Javier questioned why fulfilling the criteria of self-realization and earning one's own money with it was not enough in order to pass for normal. While others did not necessarily agree with him about what constituted proper work, he had a clear idea of what 'normal' work would look and feel like. For him, it was associated with a double identity, a public one at work and a private one outside of it. The professional identity implied playing a role, performing according to corporate standards. It meant losing control over and accepting alienation of one's own personality and feelings. It would only be after work that one could recover one's real and authentic self. His account reveals the clash of different, partly generation-specific societal discourses. While his parents had been shaped by what Reckwitz (2020: 142–3) referred to as the *social logic of generality*, Javier's generation was influenced more strongly by the *social logic of particularity or singularities*. The former, according to Reckwitz (2017), involves notions of standardization and favoured the general: mass production, consumption of standardized goods and the standard working day of the mid- and late 20th century. The latter, in contrast, sees successful self-fulfilment as the lifestyle of the 21st century's new middle class, in which 'objects, collectives or other subjects are experienced as unique, are valued and enjoyed in their singularity' (Reckwitz, 207: 293f, author's translation). Crucial to producing the singular and unique, Reckwitz (2020: 145) argues, are practices of valorization and affective identification.

We also find these two social logics clashing in other young people's narratives. For Nuria (28) and Natalia (30), for example, it translated into questions about the 'normal' work and into perceptions of different notions of affective identification existing in society, their family and their own peer group. Both were working as freelancers in the field of design after having gone through several "normal" jobs, as they referred to them. Yet, paid projects were few and far between and were not exactly enough to enable them to lead independent lives. Nuria therefore lived with her parents, while Natalia rented a small flat which, during the day, doubled as the collective's workplace. For them, the term 'normal job' was charged with assumptions and expectations. It characterized the social pressure they felt that became a heavy burden in terms of what their work should look and feel like:

'We use "normal" to describe what many people in our society, such as our mothers, assume is what we have to do to earn a living … You have to have a permanent job that is forever, stable.' (Natalia, 30)

For Nuria and Natalia, the social pressure was created primarily by the discrepancy between social expectations on the one hand and actual working conditions on the other. They talked about how people in their close and wider social environment approached them with the expectation that, given their high educational capital, they could (and should) be performing a 'normal' job and earning a salary commensurate with their qualifications. However, what was often overlooked here was that fewer and fewer of these 'normal' jobs were available and that 'adequate' pay was no longer a reality.

What made this discourse of following the 'normal' path and having a permanent position so powerful was its association with happiness. A permanent position was what ought to make Javier, Natalia and Nuria as well as those in their social environment happy. Happiness, here, became a powerful way of reinforcing and legitimizing what was considered normal, as the following statement from Nuria illustrates particularly well:

'I was working at a company … but I wasn't motivated at all. So suddenly I found myself in this situation, thinking: "OK, I've got stability, I've got a very good job, I spend a huge number of hours here, it takes over an hour to get here and over an hour to get home. I'm dedicating much more than half of my life to this and I don't even have the time to spend the money I'm earning. But it's the job they wanted to teach me that I have to do." So you are continuously moving the balance like: "My mum is very happy, society is very happy and pleased with me, I've got a steady salary. I'm not supposed to be worrying about anything." So the balance starts to move in one direction and then suddenly: "Right, but I don't have any time to spend this money, I'm not happy with what I'm doing." … Suddenly the balance is moving more in the other direction … I don't know. Personally, I'm quite confused.' (Nuria, 28)

Nuria talked about how she felt that being in stability and having a steady salary was linked to (other people's) feelings of happiness. Whose happiness she referred to remained both extremely vague ("society is very happy") and very precise ("my mum is very happy") at the same time. In either case, it seemed like an orientation to her, a moral guide as to how to live and work well and in the 'right' way. But in saying "My mum is very happy, society is very happy and pleased with me", Nuria also reveals that she felt responsible to a certain extent. Adhering to the norm of permanent employment was supposed to make her happy. Any deviation from this path would risk everyone's happiness, supposedly hers, but especially her mother's and that of wider society. As Ahmed (2010: 9) argues, it is assumed that 'we have a responsibility to be happy for others, or even … that there is a necessary and inevitable relationship of dependence between one person's happiness and the happiness of others'. That conditionality of happiness is what makes it so powerful. Happiness is not necessarily an individual concern but may also imply a duty towards other people's happiness. Yet it was precisely the mismatch between Nuria's own happiness and that of others that caused her confusion ("I'm quite confused"). Doing 'normal' jobs did not bring her closer to happiness – or at least not to her own.

Against the background of these experiences, Nuria and the others tried to redefine what work meant for them and in order to do so, they mobilized the idea of emotional fulfilment. If they were stuck in precarity, then at least they were doing something they passionately enjoyed. This narrative can, without doubt, be seen as the 'successful' internalization of the neoliberal discourse of the happy entrepreneurial self (at least to a certain extent) (Bröckling, 2007; Binkley, 2014). At the same time, it would be too easy to depict them as mere victims of it. For Natalia, Javier and the others, referring to emotionally fulfilling work was also a way of detaching happiness from the good-life fantasy of standard employment. While they did not deny that having material stability is a good thing, they did contest that only standard employment can provide happiness:

'When my family tells me that this is not real work, for my part, it requires a level of analysis and maturity to say: ... "Hey, what do you want me to say? My dear cousin, you work in a bank, you're very happy selling mortgages, perfect, I'm not going to change your mentality. And you, Mom, you love me, you want me to be happy, don't you? Or do you want me to be married with children and a mortgage and filled with bitterness every day because I come home in a bad mood? Well, you would rather want I were happy, wouldn't you? Well, this makes me happy. So now get used to it, and if you can't get used to it, we can talk about something else, we can talk about the weather, we can talk about your grandchildren or about whatever you want."' (Javier, 35)

Javier used happiness here as a moral argument in order to legitimize his definition of work. To strengthen his argument, he thus referred to the expectations of others about which emotions ought to be linked to which social ties: his family should want him to be happy. In doing so, he reminded his parents of their role by invoking a feeling of obligation (Clark, 1990: 324). As parents, they should care about his emotional wellbeing and therefore accept the way in which he achieved it. While he re-appropriated happiness and linked it to his form of work, at the same time he associated feelings of unhappiness with what his parents and wider society considered to be the normal path to happiness: a stable job, a mortgage and a family. In this way, he built a counternarrative to the cultural standard of happiness. This redefinition can be seen as a form of emotional liberation as defined by

Flam (2005). By re-appropriating and redirecting emotions, social actors 'not only challenge the existing order but, more importantly, challenge and redefine the dominant feeling rules' (van der Graaf, 2015: 21). This is done by reassessing and re-evaluating parts of everyday life. For Javier, Nuria and Natalia, this meant emphasizing to themselves and others that navigating within the labour market had changed and that new forms of work had emerged. It also meant reminding themselves again and again that even in the world of 'normal' jobs, material security and emotional security were by no means guaranteed and were often the exception rather than the rule. In this way, they tried to deconstruct the dominant happiness standard:

'But then you look around and think: "But who has a damn permanent job? (laughs) I mean, you're asking me to do something serious – I shouldn't say that – but they just fired my cousin from that bank (laughs). You know? He is unemployed now, I mean, he was the one who has been working all his life in the bank with fucking security and here I am still employed and getting my daily income."' (Javier, 35)

'Well, traditional architecture, so to speak, that of architecture offices … is poorly paid with few contracts. Almost everybody is doing bogus self-employment because they are self-employed but work only for one company.' (Nuria, 28)

'And then there are the interns. The law of the happy intern. Sure, [architecture offices] are, of course, very interested in interns … The problem is that they give them a lot of work and pay them very little.' (Natalia, 30)

By revealing the fragility of the supposedly safe path to happiness, they challenged the notion of the pursuit of a 'normal' job and a permanent position at a company and hoped in this way to better legitimize their own form and definition of work. This process mirrored what Gordon (1990: 164) described as the negotiation of emotion norms where 'people and groups debate, negotiate, and bargain over a norm's exact content and situational applicability'. Within this process of negotiation, drawing on emotionally fulfilling work was thus a way of mobilizing against the constraints of the norm of the standard employment relationship by pitting individual happiness against the normative normalcy (Misztal, 2001). As a result, the societal constraints, which norms tend to create, lost some of their relative power within the context of this group of young people. This shows that especially for middle-class youths, the emotionally fulfilling work helped to signal and maintain their social position in situations in which they had limited scope to do so.

When emotionally fulfilling work reinforces the impasse

Emotional fulfilment also featured in narratives of working-class youths, that is, those who were mainly stuck in provisional jobs or in seemingly endless training loops. And yet, while young people from the middle class could use emotional fulfilment for (re)positioning, for the young people in the following section, this was far less possible and in some cases could even reinforce their impasse.

Let us look again at Jacobo (30). At the time of the interview, he was taking part in a socioprofessional reintegration programme consisting of carpentry training. While he enjoyed learning this new craft, he felt that his passion lay elsewhere. When we discussed his previous positions and his ideal future job, he was excited by the idea of working as a waiter:

'Waiter. I really like to serve, I really like to serve customers. As a waiter, you don't get bored; as a salesman, you get bored, I've checked (laughs). As a waiter, you have to be constantly doing something, you have to be constantly on the move, and I'm a very hyperactive person; I need to move, I need to do something, otherwise I get bored, I get bored very easily. And bartending has always been my thing, and … It's a job that has fulfilled me.

I see myself as a waiter, I just can't help it … I see myself as a waiter because it has been so many years and it's a job that fulfils me.' (Jacobo, 30)

Like the young people in the previous sections, Jacobo talked about how working as a waiter fulfilled him. He considered it a lively and active role, and one which involved being constantly on the move, fitting his character as "a very hyperactive person". The quote "bartending has always been my thing" is a reference to a vocation and reveals that drawing on emotional fulfilment in and through work was not necessarily related to years of investment in education and was not only present in middle-class narratives.

However, unlike Javier, Vanesa and Nuria, Jacobo was far from able to pursue his ideal job once again. For the past six years, he had been looking for new employment. Sometimes he dropped off his CV in person and occasionally witnessed it being thrown in the bin:

'They don't see you as young. When I was 18 years old, I had a job and after a fortnight I changed jobs and got another one. It didn't take long to find a job but now you search but don't find anything. You don't stop but they don't call you either to say: "Hey, come on, we're going to give you a personal interview." No, no, no, no interviews or anything. Well, now I've been called up for an interview as a waiter's assistant and I've said: "Yes, yes, yes", because these opportunities can't be missed. Because this … For me, this, if I'm called for an interview is … it gives you encouragement. There are places where I've handed in CVs and when I've turned around, they've ripped them up and thrown them in the bin … Yes, yes. And then I was telling my previous teacher … "Sure, if they rip it up in front of your face, how are you going to apply for a job afterwards? … How are you supposed to do that?" Well, personally, I feel like my spirit is at rock bottom.' (Jacobo, 30)

This quote illustrates the different difficulties (including emotional ones) Jacobo was facing in looking for a job. In addition to the general decline in job opportunities in the aftermath of the crisis, his age was also becoming a problem for him, a feeling several of my interviewees shared. He also noticed that the new currency for being employed as a waiter was increasingly (educational) qualifications and, to a lesser extent, years of professional experience. As we saw in the Introduction, it was not only Jacobo's personal impression that reflected the structural mismatch between level of education and possibilities to enter the labour market. For the young people with low levels of education, this mismatch appeared as underqualification. Jacobo's case is thus a typical example of how, with the crisis, the demand for higher educational qualifications was penetrating even into low-wage employment sectors, thereby placing those who no longer appeared to be sufficiently qualified in an even more vulnerable position.

Against this background, drawing on emotional fulfilment was thus a way for Jacobo to show how much he had embodied this profession and was a waiter at heart, even without having a higher level of education. This mirrors what Bailey (1983) identified as the tactical uses of passion where its strategic display can demonstrate a person's deep commitment to a certain expectation. Jacobo's quote thus illustrates that the reference to emotionally fulfilling work was a double-edged sword for him: while it temporarily functioned as a form of emotional reservoir and future hope, at the same time it reminded him how far away he was from reaching this goal. It made the various structural barriers tangible, which prevented him from getting closer to the object of emotional fulfilment. Using this narrative to emphasize his agency was therefore hardly possible.

Drawing on emotional fulfilment can thus contribute to a person having a greater awareness of their own impasse. It can also add to its reinforcement. We see this most clearly in the example of Antonio (26). As a trained electrician, he went from one temporary job to the next. In most cases these did not last longer than a year. What is in itself a structural problem was built into Antonio's narrative of emotionally fulfilling work:

'The daily routine is what eats me up, not doing things, doing the same thing every day … That's why, more or less every year – I … Many companies offer me the chance to renew and so on, but I prefer not to renew … It's not easy because, on the one hand, uh … you have, you gain that freedom again but, on the other hand, you have to recreate your day-to-day life and be able to make a living, or … Uh, I don't know, but what I wanted to say is that if I'm getting to that point, I find myself trying to quit before my mind gets completely saturated, changing the scene before … Because, when you're new to a company, it's always easier, because it's all newer, it's like more exciting, more … And then, day by day, when it becomes routine, you start asking yourself: "What am I doing with my life? Is this what I want to do with my life? Is this what I'm going to do?" But, of course, I'm perfectly aware that I can do this now and that what I do now will take its toll on me in the future, because … because I can't come to a company in ten years' time and say: "Hey, look, I've been with every company for a year." I can't, they'll … they'll tell me to get stuffed (laughs). As easily as I can find a job now, when that time comes it's going to be impossible to find.' (Antonio, 26)

Keeping boredom at bay and doing something challenging for his mind made Antonio switch jobs on a regular basis. His emotions informed him when the right time to change jobs was approaching again: continuing to work there was "detrimental to the relationships I have with friends or people, I see that my negative feelings start to affect them too". In order to "be happier and be able to enjoy" himself, he left his old job behind and looked for a new one. Yet it was rarely the jobs themselves that enabled Antonio to draw on the narrative of emotional fulfilment. Many of the temporary jobs he had consisted of simple activities. He reported, for example, that he had been hired by his current employer to carry out maintenance and installation work, but that in most cases he was asked to "open some doors or bring paper upstairs and downstairs or do very basic things like that". The change itself, which entailed familiarizing himself with a new working environment, thus became the source of certain mental and emotional stimulation. Yet he was well aware that allowing himself this room for manoeuvre would at the same time severely restrict him in the future. His opportunities to position himself on the job market, as he admitted, would diminish, at the latest when he was at an age where he could no longer afford to do so, implying that switching jobs was something one could do when being young, but not at an older age.

Unlike the middle-class youths, especially those that were self-employed, Antonio did not have the opportunity to tie into existing discourses. While Javier and Nuria could legitimize their new way of working by setting themselves apart from conventional good-life fantasies, such a discourse was not available for Antonio. Even though most of the young entrepreneurs met with incomprehension or suspicion, their work, driven by emotional fulfilment, did not exclude that it could be converted into some form of (economic and symbolic) capital at some point. However, Antonio's way of seeking emotional fulfilment by switching jobs on a regular basis came with a risk. He did not have any long-term professional experience and employers could also interpret his quick job changes as a sign of an erratic and thus unreliable personality, which would reduce his scope to move within the labour market. While Antonio felt that being guided by emotional fulfilment made his impasse, to a certain extent, more bearable for him, in the long run, it could actually reinforce it.

Conclusion

This chapter has examined the role that emotions can play in young people's (re)positioning and their sense of 'placing' (Bourdieu, 2020: 339) when faced with changing conditions in a post-crisis setting. Focusing on emotional fulfilment, I have demonstrated that in situations with fewer job opportunities and limited possibilities to draw on educational capital, emotions played an important role for the young people to carve out some room for manoeuvre and to emphasize their agency. Emotions worked both as 'place markers' and 'place claims' (Clark, 1990: 310–16) as they informed young people about where they were positioned and served to communicate to others where they wished to stand.

Against this background, I demonstrated that the work which the young people wanted to do but could not afford to live off was tied to imaginations and idealizations (as with Jacobo) or emotional rewards, joy and fulfilment (as with Vanesa and Begoña), while, at the same time, class habitus was defended by disdain and contempt for the work which they had to do to earn a living (Vanesa and Begoña) or concealed by adopting a middle-class narrative of fulfilment (Jacobo). It highlighted how the young people engaged in the struggles over desirable field positions by creating distinctions and boundaries through emotional conditions used as resources, and how in some cases this was not possible. I identified the creation of emotional hierarchies as an important mechanism here, in particular for middle-class youths, through which the job matching their habitus was bound up with emotional fulfilment and those not fitting with frustration. While it became part of their coping and defence mechanism against the experience of status inconsistency, setting up an emotional hierarchy also enabled them to draw social (class) boundaries in order to defend their middle-class habitus by distancing themselves from the workplaces with which and colleagues with whom they did not feel comfortable.

Drawing on emotionally fulfilling work helped also those (middle-class) youths who were self-employed to detach from the idea that (only) the standard employment relationship constituted valuable work and was able to lead to happiness. By re-appropriating happiness and linking it to their own way of doing and thinking about work, they engaged in negotiations over emotion norms. But here too, emotional fulfilment served to differentiate their work from that of others and to see it as valuable. This clearly shows that people had to be able to 'afford' to draw on emotional fulfilment. They needed a professional activity that enabled them to apply this narrative in the first place. For those young people for whom this was not the case, drawing on emotional fulfilment meant fixing them in place and in some cases even reinforcing their impasse (as with Antonio).

7

Anger and Work

Where the young people perceived their scope of action and position taking as limited, anger proved to be a way to carve out some room for manoeuvre and allowed them to a temporarily refuse to feel powerless. Having seen in the previous chapter how young people drew on emotional fulfilment to negotiate their social position in the face of major change, this chapter focuses on anger and the ways it was used to make place claims (Clark, 1990: 314).

Anger is often a reaction to an existing or anticipated risk to a person's physical or social condition and conveys that a person's rights and sense of entitlement have been violated. This usually involves the feeling that something is being denied or taken away from a person which they regarded as being rightfully theirs. Anger can thus communicate where one desires to stand. While anger is directly connoted to power over the other and it is therefore people in power who get angry and display it openly (see, for example, Bergman Blix and Wettergren, 2018: 12), collective anger can also become an energy of self-assertion and empowerment from positions of less power and lower status (Goodwin et al, 2001; Flam and King, 2005; Lorde, 2007).

In this chapter, I examine the ways in which drawing on anger did or did not become useful to the young people to communicate and negotiate where they wished to stand. In doing so, I consider anger in its different forms (collective, isolated and absent) and the ways in which it intersects with class, race and gender.

Collective anger

Collective anger, as it came across in my data, was based primarily on two aspects. The first included the framing of anger not as an individual and isolated experience, but as a shared one (as we saw in Chapter 5). The second implied support by a collective of any form that shared common ideas, values and stories. These collectives were either organized, as in the case of social movements, institutionalized, such as trade unions, or neither when seen as (shared) frames of understanding, as in the case of feminism. The following two stories are prime examples of how the young people in this book used collective anger for (re)positioning.

Lara (32) described how anger fuelled her efforts to become self-employed and served as a source of motivation and energy to face all the obstacles involved in setting up her own business. In her former company, she had openly expressed her dissatisfaction with the practices of her former supervisor, who had dismissed her shortly afterwards. She then founded a small company with her good friend Roberto supporting other companies in their efforts to become (more) sustainable:

'I was fired from my last company because … The official story is that they didn't have the financial resources … but really it was because I was causing them headaches because I wasn't aligned with them and many things didn't seem right … so there was a strong shock and they dismissed me. But they did it in a very bad way, come on, they told me: "Take the sheet and go." Well … I mean, it generated a lot of feelings: anger, frustration, hatred, humiliation … and I still harbour those feelings.

They're very bad businesspeople … They still exist and I want the system to kill them because the system legitimizes them so much. I mean, I need that company to go bankrupt. They make me very nervous, I've removed them all from my LinkedIn account, I can't stand it anymore … I've deleted my work history with them, I've deleted that job, I've deleted them all… I despise them deeply.' (Lara, 32)

The dismissal had happened one-and-a-half years ago and yet the emotional experience had engraved itself into Lara's memory in such a way that when she recalled what had happened, the anger-related emotions resurged. The nervous state in which she found herself on account of the remembered, ongoing or anticipated social encounters associated with this company made her want to see "the system ruin it" and the company "crash" and "disappear". Even though she could not erase the experience from her memory, she erased it from wherever else she could: her LinkedIn page, her CV and her list of contacts. Her anger was fuelled by the lack of respect she encountered as a former employee whose opinions were ignored and who was dismissed in "a very bad way" when her employer considered her no longer of use. In this sense, her anger was a form of 'resistance of relations of power and respect' (Holmes, 2004: 214). She therefore perceived anger as something empowering:

'They're the exact antithesis of what I would like to contribute to business, so it [the anger] actually motivates me. I mean, if it's of any use to me, it motivates me because they're the antithesis … I mean, I would report them because they deserve it, things they do are punishable, I mean, really; those people should have fines everywhere because it is the least responsible thing in the universe. But it makes me very angry that companies that want to do things properly encounter obstacles, not us in this case, but other companies that want to do things properly, that do not have money to invest in what they believe, that is, being responsible and sustainable and contributing to society in general … And the idea that these people … that society applauds them really rattles me.' (Lara, 32)

Lara's words reveal how anger can be both 'productive of, as well as produced by, social relationships' (Holmes, 2004: 212). The disagreements between her and her former line manager, which, due to the different positions of power, led to her dismissal, made Lara angry. At the same time, anger formed the basis of and the driving force behind the creation of new social relationships as her anger fuelled her efforts to set up her own company, despite the financial and symbolic challenges involved (see Chapter 6). Anger thus led to social action, allowing Lara to reclaim her agency, which she had perceived as highly limited in her previous job.

The excerpt further illustrates that Lara's anger was not only about the way she was treated personally, but was also about the way in which the employer and his management style violated her sense of justice and idea of 'good' business. When Lara reported that companies that "invest in what they believe, that is, being responsible and sustainable and contributing to society in general" have a hard time, it reveals that her anger was embedded in a collectively shared frame of understanding – more precisely, in that of social entrepreneurship – in which values of socioecological responsibility and sustainability were held high. According to Eyerman (2005: 42), collective framing and action are 'social forces grounded in values … [and] articulate structures of feeling'. Against this background, anger is not experienced as an isolated case, but as an appropriate response to the violation of common beliefs. The domain of social entrepreneurship thus functioned similarly to social movements. It provided Lara with a collective framework or backup that helped her to overcome the fear of repression and validated her anger as legitimate and well grounded (Flam, 2005: 26–7). Lara did therefore not hesitate to display her anger during the interview, nor did she feel guilty about it. She felt what Collins (1990) described as righteous anger. This form of collective anger 'is the emotional outburst, shared by a group … against persons who violate its sacred symbols' (Collins, 1990: 44). It is particularly intense because individuals can be sure of receiving support from the community. That is precisely where anger can help to make one's voice heard and communicate where one desires to stand when framed as part of and supported by a collective, even if an individual is in the position of less power.

Lara's account also shows how collective anger enabled her to adopt a position on the violated values and thus on morality. She saw her former company as the "antithesis" of her own company. As a result, she positioned them both as moral opposites and thus created distinction between a morally responsible and a morally irresponsible way of doing business. From this position of moral superiority, she could then afford to describe her previous company as "punishable" and one which "should have fines everywhere". Yet, her disapproval was directed not only at her former employer but also at the system itself, which made such behaviour possible in the first place. Her anger thus went beyond the situational experience since she interpreted it less as a singular and isolated event and more as a metaphor for general structural inequalities (Eyerman, 2005: 45; see also Amin, 1995).

The way people, even from a subordinate position, can turn individual experience and memory into collective stories that makes anger powerful was particularly evident for those young people who were politically active and embedded in institutionalized collectives. This was, for instance, the case with Jesus (34).

Jesus was working as a temporary employee for a public company. This meant that he was supposed to occupy the post for a limited period of time until the recruitment department had found a definitive candidate. However, at the time of the interview, he had already been on the job for six years. Having a temporary contract also meant that he was entitled to fewer benefits and rights than most of his colleagues in permanent employment (for example, no obligatory compensation or advance notice in the event of contract termination). In addition, his work schedule included weekends and public holidays and was spread over 365 days of the year. Sometimes, he worked during the day, sometimes he had to do night shifts. Jesus made no secret of his aversion to the current economic system in general and to his employer in particular, whom he described as corrupt in all practices, from recruitment procedures to the payment of bonuses and the allocation of shifts. He described how his standpoint ruffled feathers as he reported unfair and illegal practices and did not shy away from conflict:

'Well, I like fighting and know that I'm fighting for something that's fair. I mean, when, in my day-to-day work, I see little things that are unfair, like this thing I told you about, that certain colleagues are being treated differently and discriminated against. Well, I speak out and go to the boss and tell him to his fucking face. And the boss is shocked because he says: "It happens to me that a shitty worker comes to tell me that this isn't right" ... And I don't care if he's my boss and if he's going to cut my productivity benefits for the rest of my life, I don't

care if he wipes his ass with that money. I mean, I'm not moving for
the money, I work for the money because I have no other choice,
because we live in a capitalist system where you have money to live
on and that's it. But within that margin, I fight within my possibilities
and I know where I stand and I know I need the money to live on.'
(Jesus, 34)

Jesus' upper body was leaning forward and he was clenching his fists as he
talked about how he "put a squeeze on them" and "stirred up the hornets'
nest". His remarks were not intended to show resignation, but emphasized
his own agency at every point. Anger played a central role in this. It helped
him to mobilize the necessary strength to assert himself. His account describes
the energy and empowerment of anger that fuelled his engagement in major
conflicts (for example, he sued his employer over his employment contract).

As the last lines of the quote demonstrate, Jesus was aware of the limitations
of his agency. He was also aware of his difficulties in positioning himself in
the job market. He had the lowest level of vocational training in mechanics
and graphic arts. He had never worked in the former since completing his
apprenticeship and, as Jesus described, employment in the latter was "very
precarious, with a lot of overtime, I mean, really shitty". He had numerous
temporary jobs in this area until 2008. When the economic crisis struck,
he was among the first to lose his job and several years of unemployment
followed. He was thus very much aware of his dependence on the system
that he rejected, as the last sentence of the quote illustrates ("But within
that margin, I fight within my possibilities and I know where I stand and
I know I need the money to live on"). Nevertheless, he refused to conclude
that the unequal power relations implied that there was no alternative and
that he had to accept the given conditions. Drawing on anger enabled him
to reject this (sense of) powerlessness and the limited scope of action. The
fight against corruption and injustice, which was driven and sustained by
his anger, thus opened up an alternative possibility for personal expression
and social recognition. The fight at work and not work itself became the
source of meaning and self-esteem. Fighting provided joy to some extent
and made him feel powerful in a certain way. The imagery of resistance
fighters during the Spanish Civil War underpinned the metaphor of combat:

'Well, I think of the hatred I have for them (laughs). Yes, the hatred
I have for fascists, I don't know, it's something I've had since I was
a child. I can't stand fascists, and so I imagine, when I feel down,
I imagine myself there crushing them and I draw strength from it, and
that's it, I can't give up. Where did our grandparents get their strength
from in the Civil War, when they were shooting with guns that were
from 1896 that didn't even shoot? ... Where did they get their strength

from? … From class consciousness, and that's it, there's no more, we don't need to ponder it any further either because … For the struggle of an ideal, for wanting to change this world, because either we change this world or we'll go to hell. Well, that's where [my energy comes from], when I think if I stay quiet … they're going to kill us anyway, they're going to kill us anyway, sooner or later they're going to kill us anyway, if not with a disease, then with a war. So, then … Well, before they kill me, I try to avoid being killed … Well, I try to pass to the offensive, not to be on the defensive because the comfortable thing is to stay in the job … to get along with the scabs, to say yes to the boss all the time.' (Jesus, 34)

The imagery of the resistance fighter provided a point of reference and allowed Jesus to inhabit a certain style of masculinity: fearless, active and combative. In this way, the anger narrative was also given a historical grounding. It was not a spontaneous outburst of emotion, but an ongoing pent-up feeling of oppression that mobilized him and which he saw as a continuation of the struggle of his grandparents' generation. As we saw with other interviewees in Chapter 5, instead of framing his situation as personal fate, he defined it as a structural problem, an analysis that helped him to see his situation in the light of structural inequalities. Therefore, his anger did not constitute a purely individual resource, but was embedded in a collective struggle, one which Jesus continued as an active member of a trade union. The union provided a platform for his anger that allowed him to 'reverse one important social norm or "feeling rule" which constitutes anger as prerogative of the powerful and labels it as deviant when displayed by the powerless' (Flam, 2005: 26). By receiving the collective support of the union, Jesus could not only validate but also openly express his deviant emotions of anger. As Collins (1990: 43) highlights, 'it is only when there are enough social bases of support to generate EE [emotional energy] that one can react to a frustration (in this case, being dominated) by mobilizing anger'.

Jesus' quote also shows that his anger constituted a mode through which he lived his class position. The conflicts arising from the unequal distribution of power and resources fuelled his anger, which led him to believe that "sooner or later they're going to kill us anyway". It also mobilized him for the conflict from an offensive position. And it was not only an emotion he had as an individual, but rather was inherent in the unequal structure of social relationships and interactions of which he was a part. It was in this context that the symbolic boundary drawing took place, whereby Jesus drew boundaries between those people who, according to him, endangered class consciousness ("the scabs") and those people which he considered to be responsible for the suffered inequalities ("they"). The latter encompassed those who occupied positions of power and dominated the game in which he knew he had only limited possibilities to play. These included "fascists", the economic elite, especially big employers, and the political establishment, in particular the Partido Popular conservative political party which was responsible for numerous post-crisis austerity measures and was involved in a major case of corruption at his company.[1]

Among the former were those who tried to gain an advantage in this unequal game and "betrayed" their (working-class) position. For Jesus, these were "scabs", "strike-breakers", "bootlickers" and "the armed arm of the boss". This form of distinction served to validate his anger, as some were seen as the cause of the unfair game (and therefore his anger) and others as the ones who kept the game going. But the distinction also helped to create a sense of distance from the power structures and patterns of dominance that he rejected, but of which he was still a part. As the first quote suggests, he was aware that there were no serious alternatives for him in terms of evading the game and its rules. To sustain his livelihood, he was reliant on work, even if he considered it exploitation under the given (precarious) circumstances. As much as he supported alternatives (for example, self-sufficiency, local autonomy), "in the end", he stated, partly disillusioned, partly bitterly, "you enter the capitalist system, where you have to use your resources to fight with them".

We can see here that Jesus' narrative of anger involved contradictions. Drawing on anger did indeed allow him 'momentary refusals of powerlessness', yet, as Skeggs (1997: 11) notes, 'to challenge powerlessness does not mean that one automatically shifts into positions of power. It means, straightforwardly, that one is refusing to be seen as powerless or to be positioned without power'. While the collective backup helped him to use his anger, even from a position of low power and status, it came at a cost. Jesus talked about how the constant struggle made him feel exhausted. The arguments with his line manager were the reason, he assumed, for his particularly frequent shifts on public holidays or weekends and unequal treatment for bonus payments. Moreover, he felt alienated from colleagues who, in most cases, did not share his anger due to fear of the consequences. Although Jesus generally perceived anger as empowering, it also caused social stress, which at times affected his mental health, resulting in insomnia, anxiety attacks and sick leave.

These examples therefore indicate that drawing on collective anger was not a limitless possibility and that it had moments of rupture and could lead to consequences. They highlight once again the power dimension of anger and emphasize the fact that one must be able to 'afford' it without having to fear symbolic or material consequences. As such, communicating and negotiating where one wishes to stand by drawing on collective anger can still be risky if one does not have the necessary symbolic capital to legitimize its use.

Isolated and absent anger

Whether or not the young people in my study openly displayed anger was thus dependent on whether they could 'afford' to. Limits on using anger for position taking were most common where people had little power or status. This was particularly the case for those young people who were (stuck) in multiple dependencies. The following two sections illustrate how (re)positioning with anger were risky when young people did not have the necessary symbolic capital to legitimize its use depending on the intersections of class, race and gender. While anger could still become useful from a subordinate position if framed as part of and supported by a collective, not everyone perceived anger as a shared experience. Anger could also be perceived as individual and situational, and would therefore not be interpreted in the light of structural inequalities.

Isolated anger

We find an example of isolated anger in the case of Paulina. She experienced this form of anger upon being dismissed from her last job. She suffered from an illness which required her to have regular medical checkups. Not long after she had started working as a sales assistant at a bakery, she asked her manager if he could allow her to leave work slightly earlier to attend a medical appointment. However, her employer was not very pleased about this and accused her of making illegitimate demands for days off only shortly after being hired:

'Well, I had just started [that job] a few weeks earlier and I had an appointment with the neurologist. I have had to go to the neurologist for some time now and I can't just say: "I can't because it's a check-up that I have to have, no matter what". So I told the boss that I had a doctor's appointment, that I was going to leave a little earlier, and he responded by saying: "Yes, you just started and you're already asking for days off." I said: "I'm not asking out of pleasure, it's an appointment I have to attend" and he asked: "Well, what do you prefer, your health or your job?" And so, of course, I went into the changing room to cry as if to say: "How dare you? Do you even have any idea about my life, what I've been through or why I have to go, for you to ask?" Well, what do you prefer, your health or your job? And so, I started to cry and my colleagues said: "Don't pay him any attention", and of course, I was like, I even had a headache, I was about to explode. I said: "Look, I'm going, I can't stand it." I think there was an hour left until the end of my shift but I was going to leave an hour earlier, I said: "I'm going,

I'll come back to return the uniform ... but no, I can't bear it" and I went home crying.' (Paulina, 29)

Paulina was accused by her employer of making exaggerated claims and was forced to choose between having a job or looking after her health. This request violated her sense of self-determination and even though she was placed at the bottom of the professional hierarchy, she was not willing to put up with the arbitrariness and lack of respect which people in lower positions are more likely to experience. Although she was not in a position of power, her anger communicated that she refused to be automatically seen as powerless and refused to accept the way she was being treated. Isolated anger therefore did not involve relating the anger to herself or considering herself to be the cause of it. As with collective anger, she saw the agent of her power disadvantage in the other (her employer). In this case, according to Kemper (1978: 57), fear is expressed as anger. 'When the other is in a position of authority', he (1978: 58) continues, 'the anxiety response is manifested in rebelliousness against orders, commands, and requests, which are ignored, disobeyed, and avoided.' Paulina refused to comply with the indirect request to adhere to her work schedule without exception. She did attend the medical appointment and left work earlier.

Yet Paulina's anger-fuelled assertion was not an open one. Whereas she indeed verbalized the anger-laden responses "How dare you?" and "Do you even have any idea about my life?" in the interview, she did not express them in the situation itself. While she directed her anger towards her manager, she did not openly express her contempt for his humiliating behaviour. There was no open confrontation, as in the case of Lara or Jesus. Without the collective framing or support, it was much more difficult for Paulina to overcome the fear to react with anger from a subordinate position. Her anger was isolated and she considered it to be situational, which explains why her anger was not as fierce as that of Jesus or Lara and accompanied by fear and shame, as her tears and the retreat into the changing room indicate. As Collins (1990: 46) points out, anger and fear tend to be mobilized together 'in cases where a person is able to mobilize anger, but has low confidence in being able to win positive results from its expression'.

Absent anger

Anger was mostly absent when dependencies were so extensive and marginalization so profound that drawing on anger for position taking was hardly possible. Here, the intersection of class, race and gender was particularly evident. As Brody et al (1995) note, people in positions of little power and low status are more likely to be perceived as less entitled. Whether they have internalized this general societal perception or not, it impacts their sense of entitlement and whether they feel it is appropriate for them to react if their entitlements are violated. The following two cases involving Teresa (22) and Jorge (26) illustrate how this can translate into an absence of anger.

Both were taking part in a socioprofessional reintegration programme when I met them. Their social workers had informed them about this training opportunity, which is how Jorge got on to a wood processing course and Teresa a customer service course. Jorge described his participation as "the only way out" of his impasse and both were generally confident that the training certificate would increase their chances of getting a job interview. While both framed the programme as an opportunity, their participation was conditional. As these programmes were usually activation measures as part of the job-seeking process, it was a prerequisite to participate in order to continue to receive benefits. Both depended on these: Jorge to contribute to the livelihood of his partner and child; Teresa to keep her accommodation as a political refugee from Latin America who came alone to Spain and did not have a local support network of family and friends.

The material struggles were joined by symbolic struggles. Like many women from Latin and South America, Teresa experienced the devaluation of the educational capital that she had accumulated in her native country. Despite completing vocational training in business management and having a range of professional experience in customer service, she could only find informal cleaning and babysitting jobs. Like the vast majority of Latin American migrant women, she found herself in the global care chain (Hochschild, 2000), which developed between Latin America and Spain, especially from the 1990s onwards. Migrant women took over the invisible and mostly informal care and domestic work of middle-class and upper-class women, who themselves had integrated into the formal labour market (Oso, 2007; Araujo and González-Fernández, 2014; López Hernán, 2020).

Jorge also experienced discrimination based on his origins. He belonged to the Romani, who historically have suffered multiple forms of discrimination and marginalization in Spain, with resulting inequalities still visible in all parts of everyday life: their access to housing, healthcare, employment and education (Poveda and Markos, 2005). For instance, Romani in Madrid have time and again been subjected to public resettlement programmes towards the south of the city in neighbourhoods that tend to rank high in statistics on poverty, migration and crime (Gay y Blasco, 1999: 7–9). Jorge himself was living in one of these districts, which in public discourse was considered a troubled and dangerous area.[2]

All of the aforementioned aspects meant that Jorge and Teresa experienced discrimination and felt out of place, as their following quotes illustrate:

'I don't know how to explain it. I feel bad when someone who is not the same race as me looks at me badly, as if to say: "Man, you don't fit in here, please go away" and that hurts. They don't say it but you understand it just from their look.' (Jorge, 26)

[This neighbourhood] has a very bad reputation … For the Community of Madrid,[3] it is very condemned, they treat it as a bad neighbourhood but it's not really like that. People from outside think it's bad but they should come and see that it's not as bad as they think.' (Jorge, 26)

'People are often nice, sometimes not, but you get used to it and deal with it.' (Teresa, 22)

These accounts demonstrate that both experienced racist exclusion, yet there was no (overt) anger in their words. Teresa's statement instead reveals the situational normalcy (Misztal, 2001) of these experiences. Jorge's account reveals his pain and shame at being treated unfairly and without the due respect, as the comments "that hurts" and "I feel bad" illustrate. He reacted with sadness when society shamed him for his (racial) ethnicity and place of residence.

The experiences of Jorge and Teresa are similar to those of the working-class women documented by Skeggs (1997) who linked feelings of discomfort and unease to the positions they could inhabit. Most of the women's practices and narratives were informed by trying to get it 'right': the 'right' education, the 'right' bodily appearance or the 'right' furniture. It was about trying to pass for normal and to prove respectability. This was also true for Teresa and Jorge, who were putting a lot of effort into constructing respectability and trustworthiness:

'We learn here [on the training course] how to be a good employee, err … how to be … serve the company, you know, how to support it.' (Teresa, 22)

'We all [referring to her friends and herself] have a very open mind, you know, to get experience in the beginning so that later on when you finish your education or when you embark on a career you already have a lot of professional experience, you already have knowledge about what it's like to be an employee.' (Teresa, 22)

'I am not an alien, as they say here. I am an equal person, I can help a company grow, I can do lots of good things.' (Jorge, 26)

'We are a normal family, like the others. So, we Spaniards are fighting to grow, and I am like those people.' (Jorge, 26)

Both Teresa and Jorge stressed their abilities and motivation for contributing to a company, society or the country, and emphasized that they were no different from other people. As for the women in Skeggs' study, their 'consciousness of their classifications, their devaluing, their inability to get it right and their inability *to be* without shame, humiliation and judgement is part of the reason why they turn[ed] to respectability and responsibility as a means of establishing a valued and legitimate way of being and way of being seen' (Skeggs, 1997: 95, emphasis in original). Within this process, anger was not considered useful as it could have endangered the whole effort involved in becoming or being seen as respectable. There was too much at stake for them not to pass as a 'normal citizen' and a 'good employee' and so (overt) anger did not fit here.

Moreover, Teresa and Jorge could not evaluate their claims to entitlements independently of their class background and racial ethnicity. As both were in a position of low status and little power, it was very likely that their expressions of entitlements – and expressions of anger if these entitlements were violated – would be perceived not only differently but also as less deserving than those of the dominant groups. This illustrates how 'structural features set up the circumstances for different ways in which … [people] understand their place and develop expectations for the consequences of their circumstances' (Shields, 2002: 153).

This is not to say that Teresa and Jorge could not have felt angry about their situation of impasse and limitations in position taking. But because of the way they were positioned and 'othered', they were more likely to suppress these feelings by pushing them below their conscious awareness. This (often unconscious) process – which may include, for example, emotional numbness (Mills and Kleinman, 1988: 1012) or self-censorship (Eddo-Lodge, 2017: xii) – allows people to bear situations that are unpleasant, humiliating or even life-threatening. While Kemper (1978: 66) argues that people tend to react with anger when they are denied approval, respect or recognition in social interactions, he also notes that if the denial is structural – as is the case for both Teresa and Jorge – anger can be turned inwards. In that case, expressing anger towards the other is not an option 'if the other is powerful by virtue of our dependence' (Kemper, 1978: 66). Since they were stuck in a network of multiple dependencies where (historical) intersections of class, race and gender played out, drawing on anger may have increased their impasse and further marginalized their social position.

Gender and anger

As categorical intersections played a crucial role in terms of whether anger could be used as place claim or not, the last section of this chapter takes a closer look at this issue, focusing in particular on gender and anger.

Drawing on anger was not exclusive to the young men in my study. Women also drew on anger to assert themselves and communicate where they wished to stand. This is in line with findings of psychological and sociological studies highlighting that all sexes experience anger with equal frequency (Kring, 2000; Simon and Nath, 2004). Yet, the difference in most cases compared to the male interviewees was the way in which these anger episodes were perceived. While all genders may express an equal amount of anger and with the same intensity, women are more likely to be seen as reacting inappropriately and to be subjected to social pressure to keep their anger low (Kring, 2000: 222; Simon and Lively, 2010). Many scholars have demonstrated how this gendered view on emotions is linked to sociostructural inequalities (for example, unequal access to power and resources) and in particular to the normative divide of male/public/work and female/private/family (Hochschild, 1983; Lupton, 1998; Shields, 2002). Men are more likely to be seen as rational and unemotional, while women are more likely to be seen as irrational and emotional. The same is true for anger. Whereas women's expression of anger is more likely to be labelled as irrational and emotional, men's anger tends to be read as (legitimate) expression of masculinity (Salerno and Peter-Hagene, 2015). It therefore allows men to tie in with cultural conceptions of masculinity when drawing on anger, while women have more difficulties in doing the same.

Now, various studies have shown that the intersection of gender, race and class has an even stronger influence on whether or not one is perceived as deserving and hence able to express anger openly. Lorde (1984), hooks (1996) and Eddo-Lodge (2017) have demonstrated how anger expressed by women of colour did not have the same value as that of white women. Even though they had framed and experienced their anger as collective, its acceptance and visibility was very limited. Salerno et al (2019) made similar findings when they analysed group decision-making processes. They discovered that when women or African Americans expressed anger, it was more often discredited as emotional and therefore had less chance of becoming resourceful in social interactions. Their study confirms earlier (psychological) work which showed that the lower the status of an individual or social group, the less people regarded them as entitled and saw their anger as an appropriate reaction (Brody et al, 1995; Motro et al, 2021). This also affects how women (and in particular (working-class) women of colour) tend to feel after anger episodes. hooks (1996: 16) writes, for instance, how she 'felt like an exile' after expressing her anger and Kring (2000: 222) notes that women are more likely to feel 'more embarrassed, ashamed, and bad about themselves', even though this has been changing in the last years with movements like #BlackLivesMatter and #MeToo (see Cooper, 2018; Lloyd, 2019 for an overview of the historical development of 'Black anger'; McCormick-Huhn and Shields, 2021).

We can see this in the way that some of my female interviewees talked about their anger. Even though they felt that anger was an appropriate feeling with regard to their impasse, they also felt uncomfortable with its persistence and intensity. Lara talked about how she associated anger-related emotions with her previous professional experience. She admitted that, at some point, she would need to come to terms with them:

'It is a very strong feeling that I still harbour, in fact, that I should let go of at some point … Ideally, they [these feelings] wouldn't exist, but I can't (laughs). Not yet.' (Lara, 32)

Similarly, Begoña believed that she struggled to manage her anger, which emerged in particular work situations:

'They generate violence, anger, in me … And, for example, it's true that, when it comes to frustration, I think I'll handle it, but anger … Uff … For me, uff, it's … I don't think I've ever really dealt with it, you know, like, my anger has always turned a lot into sadness. When I see a situation of anger, I start crying, like I've focused a lot on it and I still don't know how to handle it, you know? I get angry, I get angry, but I still can't control it.' (Begoña, 29)

Begoña's remark reveals that she believed there was a better way of dealing with anger more appropriately, one that would allow her to control the anger without turning it into sadness or crying. As we saw in Paulina's case earlier, tears can be part of an expression of anger. Yet people often associate tears with shame and perceive them as a sign of weakness, especially when women cry. When men weep, particularly in positions of higher status and power, their tears can help them to gain sympathy (Labott et al, 1991), while women risk being labelled as unstable, emotional or manipulative when acting in the same way (Lutz, 1999). Shields (2002: 162) therefore notes that a 'woman who expresses anger through tears may not be acknowledged by others present as having a legitimate claim to anger or its redress. She may then interpret the failure of others to recognize the anger as condescension and become even more angry, even more tearful'. Begoña's anger thus appears less serious and less dangerous when she expresses it through weeping. This is related to the fact that many women tend to be socialized not to be angry, but rather sad (Shields, 2002: 93). Expressing anger therefore breaks a norm and, as such, is a failure of the habituated feeling rule that women ought to keep their performance of anger low. Displays of sadness and shame then occur when one becomes aware of having breached this rule. This awareness can come from the internalized feeling rules as well as from rule reminders from outside, as we will see now.

The women who did draw on anger reported, in most cases, that family members or friends met their anger with incomprehension and reproaches.

In Lara's case, for instance, her colleague was surprised at the persistence of her intense anger. When she started talking about how she still harboured feelings of anger, he threw in the following comment:

'Holy shit! Seriously? I thought we'd forgotten about that [anger].' (Roberto, 33)

It seemed to her colleague that she had kept the feeling for too long and that she should have got over it a long time ago. His comment was an overt reminder of the feeling rules and a form of shaming. In other accounts, we find mothers discouraging or criticizing the anger of their daughters:

'She says to me: "Well, you should have waited for the end of the shift, you would have been paid … but now it's as if you left work." I tell her: "Yeah, but you don't know the pressure I was under there."' (Paulina, 29)

'She told me many times, then, to bear it [the impasse], to keep quiet and calm, not to get agitated.' (Dorotea, 35)

These comments worked as reminders for their daughters of how they should react, that is, by keeping their temper and knowing 'their place'. Paulina's mother accused her daughter of having put herself in a precarious situation by acting in anger. Dorotea's mother formulated her remarks in anticipation of her daughter's actions and can be seen as a way of discouraging her from drawing on anger and reacting to it. It is, of course, quite possible that Jesus' mother also encouraged him to moderate his anger, but in the interview, he did not talk about this. This absence of any comments as to how his friends or family members reacted to his anger points to something that also became apparent in other narratives, namely that female interviewees mentioned the (reprehensible and delegitimizing) reactions of those in their immediate social environment much more often than the young male interviewees did.

This is in line with studies that have shown how expectations regarding social sanctions for display of anger-related emotions are distributed unequally among men and women (Stoppard and Gunn Gruchy, 1993; Timmers et al, 1998). While men are less likely to expect sanctions if they express anger, the opposite is true for women. They are reported to feel more pressure to display 'positive' emotions like pleasure or happiness and expect higher costs if they fail to do so. This can be traced back to the aforementioned feeling rule that reminds women to keep their performance of anger low. But it is also related to the historically shaped social role of women as principal caregivers, for whom nurturing emotions and likeability are seen as essential for ensuring social reproduction (Federici, 1975; Hochschild, 1983; Jónasdóttir, 1991; Weeks, 2017). Dealing with anger by internalizing it, withdrawing or self-blaming (see Saarni, 1999) rather than expressing it openly is therefore not the result of an inherently female behaviour, but in fact the social consequence of their anger being consistently seen as irrational and illegitimate and being sanctioned more frequently.

This did not necessarily mean that the young women could not draw at all on anger for (re)positioning. As we have seen to some extent in Paulina's case, but particularly in Lara's account, they perceived anger as an empowering emotion, which allowed them to assert themselves, to be motivated and to refuse being seen as powerless or not worthy. But this depended on the intersection of gender with class and (racial) ethnicity. As we saw with Teresa, these categories provided the framework within which she could (not) develop her sense of entitlement and which informed her of the extent to which it was appropriate to react with anger when entitlements were violated. This may explain why anger-related emotions in particular were almost entirely absent in the accounts of Latin American migrant women with a working-class background. It also made a difference – like the young men in my study – whether the young women experienced their anger as isolated or supported by a collective. While Paulina perceived her anger as isolated, that is, it was primarily 'her' anger, for Lara it was rather 'our' anger. She saw this anger in the light of structural inequalities and as a reaction to the violated entitlements of collective positions and values. Framed as part of and supported by a collective, her anger could become powerful.

Conclusion

Focusing on anger, this chapter continued to illustrate how emotions work in position taking. We saw that anger was emanating from hysteresis and the precarious structural conditions and that the young people dealt with it in different ways depending on 1) intersections of class, race and gender, and 2) whether the anger was supported by a collective (for example, the union) or whether it was experienced as an individual emotion that could not be expressed openly (as in Paulina's case) or could not be afforded (as in Jorge's and Teresa's case). Anger thus existed in various forms, which I have described as collective, isolated and absent. When emerging in the first form, anger helped some of the young people to refuse the sense of powerlessness that is often associated with both their impasse and their precarious working environments. As a result, anger became a source of empowerment and a mobilizing force for individual or collective action. In the case of Lara, for instance, anger had a motivating effect as it pushed her to start her own company, and with Jesus it made him actively get involved in the union and report any grievances in his company. When framed as part of and supported

155

by a collective, drawing on anger could become a resource to them, even though they were in positions with relatively low power and/or low status.

But mobilizing and expressing anger was risky for those young people without the necessary symbolic capital to legitimize its use due to their social class, race and/or gender. They could then experience symbolic consequences (for example, shaming by colleagues or family members) as well as material consequences (for example, losing one's job). While collective anger had an empowering effect even from a subordinate position, isolated anger was less likely to be as helpful in communicating where one wished to stand. It required that people could 'afford' to be angry. Because even though anger is generally associated with experiences of injustice, not everyone is seen as equally deserving or entitled. In contrast to the young men, the female interviewees, for example, had fewer opportunities to link their anger to cultural conceptions of femininity, which would have validated its use. Despite the fact that anger, when framed as part of and supported by a collective, helped them in (re)positioning to some extent, rule reminders of a classed and gendered nature made it more difficult. These 'politics of entitlement' (Shields, 2002: 165) had the greatest controlling effect on those in positions of little power and low status where social class, race and gender intersected, and even more so when the anger was interpreted as isolated and situational. This explains why anger was mostly absent in the accounts of Latin American migrant women with a working-class background (as in Teresa's case) and in the accounts of those young people who were (stuck) in situations of multiple dependencies, such as those who were dependent on social workers, the job centre or the family (as in Jorge's case).

Anger here was thus indicating both subjective and objective social positioning. While the objective position influenced the way in which people could draw on anger or not, feeling anger was a subjective experience of young people's entitlements being impeded by external barriers. This highlights how anger both constitutes and is constituted by inequality and is surrounded by very closely regulating (gendered, classed and racialized) feeling rules in contemporary society due to its political force when turning from 'an individually-based, diffuse experience into a focused, collective one' (Eyerman, 2005: 46). The way in which drawing on anger (or on emotional fulfilment in Chapter 6) either became helpful in young people's (re)positioning and their sense of 'placing' (Bourdieu, 2020: 339) or was experienced as a boundary thus illustrates that emotions play a decisive role in reproducing but also challenging social structures and existing inequalities.

Conclusion

In this book, I have examined the relationship between structural change and emotions. Emotions, I have suggested, are not a personal, detached experience; they are profoundly structured by the way in which society is organized. Young people involved in this study felt the changes brought about by the economic crisis – in particular the difficulties of getting into and ahead within the labour market – in their physical and mental health: they had feelings of uncertainty, anxiety, frustration and resentment. These emotions were the product of a mismatch in which expectations and perceived entitlements were largely out of line with existing opportunities. They were emotions of hysteresis (Bourdieu, 1977, 1979), whereby the individuals in question found it difficult to fit into and adjust to the changing environment. The young people interpreted and dealt with their emotions in relation to existing explanatory frameworks, norms and reference points. Facing change therefore involved working on their emotions, for instance, by adjusting, suppressing or validating them. After all, the young people's emotions were not only reactions to the socioeconomic transformations, but were also means and practices (Scheer, 2012, 2016) in young people's (re)positioning and their sense of 'placing' (Bourdieu, 2020: 339) in a changing environment in post-crisis Spain.

In this concluding chapter, I reflect on the conceptual framework and main findings of the analysis and discuss their wider implications and social relevance.

Emotions of hysteresis and emotion work

Having a 'feel for the game' was Bourdieu's metaphor (2020: 25) for capturing the idea that someone has practical knowledge about how the world around them functions, allowing them to navigate their way around it without feeling out of place. This sense of understanding of how to play the game and knowing one's possibilities and constraints is what Bourdieu (1977) called the habitus. If the habitus is in line with the field in which the game is played, it produces feelings of confidence and security: confidence about how to behave and act as the world seems predictable and readable, and certainty about one's position therein, as the amount of status and power are perceived as adequate (Kemper, 1978). Habitus which is at odds with the field – that is, hysteresis – is most likely to produce the opposite emotions, such as uncertainty, anxiety, frustration and resentment. Like habitus, hysteresis both structures and is structured by emotions, as my analysis has demonstrated. Bridging Bourdieu's theory of practice with emotion-sociological theory has helped here to show that hysteresis produced very specific emotions and why.

Uncertainty

Hysteresis disrupts familiarity and the sense of predictability that habitus tends to provide. For the young people in post-crisis Spain, this led to uncertainty about how to read the changed environment and the new rules of the game. The difficulties they experienced in converting educational qualifications into employment and the far-reaching precarization of work (job instability, overqualification, etc.) made them uncertain as to how they could overcome their financial and professional impasse, despite further investment in and accumulation of educational capital. They were concerned about their own mental and physical limitations. If obtaining decent work implied accumulating more and more educational capital, some feared being left behind and being unable to keep pace, regardless of their experience and/or education. Connected to the uncertainty about how to read the changing field was the uncertainty of how to assess one's own chances of participation. As habitus and field became less harmonized, the freedom and opportunities available to the young people for occupying their social position decreased. Uncertainty here related both to their possibilities in the present and to their expectations of and emotional orientation towards the future. Both are guided by the habitus, which informs about what is considered achievable and appropriate, and what is not (Bourdieu, 2020: 259). However, uncertainty arises when young people are guided by views that have become fragile and invalid, as was the case in this book. They felt uncertain about whether and how opportunities would develop in a way that would make it possible to recover certain expectations or whether they had to be largely adapted or dropped completely. So, while hysteresis produced uncertainty, uncertainty also shaped hysteresis. As this book has demonstrated, uncertainty often reinforced the state of being stuck in an impasse. Due to uncertainty as well as fear of unemployment and financial difficulties, young people held on to jobs that they actually wanted to give up and had considered only as a temporary stopgap. Uncertainty and insecurity were thus linked: while uncertainty was related to a lack of insight or knowledge of what to do and what decisions to make about an unknown future, hysteresis also produced insecurity which was related to a lack of reliability and an absence of secure (financial and professional) circumstances.

Anxiety

When hysteresis extends over a longer period of time and both present and future events are met with pessimism, anxiety is likely to develop (Kemper, 1978: 74–5). For the young people in this book, anxiety was the product of a loss of future prospects and lack of perspective. As uncertainty and situations of impasse often stretched over several years, they feared that they would be stuck indefinitely. Since they had difficulties reading and participating in a changing game, many young people perceived their room to manoeuvre as (too) small and therefore felt that they had no or only very limited influence on the future. This resonates with Kemper's model in which it is argued that people feel anxious if they perceive the amount of power that they have as decreasing and hence insufficient (Kemper, 1978: 50–70). The same applies to status. If people feel that their status is declining or is at risk of declining, they are likely to feel anxious about it. The economic crisis had brought about a general visibility of professional and social downward mobility (Alonso et al, 2016), and this led many of the young people to perceive their class position as more fragile and vulnerable, regardless of whether or not they themselves were affected by declassing.

Against this backdrop, their anxiety was also bound up with different forms of dependency. Job insecurity and high youth unemployment translated into constant worries about financial difficulties and the (im)possibility of emancipating themselves from the parental home or of coming off welfare benefits. Difficulties in dealing with this anxiety were linked not only to the lack of room for manoeuvre but also to the moral connotation that (financial) dependence often implied. For many, the latter translated into additional social pressure and thus reinforced feelings of uncertainty and anxiety. Both the objective deterioration in working conditions and the subjective feeling of insecurity exposed the young people to the risk and in some cases the reality of developing poor mental health.

Frustration and resentment

Frustration arose from the disappointment that the young people felt because they did not receive awards in the way they had expected. Acquired educational qualifications had come with expectations, notably in relation to income and status, which proved difficult to fulfil. As Benedicto et al (2014: 155, author's translation) point out, 'with regard to the ideal of society on which the promise of the future was based, there has been a shift from a linear and proportional relationship (the higher the level of education, the greater the opportunities for qualified integration into the labour market) to a relationship perceived as being deceptive and false, thus increasing feelings of frustration'.

Based on Kemper's theory (1978: 80ff), frustration here was a 'consequent emotion' that resulted from the young people's expectations about their possibilities in relation to their prior investment – expectations which were refuted by hysteresis. I demonstrated that comparison produced frustration. In addition to comparing their personal expectations with their actual reality, the young people also compared their own situation with that of others. Their comparison was directed at 1) those who shared a similar social position and educational capital and were moving forward despite the economic crisis, and 2) those who were viewed as not prepared or trained enough, but were still moving forward 'undeservingly'. Hysteresis was relational: whereas frustration and disappointment were directed at the mismatch between the expectations and actual opportunities of the young people themselves, frustration and feelings of unfairness were directed at the mismatch between the expectations and actual opportunities of others.

Comparison and frustration led, as Marshall (1973) argues, to resentment: an emotion that arose because the status allocations of others were perceived as excessive and undeserved (Kemper, 1978: 111). The young people felt resentment as they saw norms of fairness and meritocracy violated in the way they were treated. The sense of resentment was even more prominent when the young people felt that the unfair advantage of others was at their expense (Barbalet, 1998: 137). We saw this, for instance, in Jacobo's case, whose feelings of frustration and resentment were most intense when he had the impression that employers preferred 'migrant others', thus making him feel disregarded and put at a disadvantage when seeking employment. Resentment hence resided in the unequally structured power and status relationships between different social groups produced and/or reinforced by hysteresis.

Hysteresis, then, brought with it a very specific structure of feeling (Williams, 1977), in which the mismatch between objective and incorporated structures produced feelings of uncertainty, anxiety, frustration and resentment. Embedded in and produced by the (changing) social structures, emotions of hysteresis were thus primarily social emotions and not attributes of character or personal experiences. They were shared and, to some extent, collective, even if they were felt and dealt with individually. Analysing emotions thus clarifies Bourdieu's argument that habitus and hysteresis are at the interface between individual agency and social structures. Hysteresis is an embodied experience of change in which the transformations in social structure are felt and processed cognitively, emotionally and physically. This was evident in the way hysteresis and impasse affected the young people's mental and physical health (see Chapter 3), but also in the way they dealt with them (see Chapters 5 and 6). What I have identified as emotive-cognitive reframing (Wettergren, 2019) and bodily techniques comprised a set of practices through which the young people tried to explain, organize and deal with their experiences of a fragmented and ill-adjusted habitus (Silva, 2016). They reframed both ideas and expectations of social reproduction and mobility, as well as the emotions that went along with them. The young people altered practices of social comparison, reconsidered the relationship to time, modified ideas of the meaning and function of work as well as good-life fantasies and ideas of happiness or shifted attributions of responsibility for hysteresis and impasse. They thus adapted explanatory frameworks that no longer matched the changed environment or replaced them with others. In this context, they either changed and suppressed or acknowledged and validated their emotions. Alongside cognitive and emotion work, the young people also used bodily techniques to work on their emotions, but not so much through thoughts as through (working on) the body. By changing somatic or other bodily sensations, they tried to dilute, reduce or detach themselves from feelings of uncertainty, anxiety and frustration.

The different bodily techniques deployed to change and adjust to hysteresis in an emotive-cognitive way illustrate the complex entwinement of mind and body. This frequently assumed and mobilized dichotomy had already been explored by Bourdieu's concept of habitus which, for him, comprised both thinking and feeling. A close inspection of hysteresis and its felt and action-inducing reality substantiates his line of thinking, and clearly shows that cognition/mind and emotion/body cannot be separated.

Hysteresis as a (unifying) generational issue?

Hysteresis, as we have seen, was a defining structural condition of many young people in post-crisis Spain. Their transition into and progress within the labour market were affected by a strong precarization of working conditions, high unemployment and the devaluation of their institutionalized cultural capital such as educational qualifications. Mannheim (2017: 104) speaks in this case of a 'generation in actuality' (*Generationszusammenhang*) that results from being exposed to and participating in a common fate within a given sociohistorical structure. Members of a social generation[1] experience an (incisive) event at the same time within their life and, based on this, according to Mannheim (2017: 94), develop a tendency towards certain ways of behaving, feeling and thinking. For the young people in this book, this tendency was expressed primarily as a sense of loss vis-à-vis previous generations which they shared almost regardless of their social position, as well as the feeling of being deprived of something they had been promised or to which they felt entitled. In public discourse, they were often referred to as 'the lost generation'[2] and also in the accounts of the young people themselves, we saw patterns of a generational experience. Many were well aware that general socioeconomic conditions were the cause for their impasse and that the reality they had prepared for no longer existed, which made it necessary for them to 'reinvent' themselves.

Alongside the sociostructural developments that revealed hysteresis to be a generational phenomenon, the cultural processes that emerged with the upheavals in the wake of the crisis were equally illustrative. Hysteresis as a mismatch between incorporated structures and objective structures inevitably involves notions of what would be normal and appropriate, and notions of values and expectations that have been violated and disappointed as a result of the changes. This involved what Gordon (1990: 146) refers to as 'emotional culture', comprising 'emotion vocabularies (words for emotions), norms (regulating expression and feeling), and beliefs about emotions (for example, the idea that "repressed" emotion is disturbing)'. The cultural aspect of hysteresis as a generational phenomenon was particularly evident in how the young people and their parents viewed work differently. I demonstrated how the young people were shaped by, shared or did not fulfil and then tried to break free from the ideas and expectations of their parents' generation, and how that affected their emotions and emotion work. Young people, who are often the first to adopt new norm structures, are not yet in the position of being locked up in the ('old') norm system, but still face the expectations of others. We saw this, for instance, in Chapters 2 and 3, where Nuria and Natalia, both freelancers, were confronted with the ideas of work and expectations of their parents which stuck to them and made them feel as though they lacked recognition. Part of the reason why this intergenerational conflict was so pronounced and intensified emotions of hysteresis was due to the historically formed dependency relationships. In studies on welfare regimes, Spain has often been described as 'familistic' (for a critique, see León and Migliavacca, 2013), that is, characterized by limited family policies and a cultural model based on traditional gender roles and family relations (Moreno Mínguez, 2007, 2008, 2010). Consequently, the family, and thus ultimately the woman, is seen as the primary institution in charge of social reproduction, that is, providing (unpaid) care and support. As such, the family is considered as responsible for the young people's welfare and as their central safety net, especially in times of hardship. In this way, pronounced interdependencies of a financial, spatial and social nature have developed between the generations. These were reflected in numerous interviews in which young people, such as Paulina, Alberta and Amelia, spoke of their fear and shame of dependency – that is, of living with and at the expense of their parents without much prospect of being able to emancipate themselves financially or spatially from them. These dependency relationships as well as the spatial proximity then acted for many as a constant mirror reflecting their own situation and often required additional explanatory work (see, for example, Javier's dual approach of working on his own emotions and those of others). All of these aspects highlight both the structural and cultural dimension of hysteresis as a generational experience.

Emotional stratification

Being a 'generation in actuality' means being bound by the same formative experiences. Yet, this bond, as Mannheim argues (2017: 92), does not necessarily result in a concrete group. The same was true in this study. While the structural change produced a generation-specific condition of hysteresis, this generation was not homogeneous. The young people differed in terms of age, gender, social class and race. I have argued that these various social categories shaped the object, direction and intensity of the individual's emotions as well as their ways of dealing with and expressing them.

In terms of age, the young people I interviewed were aged between 18 and 35. The economic crisis hit them at different points in their life – for example, some were still in training, while others had already integrated (or tried to integrate) into the labour market. Although hysteresis stemmed for all of them from the mismatch between expectations and the actual opportunities available in post-crisis Spain, it was biographically located differently. The expectations and perceived entitlements of the younger interviewees were primarily formed through habituated ideas. Within their families and circles of friends, at school and in other institutions, they encountered narratives that allowed them to develop a sense of what they could consider attainable and appropriate for themselves. Their inability to turn those ideas into reality made them feel that they were being denied something based on those narratives. In the case of the older interviewees, this sense of loss arose not only from habituated ideas concerning expectations and perceived entitlements but also from their own experiences. Most of them had already had the opportunity to convert their cultural capital into a position on the labour market which also allowed some of them to emancipate themselves financially and spatially from their parents. As such, hysteresis was for them even more evident when they lost status they had already achieved through a certain professional position or personal independence before the crisis. We saw this in Darios' story. Based on his own experience, Dario was able to make comparisons of the situation before and after which underpinned the habituated ideas fed by family biographies or public discourse. For him, hysteresis translated into a break of his biography and into what Rosen (2017) refers to as 'narrative rupture' which necessitated both the (complete) reorganization of work and life patterns, and the way in which he framed and made sense of them.

In addition to age, the dimension of social class shaped the emotions and emotion work of hysteresis. Habitus is always an expression and product of social class. If the habitus is ill-adjusted in situations of hysteresis, then dimensions of class are reflected here too. I have demonstrated that uncertainty and anxiety, which resulted primarily from instability and unpredictability concerning material security, were also directed at the loss of agency over a person's professional career and thus over opportunities for social reproduction and mobility. In particular, young people whose (middle-)class position had generally allowed scope when it came to opportunities for the present and expectations for the future articulated this sense of loss. This was particularly evident with future planning, a practice which, as I have argued, was tied to a habitus that had not only internalized ideas of planning but also feelings of confidence about the possibility of putting them into practice. This planning imperative of the middle classes, described by Schimank (2015), continued to function as a reference point during the upheavals caused by the economic crisis, which helps to explain why especially young people from the middle classes felt this dimension of hysteresis particularly strongly.

In the case of frustration and resentment, the dimension of class was revealed through the underlying mechanism of comparison. It gave people the impression that they were deprived of the same opportunities other (young) people seemed to enjoy despite their own investment. The feeling of being overlooked or even overtaken translated into a lack of social recognition for most of them. Yet, as I have demonstrated, there were different layers of nonrecognition which varied according to class position and could also overlap. While some young people suffered from nonrecognition only in one part of their way of being and doing, for others it could encompass the whole person. Consider, for example, Javier and Jacobo. Javier was confronted with normative ideas of standard employment and the corresponding expectations of his parents. He suffered from the fact that his alternative way of doing and thinking about work was not recognized. The lack of recognition in his case was primarily in the field of work. For Jacobo, it was much broader. The constant rejections on the labour market, the permanent scrutiny by state authorities on account of the social benefits he received and the stigmatization of the neighbourhood in which he lived all made it difficult for him and his whole way of being and doing to be recognized. These examples illustrate that, despite shared frustration and resentment fuelled by a lack of social recognition, their emotions were related to different objects. For young people like Javier, frustration and resentment related to the (possible) loss of status as a member of the middle class. For middle-class youths, the risk of declassing was thus at stake. For young people in marginalized positions like Jacobo, frustration and resentment were related to the nonrecognition of their respectability (Skeggs, 1997). They experienced a combination of what Smith (2001: 552) refers to as 'relegation-humiliation' and 'expulsion-humiliation', whereby people 'feel they are being held down' and 'rejected, kicked out of the game', respectively. Having grown up in a democratic society that upholds the notion of equal rights and equal opportunities for everyone, their request for respectability was therefore situated in the expectation that they would at least have equal access to some basic (human) rights and be recognized and treated humanely.

Some class-specific differences also emerged in dealing with (emotions of) hysteresis. I showed that where it had become much more difficult to signal and maintain social position and status by means of educational qualifications, salaries or the workplace, emotions proved to be an additional resource for (re)positioning and habitus defence (see Chapter 6). In some cases, however, using emotions to communicate where one wished to stand was achieved by producing distinction and (class) boundaries (Lamont and Molnár, 2002). One example was the creation of emotional hierarchies. They emerged when young people idealized and valorized work through feelings of passion and emotional fulfilment to which they did not (or no longer) had access or from which they could not fully live. At the same time, they viewed the jobs they were stuck in but needed for their livelihoods with frustration and disdain. As it was more difficult to achieve financial distinction due to the strong precarization of work and the devaluation of educational qualifications, this form of emotional hierarchy enabled symbolic distinction. Emotions served here to maintain symbolic boundaries of class. However, this form of valorization and devaluation of work(ers) through emotions of passion and emotional fulfilment was not accessible to everyone. While for some it enabled them to counteract emotions of hysteresis, for others it acted as a reminder of their (lower) status and power.

These *politics of entitlement* (Shields, 2002: 165) emerged most clearly where social categories of class, gender and race intersected. When it came to anger that emanated from hysteresis and precarious structural conditions, the young women in my study had fewer opportunities to draw on this emotion for position taking. While drawing on anger allowed the male interviewees to tie in with cultural conceptions of masculinity (see, for instance, the case of Jesus), the young women found it more difficult to do so. They could hardly draw on anger to emphasize agency, especially from positions with little power and low status. That is why, in some cases, they could not openly express anger (see, for instance, the case of Paulina) and in other cases could not even afford to feel it (see, for instance, the case of Teresa).

While more intersectional and multidimensional research on hysteresis and emotions is needed, this book suggests that there is emotional stratification within hysteresis as a shared generational condition. Ultimately, even before the economic crisis of 2008, part of the generation had only marginalized opportunities for recognition and social and economic participation. What made it a generation-specific condition was the extension of structural disadvantages as well as the feeling of being ignored and having no prospects to other social groups of young people for whom participation and personal development had been previously (more) accessible, given their social position (and amounts of economic, cultural, social and symbolic capital).

Emotions and the question of social change

Hysteresis is a condition of structural mismatch and, as such, a sign of changing times and social change brought about by structural factors such as an economic crisis. These, in turn, are embedded in contingent sociohistorical constructions of society and point towards the hegemonic world of late capitalism. The question then is: what do the findings in this book suggest for social change?

First of all, we have seen that change becomes perceptible to the individual through emotions and is thus an embodied experience. Emotions are an expression of change in that they arise from a mismatch between incorporated structures and objective structures, and signal a change in status and power relations. Since emotions inform us about how we are situated in relation to others, they also indicate when this fabric and related expectations are disrupted by (profound) change. For the young people in this book, the structural change, especially on the labour market, translated into 1) feelings of uncertainty and anxiety concerning opportunities for material and symbolic recognition, and 2) feelings of frustration and resentment about the loss of entitlements that they assumed were a given and due to the perception that others were receiving (undeserved) advantages. This was also evident in the vocabulary the young people used to describe their experiences and related emotions when they talked about feelings of "standstill", "of being stopped in your tracks", of "stagnating" and "remaining stuck". Change expressed in hysteresis was thus a form of emotional apprehension about a suspended present and an unclear future.

Second, we have seen that profound change through the crisis was not only produced at the macrolevel and then 'embraced' by individuals. Change was also 'co-produced' through social interactions at the microlevel. In this context, Gordon (1990) speaks of the individual effects on social structure that can arise through emotions, their expression or processing. He therefore advocates studying them not only as a product of social interactions but also as an '*intervening* variable in the maintenance, modification, or disruption of society' (Gordon, 1990: 170, emphasis in original). By motivating actions and communicating intentions, identities and values, emotions have an influence on social relations and can maintain or disrupt them. For Gordon (1990: 171), change in social structure occurs especially when certain emotions or 'emotional styles' take on a collective character. This is the case, he (1990: 171) says, when new 'social standards for emotional reactions' are set and 'emulated en masse'. Many of the young people in this book were not part of a social movement or necessarily analysing the bigger picture, yet their adjustments were prompted by structural change. They coped with emotions of hysteresis through emotive-cognitive reframing and bodily techniques in individual ways, but when aggregated, they had large-scale outcomes. As such, they contributed to the challenging of 'old' and the production of new feeling rules when they changed practices of social comparison (for example, qualifying their impasse), reconsidered their relationship to time (for example, concentrating on the present instead of long-term planning) or modified their understanding of the meaning and function of work (for example, seeing work as a mere income-generating activity rather than one for social recognition or self-fulfilment). In working on and shifting their reference points and expectations, the young people were thus part of the changing norm system. Their (apolitical) individual adjustments fed back into social structures and were therefore an essential component of social change.

Ultimately, we have seen that emotions can act as a catalyst for or barrier to social change. Emotions are a driving force for people to act. In many accounts, we saw how frustration and anger led young people to take action to do things differently or to initiate change, for example, by starting their own company or joining a trade union. However, collective action needs a certain emotional dynamic to develop (see Summers-Effler, 2002). The emotional dynamic involved systemic framing of a person's own situation, validating deviant emotions by turning them inside out and using collective spaces for developing awareness and collective emotion work. For the young people in this book, this meant that they interpreted their impasse situation as structurally conditioned and their feelings of frustration, uncertainty and anxiety as a product of the political, economic and social context in which they found themselves. This awareness enabled them to redirect their emotions from the individual towards external actors and structural conditions. This was how being ashamed turned into shaming out and disappointment with oneself turned into anger with the system. The emotion work involved in this (re)interpretation, which consisted of acknowledging the deviant emotions of shame and anger and validating them as appropriate, was essential not only for questioning the status quo but also for contributing to bring about a counteracting effect.

By contrast, emotions could become barriers to social change when young people saw them as a product of self-inflicted behaviour and as dealing with these as the sole responsibility of the individual. Young people then considered their impasse as a personal affair and associated their feelings of uncertainty, anxiety and frustration with their own individual character, biographical events or personal difficulties in dealing with them effectively. This often involved feelings of shame, an emotion that usually acts as a place marker (Clark, 1990) and that fixes or demotes the individual in their social position (Neckel, 1991). Dealing with the impasse thus meant adapting one's ideas and expectations to the changed circumstances. Instead of carrying the social conflict outside, the young people carried it inside and their emotion work served primarily to help them adjust by suppressing or changing deviant emotions such as uncertainty, anxiety or frustration.

Furthermore, we have seen how, in the face of structural precariousness, uncertainty and anxiety can lead to people holding on to certain things or practices. A common thread running through many of the interviews was that of young people keeping their precarious jobs and accepting exploitative working conditions for fear of being worse off after a change. All of these emotional dynamics thus contribute to the reproduction or even consolidation of existing social structures.

Future research

Having summarized and discussed the preceding findings, this book has contributed theoretically by bridging sociology of emotions with Bourdieusian theory, providing an analysis that enhances our understanding of emotions as the link between structure and agency. It has contributed empirically by applying this perspective to a recent case of hysteresis, namely that of the young generations in post-crisis Spain, and the findings in turn have provided new knowledge regarding the emotion work of hysteresis, which emotions are at play and the potential consequences. This in turn raises questions for further research, such as when and how emotions of hysteresis spur collective organization into social movements sustained over time and with an outspoken agenda for social change (and what that agenda(s) might be).

Other questions for future research concern the emotion work of hysteresis. The young people in this book invested in the future through emotion work by trying to adjust to the changed game in the hope of continuing to play eventually or by trying to transform the game altogether through collective action (in social movements, unions, etc.). Future research should focus even more on those who withdraw from the game and are unable or unwilling to use emotion work either to participate in or to change it. As Addison (2016: 187) writes, this may be because 'work on the self seems unconvincing and a fruitless effort' – efforts that, according to Bourdieu (2000: 161), 'help to plunge them deeper into failure'. A deeper analysis of the limitations of emotion work of hysteresis could then further elaborate on how inequalities are perpetuated and reinforced, and form barriers to social change.

Finally, the question arises as to whether change always produces structural conditions of hysteresis and, if so, whether the emotions evoked by hysteresis are always those of uncertainty, anxiety, frustration and resentment or whether they vary across time and space. In other words, are the emotions of hysteresis identified in this book situated in the temporal and geographical context of post-crisis Spain or can we observe similar patterns in other contexts as well?

These questions may become particularly relevant in the current context in which Spain – like the rest of the world – seems to move from one crisis to the next (for example, the global health crisis with the COVID-19 pandemic and the increasingly tangible climate crisis).

If we look, for instance, at the COVID-19 pandemic, we saw that short-term work, loss of employment and a partial collapse of public infrastructures (such as hospitals or public health offices) were some of the first tangible, material consequences. Others were more immaterial and concerned our rules and ideas on social interaction and moral behaviour, which the pandemic had exposed to far-reaching changes. What we previously considered impolite in certain spaces and around certain people (for example, covering one's face, refusing to shake hands or distancing oneself from others) had in some cases been elevated to a new expression of solidarity. Practical knowledge and habituated practices orienting behaviour and actions were partly in conflict with what the changed structures still allowed. Knowledge that we thought of as certain had started to crumble, revealing the transience and fallibility of science. There is much to suggest that conditions of hysteresis and thus emotions of hysteresis emerged in this context of (global) crisis and far-reaching change. We saw, for instance, frustration concerning lockdown measures that were perceived as unfair and a threat to personal freedom or existence, and we saw uncertainty and anxiety arising over how the global health crisis would impact us in the long run. Once again, young people constituted a particular point of focus here. For those who found that their expectations of the world as a site of study, employment, travel and sociality had changed due to the closure of borders, sites of play and encounter, schools and universities, and the loss of apprenticeships, etc., the crisis felt like a suspended future (van de Velde et al, 2022). Similar feelings start to emerge with the increasingly tangible climate crisis. So how will young people make sense of disappointed expectations and broken promises for the future? What will they do with their narratives of pessimism (McKenzie and Patulny, 2022), eco-anxiety (for an overview, see Brophy et al, 2022) and frustration about intergenerational inequalities (Simpson and Bui, 2021)?

These questions are of concrete political relevance. As the pandemic has already shown, (collective) emotions such as fear or resentment can be politically fuelled or exploited (Wettergren et al, 2020; Perriard and van de Velde, 2021). The fear of an uncontrolled spread of the virus and of the collapse of the (global) economy has prompted many governments to take radical measures within a very short time, whether to slow down industry, trade and mobility or to change and curtail (basic) laws and civil liberties. When fear is collective and perceived as acute and threatening, (rapid) political action and possibilities for change may thus be more likely (Barbalet, 1998). In addition to fear, as Wettergren et al (2020: 3) describe, political actors 'have chosen – deliberately or not – to act on and cultivate international distrust and nationalist resentment'. Here, too, emotions have been tapped into and used to justify global fragmentation, closed borders and protectionism.

These considerations suggest that the findings of this book regarding the young people's approaches to coping in a crisis setting may help us to understand the political implications of (collective) emotions and the huge effort needed by society to contain and direct emotions of hysteresis in constructive ways.

APPENDIX

The Research

The research for this book started with my interest in the economic crisis in Spain and its (long-term) impact on the lives of young people, especially with regard to their possibilities of getting into and ahead within the labour market. I did a first round of explorative interviews in 2016. The second round of data collection in 2017/2018 was more focused, moving from the young people's general perception of the crisis to their emotional experience of change.

In total, I spoke with 68 young people between the ages of 18 and 35 who lived in Madrid and had already had some experience within the labour market. As Madrid (municipality) is home to more than 60 nationalities, of which around 50 per cent have a South and Latin American origin (author's calculation based on statistical data from 2020: Ayuntamiento de Madrid, 2020), I also talked to young people with Hondurian, Colombian, Chilean, Peruvian, Ecuadorian, Cuban, Moroccan and Cameroonian nationality, some of them also with dual citizenship (Spanish/N). Often employed in precarious and temporary jobs, they were usually among the first to be affected by cutbacks and job losses in the crisis (Laparra and Pérez Eransus, 2012: 21, 97f, 146; Campos, 2018: 37).

To explore whether the emotional experience of change differed among the young people, the sampling sought to include a variety of work situations, reflecting the different forms of non/work that were subject to or expression of the changing labour conditions, especially due to the economic crisis (see Table 1).

With this form of *purposeful sampling* (Maxwell, 1996: 70f), I aimed at capturing the heterogeneity of young people's work situation in Madrid, at least to some extent. Beyond that, the sample was composed as follows with regard to age, gender, level of education and country of birth (see Table 2).

To enter the field, I used various channels and entry points. First of all, I linked up with several contacts that I had made during my stays in Madrid over a number of years (2011–13 and 2014). I shared the call for interview

Table 1: Sampling of the young people's work situation at the time of the interview

Self-employment (n=11)	Young people working as freelancers, independent shop owners or entrepreneurs (at home or in co-working spaces).
Part-time work (n=12)	Young people who had several part-time jobs in order to sustain their livelihood. Many of them tried to make a living within a field in which they have been trained, but had to combine it with one or two additional jobs. Also, young people who had part-time jobs and were in further education.
Temporary work (n=20)	Young people with temporary work contracts in the service economy. Many of them were affected by flexible working hours (for example, at weekends), outsourcing and reduction of certain rights (for example, to strike).
Unemployed (n=10)	Young people without work who received unemployment benefits. Many were doing or had been placed in further training courses (n=5) or socioprofessional reintegration schemes (n=4) by their social workers or the employment office. Here, too, the crisis led to severe cuts in public spending and the reduction of funds for these programmes.
Not in work but in (further) education or training (n=15)	Young people who were not in work but who were or went back into (further) training courses (n=4) or higher education (n=8) and lived on savings or from financial support by friends or family.
	Young people who underwent the selection process to enter the public service, called *oposiciones* in Spain (n=3). Once a field of stable and secure employment, the civil service was characterized by great insecurity at the time of the research. During the economic crisis, public spending was severely cut, which led to a radical reduction in vacancies. At the same time, the interest in joining the civil service increased at that time, which led to more competition as there were more candidates but fewer vacancies.

participation among friends, former flatmates, work colleagues and language students. Furthermore, I wrote to various citizens' and environmental initiatives as well as residents whom I had interviewed in the context of former research (Margies, 2017). In some cases the opportunity to invite people to an interview emerged spontaneously: a conversation in the fitness centre, at an event or by talking to staff at the grocery store, in the bakery or the clothes shop. Most interviewees I was able to gain through institutions where I conducted expert interviews.

The 11 expert interviews helped me in gaining a deeper understanding of the socio-economic situation of young people in Madrid in general and for different social groups in particular. I therefore selected specifically organizations and institutions that focused on young people and the labour market. They also functioned as gatekeepers to access the field and

Table 2: Sampling of the young people's age, gender, level of education and country of birth at the time of the interview

Age			
18–23 years	24–29 years	30–35 years	
n=15	n=31	n=22	

Gender			
Female	Male		
n=34	n=34		

Level of education			
Primary education	(Unfinished) secondary education	Vocational training	Higher education
n=1	n=11	n=12	n=44

Country of birth								
Spain	Honduras	Colombia	Chile	Peru	Cuba	Ecuador	Morocco	Cameroon
n=57	n=1	n=3	n=1	n=2	n=1	n=1	n=1	n=1

helped me to get in touch with young people from different social and educational backgrounds.

One of my first expert interviews was with the Spanish Youth Council (Consejo de la Juventud en España). As a platform of more than 60 youth organizations promoting the participation of young people in the political, social, economic and cultural development of the country, they gave me a comprehensive insight into the situation of young people in Spain. This included information on the labour and housing market, mobility and migration due to the crisis, as well as developments in the field of education (for example, school drop-out rates, reforms in the higher education sector and rising university fees).

In conversations with representatives of the three main trade unions (CCOO, UGT and CNT),[1] I learned about the general precarious working conditions for young people, about work-related policies and legislative changes, and about workers' rights and common practices by employers to circumvent them. This knowledge was extremely helpful later on in the interviews with the young people, as many of their experiences within the labour market were shaped by austerity measures as well as practices of employers operating in legal grey areas.

Talking to the representative of the Youth Department of the Municipality of Madrid and the directors of two public youth centres allowed me to gain an overview of the institutional infrastructure of the city's youth work. Among other things, it helped me to understand the tasks and role of the youth centres as places of lingering, leisure and learning. There were generally libraries or study rooms used by many young people who were preparing for the civil service selection exams, the *oposiciones*. It was also often a place where young people could find training courses that were offered to facilitate their entry into the labour market. At the youth centre in a northern neighbourhood with higher socioeconomic status, I spoke with young people preparing for *oposiciones*. At the youth centre in a southern neighbourhood with lower socioeconomic status, I met young people who attended further education courses in logistics and the service industry.

Speaking with two nonprofit associations that support the development and reintegration of people at risk and/or social exclusion made me aware of the extent to which austerity measures had affected social programmes, and thus also young people who were already marginalized before the crisis. On the other hand, these conversations gave me an insight into the numerous training programmes in which these young people often circulate and helped me to recognize the impasse of being stuck in training loops.

Finally, I met with two people representing or running co-working spaces (one in the centre and one in the south of the city). From them, I learned about the role of the social and spatial infrastructure of co-working spaces and the importance of community as a resource. Again, both of these people acted as gatekeepers, as they sent my request through internal distribution lists and put me in contact with those who were interested in participating in an interview.

Notes

Introduction

[1] All names of the people I have interviewed and quote in this book have been pseudonymized. Details that could allow people to be identified have also been removed or generalized as far as possible.

[2] Over a period of four years, the 15M social movement mobilized people in Spain. In 2011, in the early months, people organized numerous actions, demonstrations, occupations, gatherings, performances and marches all over the country. The central square in Madrid, Puerta del Sol, was occupied by protesters for almost a month. The participants demanded 'Real Democracy Now', meaning fundamental changes to the democratic and economic model at the time, and called for basic rights to housing, education and health (Pereira-Zazo and Torres, 2019). The movement also resonated internationally, had global links and inspired other movements such as Occupy in the US (Díez García, 2017). It also had a political impact. A number of citizen platforms and the left-wing political party Podemos, which was founded in January 2014, developed as a result of this movement. In the 2015 municipal elections, the citizen platform Barcelona en Comú came to power in Barcelona and elected Ada Colau as mayor, who was an activist and founding member of the Platform for People Affected by Mortgages (PAH). In Madrid, the citizens' platform Ahora Madrid became the second strongest force and succeeded in appointing the mayor, Manuela Carmena. At the national level, Podemos won 21 per cent of the vote in the 2015 federal elections, making it the third largest party in the country (Kassam, 2015). In the 2019 national elections, it then managed to enter government as part of a coalition with the socialist party PSOE.

[3] Bauman (2012, 2–3, emphasis in original) defines his concept of *liquid modernity* as 'the growing conviction that change is *the only* permanence, and uncertainty *the only* certainty ... it means an infinity of improvement, with no "final state" in sight and none desired'.

[4] The evictions referred to any form of building and could include primary residences, secondary residences, offices or commercial premises (*La Vanguardia*, 2017).

[5] These figures refer only to the young people who officially deregistered. They do not include all those who maintained their main residence in Spain despite emigrating. Moreover, the figures include young people with Spanish nationality as well as those of other nationalities.

[6] While this term has been widely used in Spain in the course and the aftermath of the crisis, it remains a controversial one. Especially within public discourse, it has been used to describe the young generation as an inactive one. Yet the way in which these data are often collated makes it difficult to tell whether the young people represented as being in situations referred to as NEET are indeed inactive or rather engaged, for instance, in informal or domestic labour (see, for example, Sánchez, 2012).

Chapter 1

[1] Elsewhere (for example, in his Lectures at the Collège de France), Bourdieu also mentions the 'Don Quixote paradigm' (Bourdieu, 2020: 128), drawing on Marx's use of this metaphor.

[2] Bourdieu was not the first to sociologically conceptualize this situation, as Hardy recalls (2014: 127–8). Marx and Durkheim, for example, also described similar situations with their concepts of *alienation* (1968) and *anomie* (1893), respectively. Hardy points out, however, that while Marx's and Durkheim's statements contain a moral connotation, Bourdieu 'breaks with a pre-existing moral position and suspends moralistic judgement in the interest of objectivity' (Hardy, 2014: 128).

[3] Kemper's approach can be considered close to those of structuralists, some of whom Bourdieu criticized. While 'there are ambiguities in Bourdieu's work', as Reed-Danahay argues (2005: 15–16), 'about the relative degree of freedom and constraint on human agency, as evident in the gap between readings of his work on education (viewed in its earliest forms as a theory of reproduction with no possibility of human agency) and his work on the Kabyles in *Outline* (viewed as a form of emergent practice theory exploring human agency)', Bourdieu himself criticized French structuralism and saw his way of conceptualizing habitus as moving away from this approach. He explains this, for instance, in his book entitled *The Rules of Art: Genesis and Structure of the Literary Field* (1996), in which he writes that his use of habitus enabled him 'to break with the structural paradigm' and 'to react against structuralism and its strange philosophy of action which, implicitly in the Lévi-Straussian notion of the unconscious and avowedly among the Althusserians, made the agent disappear by reducing it to the role of supporter or bearer (*Träger*) of the structure' (Reed-Danahay, 2005: 179, emphasis in original).

[4] One of the primary frameworks that Goffman identifies is that of gender. In his essay entitled 'The Arrangement between the Sexes' (1977), he demonstrates how the division of the sexes within any social field, such as the division of labour, may seem natural, but is also to be understood as a social framework for interpretation. While the '*functioning* of sex-differentiated organs is involved', he argues, 'there is nothing in this functioning that *biologically* recommends segregation; *that* arrangement is totally a cultural matter' (Goffman, 1977: 316, emphasis in original).

[5] Hochschild distinguishes between three different techniques of emotion work. Besides the cognitive technique already mentioned, we also engage in bodily and expressive emotion work. In the former, we try to 'change somatic or other physical symptoms of emotion (for example, trying to breathe slower, trying not to shake)', while in the latter, we attempt to 'change expressive gestures in the service of changing inner feeling (for example, trying to smile or cry)' (Hochschild, 2003: 96).

[6] In this context, Illouz (2015: 101) refers, among other things, to the example of the cosmetics company L'Oréal, whose turnover of sales staff selected on the basis of their emotional competence was significantly higher than that of sales staff recruited using previously applied selection criteria.

[7] The different forms which public displays of grief have taken, especially in the context of activism around AIDS, are captured impressively in the film *120 battements par minute* (Campillo, 2017). It traces the various forms of collective mourning of the queer community and the organization Act Up in Paris in the 1990s. In their struggle for visibility and recognition of grief, they organized, among other things, public funeral marches in which they paraded through the streets with white wooden crosses and then lay on the pavement in silence.

Chapter 2

[1] The figures vary according to studies and sources. While the Spanish Ministry of Education published figures showing that bachelor's and master's degrees have become around

19 per cent and 50 per cent more expensive respectively, the Spanish Confederación Sindical de Comisiones Obreras (CCOO) trade union published a study in 2016 that also took into account the number of students and thus came up with significantly higher figures. According to these figures, the costs of a bachelor's degree rose by 32 per cent and that of a master's degree by 75 per cent (CCOO Enseñanza, 2016; Sanmartín, 2016).

[2] ALMPs and social services are usually outsourced through calls for tenders by public authorities, for which nongovernmental organizations (NGOs), foundations and other institutions can submit bids. The disadvantage of this strategy, as Moreno Mínguez et al (2012: 174) note, is the lack of financial sustainability, as programmes can end at any time, even at short notice, depending on the availability of subsidies. The consequence, they continue, is that measures are designed less according to the needs of the participants and more according to the guidelines of the calls for tenders.

[3] Many of the training biographies revealed a pattern of gender stereotyping. The young women were generally placed in courses relating to care and customer service, while the young men were assigned to those relating to crafts (for example, wood and metal processing) or technology.

[4] The advice and rebukes were not exclusively based on the normative ideas of work; they were also the product of a lack of youth policies that made families the principal safety net for young people. The parents therefore guided their children towards permanent employment out of concern in order to prevent them from suffering financial hardship or experiencing parental dependence.

[5] This did not necessarily mean that they considered it to be within reach. While the standard employment relationship continued to shape ideal conceptions of work, the new parameters of flexibility were already internalized, as Alonso et al (2017) note.

[6] It was mostly self-employed people and freelancers who had previously worked in the fields of education, culture or architecture who reported these types of working conditions.

Chapter 3

[1] Yet, Schimank (2015: 14) also stresses that the planning imperative always contains a mixture of illusion and ideology, and therefore includes breaks and deviations. Nevertheless, according to Schimank (2015: 15), it continues to serve as a desirable ideal even in times of uncertainty, which can be used not least as a means of distinction.

[2] Fraser and Gordon (1994) demonstrate how the meaning of dependency has changed over time. In pre-industrial and industrial times, they argue, dependency primarily had an economic, legal and political meaning. A peasant was legally subordinated and hence dependent on his landowner, as was a slave, deprived of any political or civil rights or the housewife who was economically dependent on her husband, the male breadwinner (Fraser and Gordon, 1994: 313–19). Yet, in post-industrial society, dependency is increasingly individualized. Considered for a long time to be mainly related to structural conditions and disadvantages, its focus now shifts considerably towards individual traits and capacities. 'Fear of dependency, both explicit and implicit, posits an ideal, independent personality in contrast to which those considered dependent are deviant' (Fraser and Gordon, 1994: 332). In this way, the moral dimension has become the dominant meaning in the discourse of dependency and blaming the individual its main mechanism.

[3] However, surprisingly, very little research has been conducted into the link between the economic crisis and its impact on mental health in Spain, as criticized by many authors (Fernández-Rivas and González-Torres, 2013; Bartoll et al, 2014; Espino Granado, 2014).

[4] There are numerous possible explanations for the increased consumption of pharmaceuticals, including work-related forms of stress, such as unemployment, job insecurity or reduction of employees' rights, but also increased awareness and social acceptance of mental health

problems and certain forms of medication achieved both through awareness raising by NGOs and citizens' initiatives and lobbying by the pharmaceutical industry.

5   Jacobo received the Renta Mínima de Inserción (guaranteed minimum income), which in 2017 amounted to €375 a month in the Madrid region and could be applied for without any time limit. However, this form of social benefit was usually dependent upon participation in socioprofessional reintegration programmes.

Chapter 4

1   Spanish for 'changing one's way of thinking'.

2   See, for example, in the *Pons* dictionary: https://de.pons.com/%C3%BCbersetzung/engli sch-spanisch/cambiar+el+chip?bidir=1 and Leo: https://dict.leo.org/alem%C3%A1n-espa%C3%B1ol/cambiar%20el%20chip.

3   Natalia's statement, in which she contrasted "them" and "their objective" with herself and her own objective, suggests that her ideas (and entitlements) were still divergent and that changing or replacing frustration with an emotion with positive connotation was not necessarily possible or desirable.

4   Emotional reflexivity, as Holmes (2010, 2015) and later on Burkitt (2012) understand it, is not purely individualistic, but develops in interaction with and in relation to others. They thus distance themselves from the discourse in management and psychology, in which emotional reflexivity is usually understood as (another) tool for monitoring and managing which promises better performance through individual work on and optimization of the self (see, for example, Burkitt, 2012: 459).

5   In the case of yoga practice as one form of resonance oases, it is also important to point out the difference between the yoga industry, on the one hand, and the yoga practice and cosmology, on the other. While the former is subject to trends and profit, the latter sees itself rather as a shelter from trends and profit providing an anticompetitive space (see, for example, Godrej, 2017; Erkmen, 2021).

Chapter 5

1   While Kemper does not explicitly address it, the conviction of locating the blame outside of oneself is also linked to intersections of class, gender and race, that is, of being socialized into entitlement.

2   Regarding the circumstances under which the legitimization of feelings may occur, Thoits (1985: 238) states that 'prolonged contact between similarly affected individuals, a threshold number of such individuals, ineffective threats or incentives from external authorities for conformity, and perhaps a charismatic spokesperson may be required'.

3   In his order of the different forms of sympathy, Scheler (2008: 8–36) distinguishes between four different types: 1) the community of feeling; 2) the fellow-feeling; 3) the emotional infection; and 4) the emotional identification.

4   At this point, it is worth emphasizing that Summers-Effler's descriptions of the emotional dynamics may give the impression that these steps are linear. However, based on my empirical data, I would suggest that this process of turning emotions inside out is rather cyclical. This would be consistent with Summers-Effler's (2002: 52) aspect of 'maintaining critical consciousness', where she points out that the process does not end once critical consciousness is attained. Instead, it requires constant cognitive and emotional effort to maintain it, which can be achieved, among other things, through recurrent engagement in collective rituals and action.

5   Salmela (2012) distinguishes between weakly, moderately and strongly shared emotions.

Chapter 6

[1] I follow Bourdieu (1977, 1989) and Clark (1990) here and understand place as situational that is negotiated in everyday interaction, position as structural that is determined by a person's composition and allocation of capitals, and position taking as the practices of what people do to signal or maintain a position.

Chapter 7

[1] The Partido Popular conservative political party was in power from 2011 to 2018 and responded to the crisis (and the demands of the IMF) by implementing numerous austerity measures in the public sector, especially in education and healthcare, and by privatizing public goods (see the Introduction). During the same period, numerous cases of corruption involving the party (including the Presidents of the Community of Madrid, Esperanza Aguirre and Ignacio González, and the Spanish Prime Minister, Mariano Rajoy) were uncovered, involving the embezzlement of large amounts of public money. Jesus' company was involved in one of these cases, in which not only some of the managers but also high-ranking politicians were accused of corruption and some were sentenced to prison.

[2] This again became particularly evident during the lockdown imposed due to the COVID-19 pandemic. Policing and fining were highest in this area, even though a large part of its population not only worked in system-relevant occupations, such as nursing and housekeeping, but also in jobs where working from home was not an option.

[3] The Community of Madrid (Comunidad de Madrid) is the regional government and has been governed by the Partido Popular conservative political party since 1995.

Conclusion

[1] When I use the term 'generation' here, I refer to a cohort 'defined as people within a delineated population who experience the same significant event within a given period of time' (Pilcher, 1994: 483). By using Pilcher's (1994: 483) suggestion of 'social generation', I aim to emphasize my use of 'generation' in the cohort sense instead of a kinship sense (see also Glenn [1977] for further discussion on the terminology of generation and cohort).

[2] By institutions such as the UN (see, for example, *El País*, 2012) as well as by media (see, for example, *El Mundo*, 2011; Rivas, 2015).

Appendix

[1] The Confederación Sindical de Comisiones Obreras (CCOO) and the Unión General de Trabajadores (UGT) are two of the largest trade unions in the country, each with more than 900,000 members (Confederación Sindical de Comisiones Obreras, 2015; Unión General de Trabajadores, 2017). The Confederación Nacional del Trabajo (CNT) is one of the smaller ones, with around 5,000 members, and describes itself as an anarchosyndicalist labour union whose organizational structure is based on self-management and direct democracy, and rejects any state subsidies (Confederación Nacional del Trabajo, nd).

References

Acosta-Ballesteros, J., del Pilar Osorno-del Rosal, M. and Rodríguez-Rodríguez, O. M. (2018) 'Overeducation of Young Workers in Spain: How Much Does the First Job Matter? Social Indicators Research', *Social Indicators Research*, 138(1): 109–39.

Addison, M. (2016) *Social Games and Identity in the Higher Education Workplace: Playing with Gender, Class and Emotion*, London: Palgrave Macmillan.

Ahmed, S. (2004) *The Cultural Politics of Emotion*, Edinburgh: Edinburgh University Press.

Ahmed, S. (2010) *The Promise of Happiness*, Durham, NC: Duke University Press.

Ahmed, S. (2014) *The Cultural Politics of Emotion*, Edinburgh: Edinburgh University Press.

Alonso, L. E., Férnandez Rodríguez, C. F. and Ibáñez Rojo, R. (2016) 'Between Austerity and Discontent: Discourse on Consumption and Economic Crisis in Spain', *Revista Española de Investigaciones Sociológicas (REIS)*, 155: 21–36.

Alonso, L. E., Férnandez Rodríguez, C. F. and Ibáñez Rojo, R. (2017) 'Juventud y percepciones de la crisis: precarización laboral, clases medias y nueva política', *EMPIRIA: Revista de Metodología de Ciencias Sociales*, 37: 155–78.

Alter, J. S. (2011) 'Yoga, Modernity, and the Middle Class: Locating the Body in a World of Desire', in I. Clark-Decès (ed) *A Companion to the Anthropology of India*, Malden, MA: Wiley-Blackwell, pp 154–68.

Amin, S. (1995) *Event, Metaphor, Memory: Chauri Chaura, 1922–1992*, Berkeley: University of California Press.

Araujo, S., and González-Fernández, T. (2014) 'International Migration, Public Policies and Domestic Work: Latin American Migrant Women in the Spanish Domestic Work Sector', *Women's Studies International Forum*, 46: 13–23.

Atkinson, W. (2013) 'Economic Crisis and Classed Everyday Life: Hysteresis, Positional Suffering and Symbolic Violence', in W. Atkinson, S. Roberts and M. Savage (eds) *Class Inequality in Austerity Britain: Power, Difference and Suffering*, London: Palgrave Macmillan, pp 13–32.

Ayuntamiento de Madrid (2020) 'Demografía y Población. Población según nacionalidad. Padrón Municipal de Habitantes a 1 de Enero de 2020', [online], Available from: https://www.madrid.es/portales/munimadrid/ es/Inicio/El-Ayuntamiento/Estadistica/Areas-de-informacion-estadistica/ Demografia-y-poblacion/Poblacion-extranjera/Poblacion-extranjera-en-la-ciudad-de-Madrid/?vgnextfmt=default&vgnextoid=c289d54944580 510VgnVCM20 [Accessed 10 October 2023].

Bailey, F. G. (1983) *The Tactical Uses of Passion: An Essay on Power, Reason, and Reality*, Ithaca, NY: Cornell University Press.

Banyuls Llopis, J. M. and Recio, A. (2012) 'The Nightmare of the Mediterranean Liberalism', in S. Lehndorff (ed) *A Triumph of Failed Ideas European Models of Capitalism in the Crisis*, Brussels: European Trade Union Institute, pp 199–217.

Barbalet, J. M. (1998) *Emotion, Social Theory, and Social Structure: A Macrosociological Approach*, Cambridge: Cambridge University Press.

Barchard, K. A. (2017) 'New Section: Methods in Emotion Research', *Emotion Review* 9(3): 279–79.

Bartoll, X., Palència, L., Malmusi, D., Suhrcke, M. and Borrell, C. (2014) 'The Evolution of Mental Health in Spain during the Economic Crisis', *European Journal of Public Health*, 24(3): 415–18.

Bauman, Z. (2000) *Liquid Modernity*, Cambridge: Polity Press.

Bauman, Z. (2012) *Liquid Modernity*, Cambridge: Polity Press.

Benedicto, J., Fernández de Mosteyrin, L., Gutiérrez Sastre, M., Martín Pérez, A., Martín Coppola, E. and MLuz Morán, M. (2014) 'Transitar a la intemperie: jóvenes en busca de integración'. Observatorio de la Juventud en España, Madrid: Instituto de la Juventud.

Benford, R. D. and Snow, D. A. (2000) 'Framing Processes and Social Movements: An Overview and Assessment', *Annual Review of Sociology*, 26: 611–39.

Bergman Blix, S. (2015) 'Professional Emotion Management as a Rehearsal Process', *Professions and Professionalism*, 5(2): 1–15.

Bergman Blix, S. and Wettergren, Å. (2018) *Professional Emotions in Court: A Sociological Perspective*, London: Routledge.

Berlant, L. (2011) *Cruel Optimism*, Durham, NC: Duke University Press.

Bernardi, F. and Requena Díez de Revenga, M. (2010) 'Inequality in Educational Transitions: The Case of Post-compulsory Education in Spain', *Revista de Educación*, 1: 93–118.

Berth, H., Förster, P. and Brähler, E. (2003) 'Gesundheitsfolgen von Arbeitslosigkeit und Arbeitsplatzunsicherheit bei jungen Erwachsenen'. *Das Gesundheitswesen*, 65(10): 555–60.

Binkley, S. (2014) *Happiness as Enterprise: An Essay on Neoliberal Life*, Albany, NY: Suny Press.

Blokland, T., Krüger, D. and Vief, R. (2020) 'Leaving the House to Talk in Private. How COVID19 Restrictions Affected How and Where We Find Someone to Talk to', *SFB 1265 'Re-Figuration von Räumen'* [Blog] 21 December, Available from: https://www.sfb1265.de/en/blog/leaving-the-house-to-talk-in-private-how-covid19-restrictions-affected-how-and-where-we-find-someone-to-talk-to/ [Accessed 8 October 2023].

Blokland, T., Giustozzi, C., Krüger, D. and Schilling, H. (eds) (2016) *Creating the Unequal City: The Exclusionary Consequences of Everyday Routines in Berlin*, Farnham: Ashgate.

Blossfeld, H. P., Bertolini, S. and Hofäcker, D. (eds) (2011) *Youth on Globalised Labour Markets: Rising Uncertainty and Its Effects on Early Employment and Family Lives in Europe*, Opladen: Budrich.

Bogner, A. and Wouters, C. (1990) 'Kolonialisierung Der Herzen? Zu Arlie Hochschilds Grundlegung der Emotionssoziologie', *Leviathan*, 18(2): 255–79.

Boltanski, L. and Chiapello, E. (1999) *Le nouvel esprit du capitalisme*, Paris: Gallimard.

Bourdieu, P. (1977) *Outline of a Theory of Practice*, Cambridge: Cambridge University Press.

Bourdieu, P. (1979) *La distinction: critique sociale du jugement*, Paris: Edde Minuit.

Bourdieu, P. (1989) 'Social Space and Symbolic Power', *Sociological Theory*, 7(1): 14–25.

Bourdieu, P. (1990) *The Logic of Practice*, Stanford: Stanford University Press.

Bourdieu, P. (1996) *The Rules of Art: Genesis and Structure of the Literary Field*, Stanford: Stanford University Press.

Bourdieu, P. (2000) *Pascalian Meditations*, Cambridge: Polity Press.

Bourdieu, P. (2013) *Die feinen Unterschiede: Kritik der gesellschaftlichen Urteilskraft*, Frankfurt am Main: Suhrkamp.

Bourdieu, P. (2020) *Habitus and Field: Lectures at the Collège de France (1982–1983)*, Cambridge: Polity Press.

Bourdieu, P. and Passeron, J. C. (1970) *La Reproduction. Éléments pour une Théorie du Système d'enseignement*, Paris: Les Éditions de Minuit.

Bröckling, U. (2007) *Das unternehmerische Selbst: Soziologie einer Subjektivierungsform*, Frankfurt am Main: Suhrkamp.

Brody, L., Lovas, G. and Hay, D. (1995) 'Gender Differences in Anger and Fear as a Function of Situational Context', *Sex Roles*, 32(1): 47–78.

Brophy, H., Olson, J. and Paul, P. (2022) 'Eco-anxiety in Youth: An Integrative Literature Review'. *International Journal of Mental Health Nursing*, 32(3): 633–61.

Burkitt, I. (2012) 'Emotional Reflexivity: Feeling, Emotion and Imagination in Reflexive Dialogues'. *Sociology*, 46(3): 458–72.

Burkitt, I. (2014) *Emotions and Social Relations*, London: Sage.

Campillo, R. (2017) *120 battements par minute*, Les Films de Pierre.

Campos, R. L. (2018) 'Expansión de la temporalidad y erosión de la relación de empleo estándar en España: ¿La irrupción de un nuevo paradigma de relación de empleo?', *Cuadernos de Relaciones Laborales*, 36(1): 35–63.

CCOO Enseñanza (2016) 'Los precios de las matrículas universitarias, becas, ayudas y beneficios fiscales en Europa. La evolución de los preciospúblicos del sistema universitario español entre 2011 y 2016', [online], Available from: https://www.uco.es/ccoo/archivos/1066.pdf [Accessed 20 February 2022].

Cebolla-Boado, H., Radl, J. and Salazar, L. (2014) *Aprendizaje y Ciclo Vital. La Desigualdad de Oportunidades Desde la Educación Preescolar Hasta la Edad Adulta.* Barcelona: Obra Social 'la Caixa'.

Clark, C. (1990) 'Emotions and Micropolitics in Everyday Life: Some Patterns and Paradoxes of "Place"', in T. D. Kemper (ed) *Research Agendas in the Sociology of Emotions*, Albany, NY: State University of New York Press, pp 305–33.

Clarke, J. and Newman, J. (2012) 'The Alchemy of Austerity', *Critical Social Policy*, 32(3): 299–319.

Colectivo Ioé (2013) *La Juventud Ante su Inserción en la Sociedad. Actitudes y Demandas en Relación a la Escuela. Una Aproximación a las Causas del Abandono Escolar Prematuro*, Madrid: Ministerio de Educación, Cultura y Deporte.

Collins, R. (1981) 'On the Microfoundations of Macrosociology', *American Journal of Sociology*, 86(5): 984–1014.

Collins, R. (1988) 'Theoretical Continuities in Goffman´s Work', in P. Drew and A. Wootton (eds) *Erving Goffman: Exploring the Interaction Order*, Cambridge: Polity Press, pp 41–63.

Collins, R. (1990) 'Stratification, Emotional Energy, and the Transient Emotions', in T. D. Kemper (ed) *Research Agendas in the Sociology of Emotions*, Albany, NY: State University of New York Press, pp 27–57.

Confederación Nacional del Trabajo (nd) '¿Qué es CNT?', *Confederación Nacional del Trabajo*, [online], Available from: https://www.cnt.es/que-es-cnt/ [Accessed 12 February 2021].

Confederación Sindical de Comisiones Obreras (2015) 'Afiliación y representación', [online], Available from: https://www.ccoo.es/0106a77ec7bd5bedca76386125efd507000001.pdf [Accessed 8 October 2023].

Consejo de la Juventud de España (2013a) 'Observatorio de Emancipación', 1. Madrid.

Consejo de la Juventud de España (2013b) 'Observatorio de Emancipación. Andalucía. 1er Semestre 2013', Madrid.

Consejo de la Juventud de España (2013c) 'Observatorio de Emancipación. Canarias. 1er Semestre 2013', Madrid.

Consejo de la Juventud de España (2013d) 'Observatorio de Emancipación. Extremadura. 1er Semestre 2013', Madrid.

Consejo de la Juventud de España (2014) 'Observatorio de Emancipación', 1. Madrid.

Consejo de la Juventud de España (2015) 'Observatorio de Emancipación', 1. Madrid.

Consejo de la Juventud de España (2017) 'Observatorio de Emancipación. España, 1er Semestre 2017', Madrid.

Cooper, B. (2018) *Eloquent Rage: A Black Feminist Discovers Her Superpower*, New York: St Martin's Press.

Crespo, E. and Serrano, A. (2001) 'The Individualisation of Labour, Job Insecurity and Vulnerability: Young People's Experience of Work in Spain', *Transfer: European Review of Labour and Research*, 7(2): 289–308.

Dessy, O. (2016) 'Youth Unemployment and Health over 50: Evidence for the European Countries', in G. Coppola and N. O'Higgins (eds) *Youth and the Crisis: Unemployment, Education and Health in Europe*, New York: Routledge, pp 195–207.

Díez García, R. (2017) 'The "Indignados" in Space and Time: Transnational Networks and Historical Roots', *Global Society: Global Civil Society Participation: Insights from Social Movement and Public Participation Studies*, 31(1): 43–64.

Dubet, F. (2008) *Ungerechtigkeiten: zum subjektiven Ungerechtigkeitsempfinden am Arbeitsplatz*, Hamburg: Hamburger Edition.

Durkheim, E. (1893) *De la Division du Travail Social: Étude sur l'organisation des Sociétés Supérieures*, Paris: Félix Alcan.

Durkheim, E. (1897) *Le Suicide: Étude de Sociologie*, Paris: Félix Alcan.

Durkheim, E. (1966) *The Rules of Sociological Method*, New York: The Free Press.

Eddo-Lodge, R. (2017) *Why I'm No Longer Talking to White People about Race*, London: Bloomsbury Circus.

El Mundo (2011) 'La generación perdida', [online] 19 August, Available from: https://www.elmundo.es/yodona/2011/08/19/lifestyle/1313755 060.html [Accessed 19 March 2020].

El País (2012) 'Ban alerta de que el alto desempleo juvenil puede crear una "generación perdida"', [online], Available from: https://elpais.com/economia/2012/08/10/agencias/1344630481_318547.html [Accessed 20 March 2020].

Elias, N. (1939) *Über den Prozeß der Zivilisation. Soziogenetische und Psychogenetische Untersuchungen*, Basel: Verlag Haus zum Falken.

Elias, N. (1997) *Über den Prozeß der Zivilisation: soziogenetische und psychogenetische Untersuchungen. Zweiter Band: Wandlungen der Gesellschaft. Entwurf zu einer Theorie der Zivilisation*, Frankfurt am Main: Suhrkamp.

Erkmen, T. D. (2021) 'Flexible Selves in Flexible Times? Yoga and Neoliberal Subjectivities in Istanbul'. *Sociology*, 55(5): 1035–52.

Espino Granado, A. (2014) 'Crisis económica, políticas, desempleo y salud (mental)', *Revista de la Asociación Española de Neuropsiquiatría*, 34(122): 385–404.

Eurostat (nd) [online], Available from: https://ec.europa.eu/eurostat/web/youth/statistics-illustrated [Accessed 24 February 2016].

Eyerman, R. (2005) 'How Social Movements Move: Emotions and Social Movements', in H. Flam and D. King (eds) *Emotions and Social Movements*, London: Routledge, pp 41–56.

Federici, S. (1975) *Wages against Housework*, Bristol: Power of Women Collective and Falling Wall Press.

Fernández-Rivas, A. and González-Torres, M. A. (2013) 'The Economic Crisis in Spain and Its Impact on the Mental Health of Children and Adolescents', *European Child & Adolescent Psychiatry*, 22(9): 583–86.

Flam, H. (2002) *Soziologie der Emotionen: eine Einführung*, Konstanz: UVK Verlag.

Flam, H. (2005) 'Emotions' Map: A Research Agenda', in H. Flam and D. King (eds) *Emotions and Social Movements*, London: Routledge, pp 19–40.

Flam, H. (2009) 'Authentic Emotions as Ethical Guides', in M. Salmela and V. Mayer (eds) *Emotions, Ethics, and Authenticity*, Amsterdam: Benjamins, pp 195–214.

Flam, H. (2015) 'Introduction: Methods of Exploring Emotions', in H. Flam and J. Kleres (eds) *Methods of Exploring Emotions*, London: Routledge, pp 1–21.

Flam, H. and King, D. (2005) *Emotions and Social Movements*, London: Routledge.

Flam, H. and Kleres, J. (2015) *Methods of Exploring Emotions*, London: Routledge.

France, A. (2016) *Understanding Youth in the Global Economic Crisis*, Bristol: Policy Press.

Fraser, N. and Gordon, L. (1994) 'A Genealogy of Dependency: Tracing a Keyword of the U.S. Welfare State', *Signs*, 19(2): 309–36.

Froeliger, B., Garland, E. L., Modlin, L. A. and McClernon, F. J. (2012) 'Neurocognitive Correlates of the Effects of Yoga Meditation Practice on Emotion and Cognition: A Pilot Study', *Frontiers in Integrative Neuroscience*, 6: 48.

Fundación 1º de Mayo (2012) 'Las reformas laborales en España y su repercusión en materia de contratación y empleo. 52 reformas desde la aprobación del estatuto de los trabajadores en 1980.' Madrid: Fundación 1º de Mayo.

Gamberoni, E., Gradeva, K. and Weber, S. (2016) 'Employment Subsidy Schemes: Firm-Level Evidence from the 2012 Spanish Labour Market Reform', *VoxEU.Org* (blog) [online], Available from: https://voxeu.org/article/employment-subsidy-schemes-evidence-spain [Accessed 3 November 2023].

García Dauder, S. and Pérez Sedeño, E. (2017) *Las 'Mentiras' Científicas Sobre las Mujeres*, Madrid: Catarata.

García López, J. (2011) 'Youth Unemployment in Spain: Causes and Solutions', Working Papers. BBVA Bank, Economic Research Department.

Gard, T., Noggle, J. J., Park, C. L., Vago, D. R. and Wilson, A. (2014) 'Potential Self-Regulatory Mechanisms of Yoga for Psychological Health', *Frontiers in Human Neuroscience*, 8: 770.

Garfinkel, H. (1963) 'A Conception of, and Experiments with, "Trust as a Condition of Stable Concerted Actions"', in O. J. Harvey (ed) *Motivation and Social Interaction. Cognitive Determinants*, New York: Ronald Press, pp 187–265.

Garfinkel, H. (1967) *Studies in Ethnomethodology*, Englewood Cliffs, NJ: Prentice Hall.

Gay y Blasco, P. (1999) *Gypsies in Madrid: Sex, Gender and the Performance of Identity*, Oxford: Bloomsbury Academic.

Gili, M., García Campayo, J. and Roca, M. (2014) 'Crisis económica y salud mental. Informe SESPAS 2014', *Gaceta Sanitaria*, 28(S1): 104–8.

Gille, C. and Klammer, U. (2017) 'Wohlfahrtskapitalistische Regime und Handlungsfähigkeit erwerbsloser junger Menschen in Spanien und Deutschland', *Soziale Passagen*, 9(1): 43–63.

Glenn, N. (1977) *Cohort Analysis*, London: Sage.

Godrej, F. (2017) 'The Neoliberal Yogi and the Politics of Yoga', *Political Theory*, 45(6): 772–800.

Goffman, E. (1952) 'On Cooling the Mark out', *Psychiatry*, 15(4): 451–63.

Goffman, E. (1959) *The Presentation of Self in Everyday Life*, Garden City, NY: Doubleday.

Goffman, E. (1974) *Frame Analysis: An Essay on the Organization of Experience*, New York: Harper & Row.

Goffman, E. (1977) 'The Arrangement between the Sexes', *Theory and Society*, 4(3): 301–31.

Goffman, E. (1993) *Rahmen-Analyse: Ein Versuch über die Organisation von Alltagserfahrungen*, Frankfurt am Main: Suhrkamp.

Goffman, E. (2010) *Relations in Public: Microstudies of the Public Order*, New Brunswick, NJ: Transaction Publishers.

Goffman, E. (2012) *Wir alle spielen Theater: Die Selbstdarstellung im Alltag*, Munich: Piper.

Goleman, D. (1995) *Emotional Intelligence: Why It Can Matter More Than IQ*, New York: Bantam Books.

Goodwin, J., Jasper, J. M. and Polletta, F. (eds) (2001) *Passionate Politics: Emotions and Social Movements*, Chicago: University of Chicago Press.

Gordon, S. L. (1990) 'Social Structural Effects on Emotions', in T. D. Kemper (ed) *Research Agendas in the Sociology of Emotions*, Albany, NY: State University of New York Press, pp 145–79.

Gould, D. (2002) 'Life during Wartime: Emotions and the Development of Act Up', *Mobilization*, 7(2): 177–200.

Gugutzer, R. (2013) 'Hermann Schmitz: Der Gefühlsraum', in K. Senge and R. Schützeichel (eds) *Hauptwerke der Emotionssoziologie*, Wiesbaden: Springer Fachmedien, pp 304–10.

Hardy, C. (2010) 'Hysteresis', in M. Grenfell (ed) *Pierre Bourdieu: Key Concepts*, Durham: Acumen, pp 131–48.

Hardy, C. (2014) 'Social Space', in M. Grenfell (ed) *Pierre Bourdieu: Key Concepts*, Durham: Acumen, pp 229–49.

Hartfiel, N., Havenhand, J., Khalsa, S. B., Clarke, G. and Krayer, A. (2011) 'The Effectiveness of Yoga for the Improvement of Well-Being and Resilience to Stress in the Workplace', *Scandinavian Journal of Work, Environment & Health*, 37(1): 70–76.

Heller, Á. (1979) *A Theory of Feelings, Dialectic and Society*, Assen: Van Gorcum.

Heritage, J. (1984) *Garfinkel and Ethnomethodology*, Cambridge: Polity Press.

Herrera Cuesta, D. (2018) 'Employability versus Overqualification. Mismatch between Training and Employment in the Laboral Trajectories of Young Graduates in Spain', *Sociología del Trabajo*, 89: 29–52.

Hochschild, A. R. (1979) 'Emotion Work, Feeling Rules, and Social Structure', *American Journal of Sociology*, 85(3): 551–75.

Hochschild, A. R. (1983) *The Managed Heart: Commercialization of Human Feeling*, Berkeley: University of California Press.

Hochschild, A. R. (2000) 'Global Care Chains and Emotional Surplus Value', in W. Hutton and A. Giddens (eds) *On the Edge: Living with Global Capitalism*, London: Jonathan Cape, pp 130–46.

Hochschild, A. R. (2003) *The Commercialization of Intimate Life: Notes from Home and Work*, Berkeley: University of California Press.

Hochschild, A. R. (2016) *Strangers in Their Own Land: Anger and Mourning on the American Right*, New York: New Press.

Hochschild, A. R. and Machung, A. (1989) *The Second Shift: Working Parents and the Revolution at Home*, New York: Viking Penguin.

Holmes, M. (2004) 'Feeling beyond Rules: Politicizing the Sociology of Emotion and Anger in Feminist Politics', *European Journal of Social Theory*, 7(2): 209–27.

Holmes, M. (2010) 'The Emotionalization of Reflexivity', *Sociology*, 44(1): 139–54.

Holmes, M. (2015) 'Researching Emotional Reflexivity', *Emotion Review*, 7(1): 61–66.

Holtgrewe, U., Voswinkel, S. and Wagner, G. (eds) (2000) *Anerkennung und Arbeit*, Konstanz: UVK.

Honneth, A. (2013) 'Verwilderungen des Sozialen Konflikts. Anerkennungskämpfe zu Beginn des 21. Jahrhunderts', in A. Honneth, O. Lindemann and S. Voswinkel (eds) *Strukturwandel der Anerkennung. Paradoxien Sozialer Integration in der Gegenwart*, Frankfurt am Main: Campus Verlag, pp 17–39.

hooks, b. (1996) *Killing Rage: Ending Racism*, New York: Holt.

Illouz, E. (1997) *Consuming the Romantic Utopia: Love and the Cultural Contradictions of Capitalism*, Berkeley: University of California Press.

Illouz, E. (2006) *Gefühle in Zeiten des Kapitalismus*, Frankfurt am Main: Suhrkamp.

Illouz, E. (2015) *Gefühle in Zeiten des Kapitalismus*, 5th edn. Frankfurt am Main: Suhrkamp.

Jasper, J. M. (2014) 'Emotions, Sociology, and Protest', in C. von Scheve and M. Salmela (eds) *Collective Emotions*, Oxford: Oxford University Press, pp 341–55.

Jefatura del Estado (2012) Real Decreto-Ley 14/2012, de 20 de Abril, de Medidas Urgentes de Racionalización del Gasto Público en el Ámbito Educativo, [online], Available from: https://www.boe.es/diario_boe/txt.php?id=BOE-A-2012-5337 [Accessed 8 October 2023].

Jónasdóttir, A. G. (1991) *Love Power and Political Interests: Towards a Theory of Patriarchy in Contemporary Western Societies*, Örebro: University of Örebro.

Kassam, A. (2015) 'Spanish Election: National Newcomers End Era of Two-Party Dominance', *The Guardian*, [online] 21 December, Available from: http://www.theguardian.com/world/2015/dec/20/peoples-party-wins-spanish-election-absolute-majority [Accessed 8 October 2023].

Kemper, T. D. (1978) *A Social Interactional Theory of Emotions*, New York: Wiley.

Kemper, T. D. (1981) 'Social Constructionist and Positivist Approaches to the Sociology of Emotions', *American Journal of Sociology*, 87(2): 336–62.

Kemper, T. D. (2001) 'A Structural Approach to Social Movement Emotions', in J. Goodwin, J. M. Jasper and F. Polletta (eds) *Passionate Politics: Emotions and Social Movements*, Chicago: University of Chicago Press, pp 58–73.

Kleres, J. (2011) 'Emotions and Narrative Analysis: A Methodological Approach', *Journal for the Theory of Social Behaviour*, 41(2): 182–202.

Kleres, J. and Wettergren, Å. (2017) 'Fear, Hope, Anger, and Guilt in Climate Activism', *Social Movement Studies*, 16(5): 507–19.

Kring, A. M. (2000) 'Gender and Anger', in A. H. Fischer (ed) *Gender and Emotion: Social Psychological Perspectives*, New York: Cambridge University Press, pp 211–32.

Kvale, S. (2007) *Doing Interviews*, London: Sage.

La Vanguardia (2017) 'España encadena seis años con más de 60.000 desahucios', [online] 3 March, Available from: https://www.lavanguardia.com/economia/20170303/42505182370/desahucios-espana-2016-ejecuciones-hipoteca.html [Accessed 8 October 2023].

Labott, S. M., Martin, R. B., Eason, P. S. and Berkey, E. Y. (1991) 'Social Reactions to the Expression of Emotion', *Cognition and Emotion*, (5–6): 397–417.

Lamont, M. and Molnár, V. (2002) 'The Study of Boundaries in the Social Sciences', *Annual Review of Sociology*, 28(1): 167–95.

Laparra, M. and Pérez Eransus, B. (eds) (2012) *Crisis y Fractura Social en Europa. Causas y Efectos en España*, Barcelona: Obra Social 'la Caixa'.

Leo, online dictionary (nd) [online], Available from: https://dict.leo.org/alem%C3%A1n-espa%C3%B1ol/cambiar%20el%20chip [Accessed 13 May 2021].

León, M. and Migliavacca, M. (2013) 'Spain and Italy: Still the Case of Familistic Welfare Models?', *Population Review*, 52(1): 25–42.

Li, A. W. and Goldsmith, C. A. W. (2012) 'The Effects of Yoga on Anxiety and Stress', *Alternative Medicine Review: A Journal of Clinical Therapeutic*, 17(1): 21–35.

Llopis Goig, R. and Tejerina, B. (2016) 'Crisis, educación y precariedad-afluencia. El rol de la educación en las condiciones de vida de la población española', *Política y Sociedad*, 53(2): 413–42.

Lloyd, V. (2019) 'The Ambivalence of Black Rage', *CLCWeb: Comparative Literature and Culture*, 21(3).

Lofland, J. and Lofland, L. H. (2006) *Analyzing Social Settings: A Guide to Qualitative Observation and Analysis*, Belmont: Wadsworth.

López Calle, P. (2012) 'Alicia y Yo. Una perspectiva socio-clínica sobre explotación y alienación del trabajo en los nuevos modelos productivos', *Intersubjetivo: Revista de psicoterapia psicoanalítica y salud*, 12(1): 166–88.

López Calle, P. (2019) 'Subjetividad precaria como recurso productivo. Crisis, trabajo e identidad en las periferias metropolitanas desindustrializadas', *Revista Española de Sociología*, 28(2): 347–64.

López Gómez, J. M. and López Lara, E. J. (2012) 'Medidas contra la segmentación laboral en el contexto de la crisis en España', *Estudios – Centro de Estudios Avanzados. Universidad Nacional de Córdoba*, 28: 15–32.

López Hernán, Y. (2020) 'Care Work in the Global Economy: The Case of Latin American Migrant Women in Spain', *Glocalism: Journal of Culture, Politics and Innovation*, 2019(3): 1–22.

Lorde, A. (1984) *Sister Outsider: Essays and Speeches*, Freedom, CA: Crossing Press.

Lorde, A. (2007) *Sister Outsider: Essays and Speeches*. Berkeley: Crossing Press.

Loughran, T. and Mannay, D. (2018) *Emotion and the Researcher: Sites, Subjectivities and Relationships*, Bingley: Emerald Publishing.

Lupton, D. (1998) *The Emotional Self: A Sociocultural Exploration*, London: Sage.

Lutz, T. (1999) *Crying: The Natural and Cultural History of Tears*, New York: W. W. Norton.

Magnusson, E. and Marecek, J. (2015) *Doing Interview-Based Qualitative Research: A Learner's Guide*, Cambridge: Cambridge University Press.

Mannheim, K. (2017) 'Das Problem der Generationen', *Kölner Zeitschrift für Soziologie und Sozialpsychologie*, 69(S1): 81–119.

Margies, N. (2017) 'Serving the Private Good through Legal Manoeuvrings', *Articulo. Journal of Urban Research*, Varia.

Margies, N. (2022) 'Emotions and the City', *Urban Transcripts Journal*, 5(2).

Marshall, T. H. (1973) *Class, Citizenship and Social Development*, Westport, CT: Greenwood Press.

Marx, K. (1968) *Ökonomisch-philosophische Manuskripte: geschrieben von April bis Aug. 1844*, Leipzig: Reclam.

Maxwell, J. A. (1996) *Qualitative Research Design: An Interactive Approach*, Thousand Oaks: Sage.

Mayer, V. (2009) 'How to Be "Emotional"?' in M. Salmela and V. Mayer (eds) *Emotions, Ethics, and Authenticity*, Amsterdam: Benjamins, pp 113–32.

Mbembe, A. and Roitman, J. (1995) 'Figures of the Subject in Times of Crisis', *Public Culture*, 7(2): 323–52.

McCormick-Huhn, K. and Shields, S. A. (2021) 'Favorable Evaluations of Black and White Women's Workplace Anger during the Era of #MeToo', *Frontiers in Psychology*, 12.

McKenzie, J. and Patulny, R. (2022) *Dystopian Emotions: Emotional Landscapes and Dark Futures*, Bristol: Bristol University Press.

Merton, R. K. (1968) *Social Theory and Social Structure*, New York: Free Press.

Mills, T. and Kleinman, S. (1988) 'Emotions, Reflexivity, and Action: An Interactionist Analysis', *Social Forces*, 66(4): 1009–27.

Misztal, B. A. (2001) 'Normality and Trust in Goffman's Theory of Interaction Order', *Sociological Theory* 19(3): 312–24.

Misztal, B. A. (2015) *Multiple Normalities: Making Sense of Ways of Living*, London: Palgrave Macmillan.

Moreno Mínguez, A. (2007) 'Incidencia de las políticas familiares en el empleo femenino en los Estados de bienestar del sur de Europa en perspectiva comparada', *Papers: Revista de Sociología*, 86: 73.

Moreno Mínguez, A. (2008) 'El reducido empleo femenino en los Estados del bienestar del sur de Europa. Un análisis comparado', *Revista Internacional de Sociología*, 66(50): 129–62.

Moreno Mínguez, A. (2010) 'Family and Gender Roles in Spain from a Comparative Perspective', *European Societies*, 12(1): 85–111.

Moreno Mínguez, A., López Peláez, A. and Segado Sánchez-Cabezudo, S. (2012) *La Transición de los Jóvenes a la Vida Adulta. Crisis Económica y Emancipación Tardía*, Barcelona: Obra Social 'la Caixa'.

Motro, D., Evans, J. B., Ellis, A. P. J. and Benson, L. (2021) 'Race and Reactions to Women's Expressions of Anger at Work: Examining the Effects of the "Angry Black Woman" Stereotype', *Journal of Applied Psychology*, 107(1): 142–52.

Munson, Z. W. (2009) *The Making of Pro-Life Activists: How Social Movement Mobilization Works*, Chicago: University of Chicago Press.

Navarro, V. (2013) 'The Social Crisis of the Eurozone: The Case of Spain', *International Journal of Health Services*, 43(2): 189–92.

Neckel, S. (1991) *Status und Scham: zur symbolischen Reproduktion sozialer Ungleichheit*, Frankfurt am Main: Campus Verlag.

Neckel, S. (2005) 'Emotion by Design. The Self-Management of Emotions as a Cultural Program', *Berliner Journal fur Soziologie*, 15(3): 419–30.

Neckel, S. (2013) 'Arlie Russell Hochschild: Das Gekaufte Herz. Zur Kommerzialisierung der Gefühle', in K. Senge and R. Schützeichel (eds) *Hauptwerke der Emotionssoziologie*, Wiesbaden: Springer Fachmedien, pp 168–75.

Ortiz, I. and Cummins, M. (2012) 'When the Global Crisis and Youth Bulge Collide: Double the Jobs Trouble for Youth'. SSRN Scholarly Paper ID 2029794, Rochester, NY: Social Science Research Network.

Oso, L. (2007) 'La inserción laboral de la población latinoamericana en España: el protagonismo de las mujeres', in I. Yépez de Castillo and G. Herrera (eds) *Nuevas migraciones latinoamericanas a Europa: balances y desafíos*, Quito: Flacso, pp 453–79.

Pereira-Zazo, Ó. and Torres, S. L. (eds) (2019) *Spain after the Indignados/15M Movement: The 99% Speaks out*, Cham: Springer International Publishing.

Perriard, A. and van de Velde, C. (2021) 'Le pouvoir politique des émotions', *Lien social et Politiques*, 86: 4–19.

Pernau, M. (2014) 'Civility and Barbarism: Emotions as Criteria of Difference', in U. Frevert et al (eds) *Emotional Lexicons: Continuity and Change in the Vocabulary of Feeling, 1700–2000*, Oxford: Oxford University Press, pp 230–59.

Peugny, C. (2009) *Le déclassement*, Paris: Grasset.

Pilcher, J. (1994) 'Mannheim's Sociology of Generations: An Undervalued Legacy', *British Journal of Sociology*, 45(3): 481–95.

Pineda-Herrero, P., Agud, I. and Ciraso Calí, A. (2016) 'Factores que intervienen en la inserción laboral de los titulados en educación en tiempos de crisis: un estudio sobre Cataluña', *Revista de educación*, 372: 141–69.

Pique, M. A. C., Pardell Vea, A. and Seres Cabases, A. (2017) 'El modelo de empleo juvenil en Espana (2013–2016)', *Politica y Sociedad*, 54(3): 733–55.

Pons, online dictionary (nd) [online], Available from: https://de.pons.com/%C3%BCbersetzung/englisch-spanisch/cambiar+el+chip?bidir=1 [Accessed 13 May 2021].

Poveda, D. and Markos, T. (2005) 'The Social Organization of a "Stone Fight": Gitano Children's Interpretive Reproduction of Ethnic Conflict', *Childhood*, 12(3): 327–49.

Prieto, C., Arnal, M., Caprile, M. and Potrony, J. (eds) (2009) *La calidad del empleo en España: una aproximación teórica y empírica*, Madrid: Ministerio de Trabajo e Inmigración.

Reckwitz, A. (2017) *Die Gesellschaft der Singularitäten. Zum Strukturwandel der Moderne*, Berlin: Suhrkamp.

Reckwitz, A. (2020) 'The Society of Singularities', in D. Bachmann-Medick, J. Kugele and A. Nünning (eds) *Futures of the Study of Culture*, Berlin: De Gruyter, pp 141–54.

Reed-Danahay, D. (2005) *Locating Bourdieu*, Bloomington: Indiana University Press.

Reibling, N., Beckfield, J., Huijts, T., Schmidt-Catran, A., H. Thomson, K. and Wendt, C. (2017) 'Depressed during the Depression: Has the Economic Crisis Affected Mental Health Inequalities in Europe? Findings from the European Social Survey (2014) Special Module on the Determinants of Health', *European Journal of Public Health*, 27(1): 47–54.

Rivas, M. (2015) 'Quién tema a la generación perdida?', *El País*, [online] 10 July, Available from: https://elpais.com/elpais/2015/07/10/eps/143653 0215_929131.html [Accessed 21 March 2020].

Robert, G., Miguel Martínez, J., García, A. M., Benavides, F. G. and Ronda, E. (2014) 'From the Boom to the Crisis: Changes in Employment Conditions of Immigrants in Spain and Their Effects on Mental Health', *European Journal of Public Health*, 24(3): 404–9.

Roca, M., Gili, M., Garcia-Campayo, J. and García-Toro, M. (2013) 'Economic Crisis and Mental Health in Spain', *The Lancet*, 382(9909): 1977–8.

Rosa, H. (2016) *Resonanz: Eine Soziologie der Weltbeziehung*, Berlin: Suhrkamp.

Rosen, E. (2017) 'Horizontal Immobility: How Narratives of Neighborhood Violence Shape Housing Decisions', *American Sociological Review*, 82(2): 270–96.

Rosenwein, B. H. (2010) 'Problems and Methods in the History of Emotions', *Passions in Context*, I(1): 1–33.

Ruiz, M. T. and Verbrugge L. M. (1997) 'A Two Way View of Gender Bias in Medicine', *Journal of Epidemiology and Community Health*, 51(2): 106–9.

Saarni, C. (1999) *The Development of Emotional Competence*, New York: Guilford Press.

Salerno, J. M. and Peter-Hagene, L. C. (2015) 'One Angry Woman: Anger Expression Increases Influence for Men, But Decreases Influence for Women, during Group Deliberation', *Law and Human Behavior*, 39(6): 581–92.

Salerno, J M., Peter-Hagene, L. C. and Jay, A. C. V. (2019) 'Women and African Americans Are Less Influential When They Express Anger during Group Decision Making', *Group Processes & Intergroup Relations*, 22(1): 57–79.

Salmela, M. (2012) 'Shared Emotions', *Philosophical Explorations*, 15(1): 33–46.

Samulowitz, A., Gremyr, I., Eriksson, E. and Hensing, G. (2018) ' "Brave Men" and "Emotional Women": A Theory-Guided Literature Review on Gender Bias in Health Care and Gendered Norms towards Patients with Chronic Pain', *Pain Research & Management*, 2018: 6358624–14.

Sánchez Becerril, F. (2019) 'El caos de los psicólogos en la pública: por qué la mayoría de la gente va a privados', *El Español*, [online] 25 February, Available from: https://www.elespanol.com/ciencia/salud/20190225/psi cologos-seguridad-social-tardan-atender-dedican-tiempo/378212578_ 0.html [Accessed 1 March 2019].

Sánchez, F. R. (2012) 'Youth Unemployment in Spain', Berlin: Friedrich-Ebert-Stiftung.

Sanmartín, R. O. (2016) 'El precio del grado en España es 20 veces más caro que en Alemania', *El Mundo*, [online] 15 April, Available from: https:// www.elmundo.es/sociedad/2016/04/15/570f9b3ce5fdea6d578b45cd.html [Accessed 8 October 2023].

Scheer, M. (2012) 'Are Emotions a Kind of Practice (and Is That What Makes Them a History)? A Bourdieuian Approach to Understanding Emotion', *History and Theory*, 51(2): 193–220.

Scheer, M. (2016) 'Emotionspraktiken: Wie man über das Tun an die Gefühle herankommt', in M. Beitl and I. Schneider (eds) *Emotional Turn?!: europäisch ethnologische Zugänge zu Gefühlen & Gefühlswelten*, Vienna: Selbstverlag des Vereins für Volkskunde, pp 15–36.

Scheler, M. (1923) *Wesen und Formen der Sympathie*, Bonn: Friedrich Cohen.

Scheler, M. (2008) *The Nature of Sympathy*, New Brunswick, NJ: Transaction Publishers.

Schimank, U. (2015) 'Lebensplanung!? Biografische Entscheidungspraktiken irritierter Mittelschichten', *Berliner Journal für Soziologie*, 25(1): 7–31.

Schmitz, H. (1990) *Der unerschöpfliche Gegenstand: Grundzüge der Philosophie*, Bonn: Bouvier.

Schmitz, H. (1993) 'Gefühle als Atmosphären und das affektive Betroffensein von ihnen', in H. Fink-Eitel (ed) *Zur Philosophie der Gefühle*, Frankfurt am Main: Suhrkamp, pp 33–56.

Scott, J. C. (1990) *Domination and the Arts of Resistance: Hidden Transcripts*, New Haven: Yale University Press.

Sennett, R. (1998) *The Corrosion of Character: The Personal Consequences of Work in the New Capitalism*, New York: W. W. Norton.

Sennett, R. (2003) *Respect. The Formation of Character in a World of Inequality*, London: Penguin.

Sennett, R. (2008) *The Craftsman*, New Haven: Yale University Press.

Sherman Heyl, B. (2007) 'Ethnographic Interviewing', in P. Atkinson (ed) *Handbook of Ethnography*, Los Angeles: Sage, pp 369–83.

Shields, S. A. (2002) *Speaking from the Heart: Gender and the Social Meaning of Emotion*, Cambridge: Cambridge University Press.

Silva, E. B. (2016) 'Unity and Fragmentation of the Habitus', *Sociological Review*, 64(1): 166–83.

Simmel, G. (1903) 'Die Grosstädte und das Geistesleben', in T. Petermann (ed) *Die Grossstadt. Vorträge und Aufsätze zur Städteausstellung*, Dresden: Jahrbuch der Gehe-Stiftung Dresden, pp 185–206.

Simon, R. W. and Lively, K. (2010) 'Sex, Anger and Depression', *Social Forces*, 88(4): 1543–68.

Simon, R. W., and Nath, L. (2004) 'Gender and Emotion in the United States: Do Men and Women Differ in Self-Reports of Feelings and Expressive Behavior?' *American Journal of Sociology*, 109(5): 1137–76.

Simone, A. and Schilling, H. (2015) 'Practices within Precarity: Youth, Informality, and Life Making in the Contemporary City', Presented at the RC21 International Conference Urbino (Italy), 27–29 August.

Simpson, L. and Bui, M. (2021) *Left behind: A Decade of Intergenerational Unfairness*, London: Intergenerational Foundation.

Skeggs, B. (1997) *Formations of Class and Gender: Becoming Respectable*. London: Sage.

Skeggs, B. (2004) *Class, Self, Culture*, London: Routledge.

Skeggs, B. (2014) 'Values beyond Value? Is Anything beyond the Logic of Capital?', *British Journal of Sociology*, 65(1): 1–20.

Smith, A. (1812) *The Theory of Moral Sentiments*, London: Cadell & Davies.

Smith, D. (2001) 'Organizations and Humiliation: Looking beyond Elias', *Organization*, 8(3): 537–60.

Stoppard, J. M. and Gunn Gruchy, C. D. (1993) 'Gender, Context, and Expression of Positive Emotion', *Personality and Social Psychology Bulletin*, 19(2): 143–50.

Streeter, C. C., Whitfield, T. H., Owen, L., Rein, T., Karri, S. K., Yakhkind, A. et al (2010) 'Effects of Yoga versus Walking on Mood, Anxiety, and Brain GABA Levels: A Randomized Controlled MRS Study', *Journal of Alternative and Complementary Medicine*, 16(11): 1145–52.

Summers-Effler, E. (2002) 'The Micro Potential for Social Change: Emotion, Consciousness, and Social Movement Formation', *Sociological Theory*, 20(1): 41–60.

Telles, S., Kumar Sharma, S., Kumar Gupta, R., Kumar Pal, D., Gandharva, K. and Balkrishna, A. (2019) 'The Impact of Yoga on Teachers' Self-Rated Emotions', *BMC Research Notes*, 12.

Thoits, P. A. (1985) 'Self-Labeling Processes in Mental Illness: The Role of Emotional Deviance', *American Journal of Sociology*, 91(2): 221–49.

Thoits, P. A. (1990) 'Emotional Deviance: Research Agendas', in T. D. Kemper (ed) *Research Agendas in the Sociology of Emotions*, Albany, NY: State University of New York Press, pp 180–206.

Thoits, P. A. (1996) 'Managing the Emotions of Others', *Symbolic Interaction*, 19(2): 85–109.

Timmers, M., Fischer, A. H. and Manstead, A. S. R. (1998) 'Gender Differences in Motives for Regulating Emotions', *Personality and Social Psychology Bulletin*, 24(9): 974–85.

Tracy, S. J. (2005) 'Fracturing the Real-Self Fake-Self Dichotomy: Moving toward "Crystallized" Organizational Discourses and Identities', *Communication Theory*, 15(2): 168–95.

Unión General de Trabajadores (2017) '¿Qué es UGT?', *UGT*, [online] 5 December, Available from: https://www.ugt.es/que-es-ugt [Accessed 8 October 2023].

Van de Velde, C. (2011) 'Indignés: les raisons de la colère', *Cités*, 47/48: 293–7.

Van de Velde, C. (2016) 'Visages et expériences des "NEET": "J'aimerais que quelqu'un m'attende quelque part"', *Revue du CREMIS*, 9(1): 27–32.

Van de Velde, C. (2019) 'Sous la catégorie des "NEET": normes sociales et parcours de vie', *Diversité*, 194(1/3): 62–69.

Van de Velde, C., Blais, A., Boudreault, S., Hardy, C., Konaté, K., Lagier, J., Lary, S., Maglioni, M. and Trigueros, P. (2022) 'Etre jeune et vivre une pandémie', *Revue du CREMIS*, 13(1).

Van der Graaf, P. (2015) 'Feeling at Home and Habitus: How Space Matters for Emotions', in J. Kleres and Y. Albrecht (eds) *Die Ambivalenz der Gefühle: Über die verbindende und widersprüchliche Sozialität von Emotionen*, Wiesbaden: Springer Fachmedien, pp 19–39.

Verdú, V. (2011) '"El 15-M es emocional, le falta pensamiento"', *El País*, [online] 17 October, Available from: https://elpais.com/politica/2011/10/17/actualidad/1318808156_278372.html [Accessed 5 November 2023].

Villa, P. I. (ed) (2008) *Schön normal: Manipulationen am Körper als Technologien des Selbst*, Bielefeld: Transcript Verlag.

Von Scheve, C. (2009) *Emotionen und soziale Strukturen: die affektiven Grundlagen sozialer Ordnung*, Frankfurt am Main: Campus Verlag.

Walkerdine, V. (1988) *The Mastery of Reason: Cognitive Development and the Production of Rationality*, London: Routledge.

Walkerdine, V. and Jimenez, L. (2012) *Gender, Work and Community after De-industrialisation: A Psychosocial Approach to Affect*, Basingstoke: Palgrave Macmillan.

Warner, L. R. and Shields, S. A. (2009) 'Status, Gender, and the Politics of Emotional Authenticity', in M. Salmela and V. Mayer (eds) *Emotions, Ethics, and Authenticity*, Amsterdam: Benjamins, pp 91–112.

Weber, M. (1934) *Die protestantische Ethik und der Geist des Kapitalismus*, Tübingen: Mohr.

Weber, M. (2004) *The Vocation Lectures*, Indianapolis: Hackett Publishing.

Weeks, K. (2017) 'Down with Love: Feminist Critique and the New Ideologies of Work', *Women's Studies Quarterly*, 45(3): 37–58.

Wettergren, A. (2019) 'Emotive-Cognitive Rationality, Background Emotions and Emotion Work', in R. Patulny, A. Bellocchi, R. E. Olson, S. Khorana, J. McKenzie and M. Peterie (eds) *Emotions in Late Modernity*, Abingdon: Routledge, pp 27–40.

Wettergren, Å., Holmes, M. and Manning, N. (2020) 'Emotions in the Pandemic: Crises and Politics of Change', *Emotions and Society*, 2(2): 115–19.

Wierzbicka, A. (1999) *Emotions across Languages and Cultures: Diversity and Universals*, Cambridge: Cambridge University Press.

Willems, H. (1997) *Rahmen und Habitus: zum theoretischen und methodischen Ansatz Erving Goffmans*, Frankfurt am Main: Suhrkamp.

Williams, R. (1977) *Marxism and Literature*, Oxford: Oxford University Press.

Yang, G. (2000) 'Achieving Emotions in Collective Action: Emotional Processes and Movement Mobilization in the 1989 Chinese Student Movement', *Sociological Quarterly*, 41(4): 593–614.

Young, I. M. (2005) *On Female Body Experience 'Throwing like a Girl' and Other Essays*, Oxford: Oxford University Press.

Zelizer, V. A. (1994) *The Social Meaning of Money*, New York: Basic Books.

Index

References to tables appear in **bold** type. References to endnotes show both the page number and the note number (177n3).

social spaces and 31
working conditions 173, 179n1 (appendix)
upper classes 104
See also declassing; middle classes; status
The Uses of Anger (Lorde) 32

V

validation work 106–7, 142
Vanesa (interviewee)
on collective spaces 108–9, 110, 113
on emotional fulfilment 123–5, 126–9, 138
on normative framework of
employment 58–9
verbal communication 6, 7
Vidal (interviewee) 46, 81–2, 84–5, 106–7
violence 4, 5, 8, 34

W

wages *See* income
Walkerdine, V. 4
Warner, L. R. 8
Weber, Max 4, 65, 124
weeping *See* crying
Wettergren, Å 26–8, 170
Willems, H. 88–9, 96
women
anger and 151–5, 165
education levels of 13
emotional hierarchies 35
employment experiences of 9, 150–1
home as front stage 30
pain, perception of 8
See also gender; men

work *See* employment; labour market
workplace hierarchies 28, 58, 148
worry 61–3
See also anxiety
writing 95–6

Y

yoga 98–100, 178n5
Young, I. M. 91
young people
economic crisis, impacts on 11
education (*See* education)
employment (*See* employment;
labour market)
hysteresis (*See* hysteresis)
impasse (*See* impasse)
individual backstages (*See*
individual backstages)
mismatch (*See* mismatch)
NEET (not in education, employment or
training) 14, 175n6
personal space (*See* individual backstages)
research 171–4, **172**, **173**
training (*See* training)
*See also different emotions (e.g., frustration,
anxiety, uncertainty); individual interviewees
(e.g., Belén, Mateo, Natalia)*
youth centres 173–4
Youth without a Future *See* Juventud sin
Futuro (Youth without a Future)

Z

Zapatero, José Lois Rodríguez 10

Printed and bound by CPI Group (UK) Ltd, Croydon, CR0 4YY

23/04/2025

14661024-0001